The Sieges of
Ciudad Rodrigo
1810 and 1812

The Sieges of Ciudad Rodrigo 1810 and 1812

The Peninsular War

Tim Saunders

Pen & Sword
MILITARY

First published in Great Britain in 2018 by
PEN & SWORD MILITARY
An imprint of
Pen & Sword Books Ltd
47 Church Street
Barnsley
South Yorkshire
S70 2AS

ISBN 978-1-52672-432-8

Typeset by Concept, Huddersfield HD4 5JL.
Printed and bound in England by TJ International Ltd, Padstow, Cornwall.

Pen & Sword Books Limited incorporates the imprints of Atlas, Archaeology,
Aviation, Discovery, Family History, Fiction, History, Maritime, Military,
Military Classics, Politics, Select, Transport, True Crime, Air World,
Frontline Publishing, Leo Cooper, Remember When, Seaforth Publishing,
The Praetorian Press, Wharncliffe Local History, Wharncliffe Transport,
Wharncliffe True Crime and White Owl.

For a complete list of Pen & Sword titles please contact
PEN & SWORD BOOKS LIMITED
47 Church Street, Barnsley, South Yorkshire, S70 2AS, England
E-mail: enquiries@pen-and-sword.co.uk
Website: www.pen-and-sword.co.uk

Contents

DEDICATION

This book is dedicated to the 2nd 95th Rifle Living History Society who have allowed me to take my knowledge of Napoleonic warfare to places I never expected.

Introduction

To take a town fortified in a regular manner according to the modem system, that is to say, a place that has the scarp walls well hid by the counterscarp and glacis, the only certain and efficacious mode is by the different parallels and sap, the ricochet and vertical fire, and afterwards from the crest of the glacis to batter in breach.

But this method seems by no means necessary against such places as Ciudad Rodrigo, Badajoz or St. Sebastian, which are fortified in the old way, and where from five to seven hundred yards some portions of the scarp of the walls were seen uncovered to their foot, or nearly so, and consequently could be battered in breach from that distance.

(*Few Observations on the Mode of Attack and Employment of Heavy Artillery at Ciudad Rodrigo, Badajoz in 1812 and St. Sebastian in 1813*, Anonymous Royal Artillery Officer)

Sir Charles Oman in his chapter on sieges in *Wellington's Army 1809–1814* opened with the statement: 'Everyone knows that the record of the Peninsular Army in the matter of sieges is not the most brilliant pages in its annals.' In that respect, views have changed little; however, the manner in which the Duke of Wellington seized the opportunity and conducted the siege of Ciudad Rodrigo, one that the other great Peninsular historian J.W. Fortescue likened to a *coup de main*, certainly shows the Peninsular Army in a favourable light and highlights what could have been, in this most brutal aspect of Napoleonic warfare.

It should also be remembered that much had changed since the classical period of siege warfare: that of Marlborough and Vauban. While developments in defences had in many cases been impossible or not undertaken at Ciudad Rodrigo, the march of artillery technology had continued. Brevet Major May commented:

The arts have given smoother surfaces and more mathematical precision to the forms of ordnance, the bore, shot, and shells: if, therefore, the foregoing premises be admitted, it follows, that while fortresses, in their construction and strength, are nearly the same as at the time of Vauban, the battering artillery has been improved four-fold and the powder fully double, and that their consequent influence on the attack of places towards their more rapid reduction ...

The city of Ciudad Rodrigo had been a centre of Spanish resistance to the imposition of Joseph Bonaparte on the throne of Spain. The Junta of Castile took up residence in the city and work was undertaken to improve the defences and its defenders when in late 1809 Marshal Ney had attempted to cajole the Spanish into surrendering during a low point in their fortunes.

Ciudad Rodrigo was, however, the scene of the opening act of the French 1810 invasion of Portugal and again in the Allied 1812 campaign. The French siege of 1810 was conducted against a background of guerrilla attacks on their lines of communication, a paucity of supplies, discord among the marshals and Napoleon attempting to conduct the campaign from Paris. Marshal Masséna's attack was deliberate, conventional and time-consuming, while Wellington's 1812 siege was almost exactly the opposite, being well-prepared and against a far less active commander than the French had to contend with. The difference between the two sieges could not be more complete.

There is also a controversy over the 1810 siege. The governor, General Herrasti, proved from the outset to be a man of determination and his single-mindedness is in distinct contrast to the divided French command during the 1810 siege, which drifted into weeks before he was forced to accept the inevitable and surrender the city. Herrasti had done well, but even though Wellington's army was less than 10 miles away, the British were still not strong enough to take on the French on ground of their own choosing. This seeming abandonment is still controversial today. At a commemorative event in Plaza Herrasti, I witnessed a Spanish army contingent making abusive gestures to British soldiers and re-enactors. They clearly believed, like their ancestors, that they were let down or even betrayed by 'perfidious Albion'. This book will, of course, be examining Wellington's decisions in detail.

In contrast to the protracted and poorly-resourced French siege of 1810, the British siege of 1812 was an example of focused command, planning, resourcing and conduct but still as far as the Royal Engineers were concerned showed plenty of room for improvement.

Ciudad Rodrigo is today a charming, friendly and compact city, still bearing the marks of battle. It is well-placed to act as a base for exploring the 1810–1812 battlefields of the Águeda/Côa area. It is well-furnished with hotels, including a parador (a state-run hotel) in the castle that was used as a headquarters by the defenders during both sieges. Delightful restaurants and bars abound on the Plaza Mayor and can be found tucked away in the alleyways and side-streets where marks of musket balls striking the walls still bear witness to events of more than 200 years ago.

As will be seen from the photographs in this book, the walls and defences of Ciudad Rodrigo, although repaired and developed for a few years after 1812, represent one of the most complete sets of Napoleonic defences of more than a trifling size to be found anywhere in the peninsula. With two sieges to compare and contrast, it is worth scheduling a full day to walk around the outer defences, along the city walls and through the streets and squares.

This book is not, however, solely about Ciudad Rodrigo and siege warfare but encompasses the equally important outpost actions, particularly those of the Light Division and Wellington's light cavalry during the 1810 siege. All those of significance on the Spanish side of the border are included. These actions show Brigadier General Craufurd, 'the master of the outposts', as both brilliant and flawed; amply demonstrating how the quality of the troops he trained in his light infantry methodology repeatedly extricated him from difficult situations!

To restrict the size of this book I have used the Spanish/Portuguese border to define the detailed content. That is to say, those on the Spanish side are covered in detail and the Portuguese side in outline only. A subsequent volume will cover the events, including Fuentes de Oñoro and the Côa, between 1809 and 1812 on the Portuguese side in detail.

Tim Saunders
Warminster,
October 2017

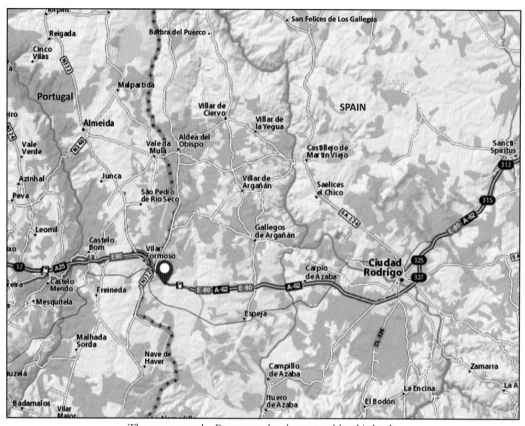

The area up to the Portuguese border covered by this book.

Chapter One

Ciudad Rodrigo

Spain, Portugal, France and Britain have shared a history of competition, conflict and alliance dating back some eight centuries by the time of the Napoleonic Wars. Much of that competition and conflict was played out across the globe as the four great nations of eighteenth-century Europe carved out empires. However, a persistent focus of fighting, one that pre-dated the Europe of Napoleon by many hundreds of years, was on the borders of Spain and Portugal, where the beautiful city and fortress town of Ciudad Rodrigo sits above the River Águeda.

Situated on the Spanish plains of Castile and León in the western part of the province of Salamanca, Ciudad Rodrigo is less than 20 miles from the border with Portugal. It has long been a crossing-point on the River Águeda, a tributary of the Douro, with Palaeolithic rock carvings on the riverbank only a short distance away at Siega Verde, which is a World Heritage Site. There is also an Iron Age carving of a boar in a square adjacent to the castle. Ciudad was established as a village on a piece of high ground by a Celtic tribe in the sixth century BC and

The Ciudad Rodrigo Boar.

was originally known as Miróbriga but some 200 years later when the Romans conquered the western part of Spain (the conquest of Lusitania) they renamed the city Augustóbriga after the emperor Octavian Caesar Augustus. The city is adjacent to the Roman Colimbirana Road and the original bridge over the River Águeda also dated back to Roman times.

The three pillars – all that is left visible of the Roman settlement – are found on the coat of arms of Ciudad Rodrigo and were a part of a temple, reputedly all that was left standing after the city was sacked during what in Britain were the Dark Ages.

The coat of arms of Ciudad Rodrigo.

The Moorish Period

The word Moors derives from the Latin *mauri*, a name for the Muslim religious fanatics from Berber/Arab tribes originating in modern-day Algeria and Morocco. They arrived in the Iberian Peninsula in 711 AD and swept across the land in just a few years before a series of checks limited their expansion, which at one stage had crossed the Pyrenees and into France. Their 700-year presence gave Spain her very different identity from that of the rest of Europe as the peoples of Iberia interbred, absorbing elements of Muslim tradition, language and culture. Moorish territory was known as Al-Andalus and for much of the period became a part of the Caliph of Damascus, then the centre of the Muslim world.

Initially all of the Iberian Peninsula, including Ciudad Rodrigo, came under Moorish rule except for the mountains of the north and north-west which were held by Christian peoples and was from where the long-drawn-out re-conquest of Iberia would originate, as early as Pelayo's victory over the Moors at Covadonga in 718 AD. The Moorish occupation of the area around Ciudad Rodrigo lasted for some 160 years, but Spain would not be entirely free of the Moors until the fifteenth century.

The Medieval Period

As the re-conquest proceeded south, Ciudad Rodrigo was rebuilt and repopulated in the eleventh century under Rodrigo González Girón, from whom the city takes its name. A century later, Ferdinando II of León ordered the walls to be built around the medieval city. These walls are 1.5 miles in circumference and are today pierced with seven gates. Work on construction of the cathedral also started during this period and like many such projects lasted for almost 200 years and therefore the cathedral demonstrates the transition from a Romanesque to a more neoclassical form. Ciudad Rodrigo's importance steadily increased, as did its role in confronting both the Portuguese to the west and the Moors to the south.

In the fourteenth century (1372), Henry II of Castile ordered the construction of the castle on the highest point in the city, which is now a National Parador and is greatly recommended as a base, albeit an expensive one. The city today very much reflects its fifteenth- and sixteenth-century heyday, which was a period of both political power and economic plenty thanks to its position on a major trade route into Portugal.

In the mid-sixteenth century, a Jewish trading community was established in Ciudad Rodrigo and attracted the brutal attention and persecution of the Spanish Inquisition. During the seventeenth and eighteenth centuries, however, Ciudad Rodrigo went into a steady decline.

During the War of the Spanish Succession (1701–1714) Ciudad Rodrigo was besieged and changed hands twice. It was taken in 1706 by a force of 40,000 Portuguese, Dutch and English soldiers under the command of Henri de Massue, Earl of Galway. It was, however, retaken in 1707 by a Franco-Spanish army under the command of Alexandre Maître, Marquis de Bay, in a three-week siege. The majority of the defences to be seen today beyond the old city wall are the result of improvements following the two early eighteenth-century sieges.

Following the brutally-repressed Dos de Mayo rebellion in 1808 against the French and the placing of King Joseph Bonaparte on the throne in Madrid, the Junta of Castile took up residence in Ciudad Rodrigo. As a result, the city had become a centre of resistance to the French invader. The creation of the additional defensive outworks described below dates from this period.

The Defences of Ciudad Rodrigo

During the eighteenth century additional protective works to defend against artillery fire, which had rendered most medieval fortifications obsolescent, was carried out around the most vulnerable parts of the fortress but by the turn of the nineteenth century Ciudad Rodrigo was still classified as a second-rate fortress. Nonetheless, with the difficulty inherent in assembling siege materials in the peninsula at the time, taking the city still represented a significant challenge to any attacking army.

Ciudad Rodrigo stands 80 to 100ft above the northern bank of the River Águeda and the bridge to the suburb of Santa Marina. The precipitate rocky slopes overlooking the river had been an intrinsic part of the settlement's defences from the earliest of times. The north-east corner of Ciudad Rodrigo, however, has a far gentler approach and access to the city. Consequently it was here that the suburban area of San Francisco and market gardens and allotments had developed. By 1810, however, the walls were protected from effective bombardment by the suburb, which had been turned into a widespread outwork with the digging of an extensive ditch and bank around it. In addition, cannon were mounted in the substantial convent buildings that made up much of the suburb and it was connected to the defences of the main fortress by palisades on either side. To the west of the city stood the isolated convent of Santa Cruz,

King Joseph Bonaparte, placed on the usurped throne of Spain by Napoleon.

the walls and gardens of which had similarly been converted into a significant outwork.

The main defences of Ciudad Rodrigo were elliptical in shape, 800 yards east to west and 500 yards north to south. The original stone and brick wall was about 30ft high but had, as a result of the sieges mentioned above, at the beginning of the eighteenth century been modernized with a faussebraye (a secondary rampart), along with protective ravelins and a glacis slope. The faussebraye was concentrated around the northern and western sides of the fortress which were now considered to be the most vulnerable as with the march of artillery technology the city walls were now vulnerable to fire from the Teson (hill) features.

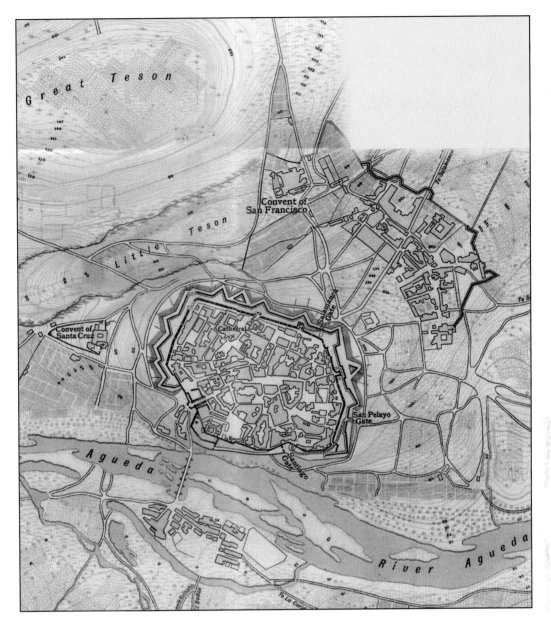

Ciudad Rodrigo and its outworks.

The Greater Teson was nearly 500ft high and about 600 yards from the walls, while the Lesser Teson was 200ft high and 250 yards from the walls. The glacis slope and faussebraye were intended to help protect the walls from artillery fire, but the problem was that the Greater Teson was at least 25ft higher than the city and therefore the faussebraye only provided partial protection. Captain Burgoyne of the Royal Engineers summed up the inadequacies of these eighteenth-century additions to the defences: 'The faussebraye, owing to its low relief and the natural

A section of the eighteenth-century defences on the northern side of the city.

fall of the ground, afforded but a poor cover to the main enceinte, and for the same reason was itself but imperfectly protected by its glacis.'

It did, however, mean that there was a pair of stone revetted 12 to 13ft deep moats astride the faussebraye which an attacker would have to cross, having first battered his way through with artillery.

To the front of the inner moat, the faussebraye and the outer moat was the open killing area of the glacis slope, complete with a stone revetted counterscarp.

After the 1812 siege the breaches were repaired, the moats deepened and two redoubts built on the Greater Teson (often confused with the 1811 Fort Renaud). In the 1820s a new gate and bridge across the moat were built at the site of the 1812 Lesser Breach.

Ciudad Rodrigo remained a significant fortification well into the nineteenth century as regular tension with neighbouring Portugal continued to be a factor.

A cross-section of the defences in the city's north-west corner.

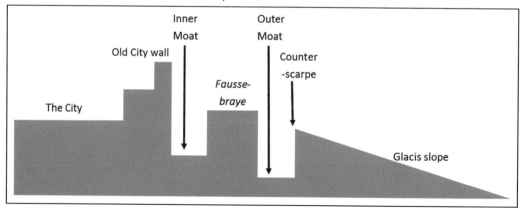

Chapter Two

The Peninsular War, 1808–1809

Fearing contagion among their own people as the energy unleashed by the French Revolution threatened to sweep aside the eighteenth-century *ancien régime*, the threatened monarchies joined the First Coalition. Those lining up alongside Britain in 1792 to oppose revolutionary France included Spain and Portugal. In 1795, however, the Bourbon monarchy signed an alliance with France, thus abandoning the coalition, but Portugal remained in alliance with Britain even when the First Coalition collapsed in 1797 and nominally continued the fight against France.

In a coup on *18 Brumaire, Year VIII* (9 November 1799), Napoleon seized French parliamentary and military power and subsequently became First Consul. With much of Europe quickly subdued, Napoleon was determined to break Portugal's alliance with Britain but when Portugal refused, France and Spain resorted to force. In 1801, a small French army entered the peninsula, joined forces with the Spanish under General Manuel de Godoy and marched against Portugal in the so-called War of the Oranges. The Franco/Spanish invasion force entered Portugal and, despite being rebuffed at the fortified city of Elvas, within eighteen days was in control of the whole country. The Portuguese Prince Regent, Dom João, was forced to accept the humiliating peace of Badajoz in which Portugal agreed to close its ports to British trade and at the same time grant commercial concessions to France. Portugal was also to hand over the long-disputed province of Olivenza to Spain and part of Brazil to France, and in addition she was to pay an indemnity to the victors.

During the next six years, while French influence in Bourbon Spain grew, Portugal navigated a course that enabled her to maintain a precarious state of neutrality without financially crippling herself by over-restricting trade.

In a series of victories, principally at Austerlitz (1805) and Jena and Auerstädt (1806), Napoleon, now Emperor, saw off the Third and Fourth Coalitions. With the defeat of the Russians at Friedland (1807), followed by the Treaty of Tilsit with Czar Alexander in July 1807, Napoleon was free to concentrate on the Iberian Peninsula and enforce his Continental System. This had been put in place to prevent Britain trading with Europe and therefore undermine her role as financial backer of the coalitions that had faced Napoleon for most of the

A young Napoleon as First Consul.

previous twelve years. Portugal and Sweden had, however, continued to trade with Britain, their most important partner, and ignored the Continental System. When Napoleon finally threatened Portugal, a reluctant Prince Regent was forced to concede and close Portuguese ports and sever ties with Britain, but at this stage he refused to detain English landowners and merchants or to seize their lands, goods and chattels.

Napoleon was determined to enforce the Continental System. To that end he negotiated the Treaty of Fontainebleau with Spain aiming to destroy the

Marshal Junot as a grenadier in the revolutionary army.

Portuguese government and promptly dispatched General Junot and a French army of 25,000 to invade Portugal. In this endeavour Junot was joined by three Spanish divisions. As the Franco-Spanish army marched, weak and mesmerized by the pace of events, the Portuguese government dithered and as a result offered little resistance to a second invasion. Consequently, Junot entered Lisbon on 30 November 1807 with ease, only to find that the Prince Regent and much of the nobility along with the most distinguished families had taken ship, fleeing to the Portuguese colony of Brazil with their own fleet and a Royal Navy escort, the latter to ensure the ships did not fall into French hands.

The French occupied much of the central part of the country and absorbed elements of the Portuguese army while disbanding others. Meanwhile, Spanish armies to the south occupied the Algarve and Oporto in the north.

While Junot consolidated the French presence in central Portugal, Napoleon had decided to remove the unpopular, corrupt and venal Bourbons from the Spanish throne. Under a pretext, he dispatched 100,000 *Grande Armée* veterans across the Pyrenees Mountains into north-eastern Spain and, having lured Charles VI to Bayonne, he forced him to give up the throne in favour of Napoleon's own brother Joseph.

The emperor had misjudged the mood of the people and, reeling from the heavy-handed insult, in 1808 Spanish temper and pride finally exploded at the outrage in the Dos de Mayo uprising. It was quickly and brutally suppressed in Madrid but had meanwhile spread to much of the country. At the same time, the Portuguese also revolted against their occupiers. In overreaching himself, Napoleon created a war that became his 'Spanish ulcer'. For the next six years the peninsula was a significant diversion of increasingly scarce French manpower and resources and ultimately contributed to his downfall.

The Spanish border fortress of Ciudad Rodrigo in the hands of the 'rebellious' Junta was soon a factor, effectively isolating the 4,000 French troops occupying its Portuguese counterpart, the fortress of Almeida, just 20 miles away. The local French commander General Loison sent messages demanding passage for a division and to establish communications with Marshal Bessières in Old Castile. The population of Ciudad Rodrigo opposed this move and had indeed already

Charles IV.

General Loison.

begun preparations to resist the imposition of a French occupation. General Loison's French emissaries were promptly driven out of the city along with French sympathizers.

The Junta at Ciudad Rodrigo began the work, as described in the previous chapter, to fortify the various substantial religious buildings as outworks to the city's main defences. Gangs of volunteer labour were belatedly sent to repair and update the city walls and a local militia was raised, numbering approximately 8,000 men.

The garrison of Ciudad Rodrigo received a small reinforcement of regular troops before, in mid-June 1808, the French, hoping to bluff the Spanish into surrendering the border defences of Fort Concepcion, offered to relieve the

Fort Concepcion, a small fortress on the border with Portugal, now restored as a hotel.

Last stand of the Spanish in the Dos de Mayo revolt in 1808.

garrison of their task. In the event the Spanish commander and his men, rather than surrender or fight, slipped away via a sally port and the French duly occupied the abandoned fort.

The British and the Peninsula

Even though the Royal Navy ruled the seas, a fact confirmed by the Battle of Trafalgar in 1805, Britain's army had been consistently unable to remain on mainland Europe, but His Majesty's government remained implacably opposed to Napoleon. The government sought to make use of the army and to that end General Wellesley assembled a force of 5,000 men at Cork for an expedition against the Spanish colonies. With the situation in the peninsula changing rapidly and Spain, the old enemy, now looking more like an ally and with Admiral Spencer's small naval and landing force already co-operating with the Spanish troops, Sir Arthur Wellesley's force, increased to 8,000, was tasked to sail to the Iberian Peninsula. According to Fortescue:[1]

> ... on the 30 of June Wellesley received his instructions ... Since the government's information as to the strength of the French was uncertain, Sir Arthur was to go forward to Coruna to ascertain the state of affairs both in Spain and Portugal; and, if he judged himself strong enough, when joined by Spencer's corps, to begin operations at once, he was authorised to do so.

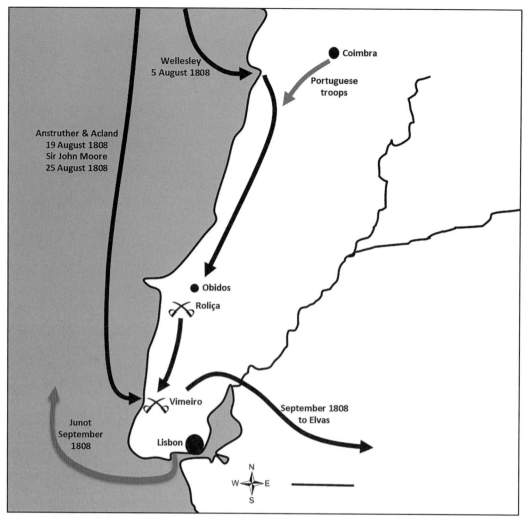

The 1808 campaign in Portugal.

If not, he was to wait, with permission of the Galician Junta, at Vigo, until ten thousand additional men could join him from England.

The scale of the expedition was steadily increased with brigades from the south of England being prepared to sail, with the addition of the 8,000 men of Sir John Moore's abortive expedition to Sweden once more available.

Having gathered information at Corunna and Oporto, Wellesley landed his force at Mondego Bay where disembarkation of his force began on 1 August. Ten days later a 15,000-strong force marched for Lisbon on the coast road, divided into six brigades. They clashed with French outposts at Óbidos before attacking and defeating Delaborde's outnumbered French troops at Roliça on 17 August.

In the meantime, a cautious General Burrard, who was senior to Wellesley, had arrived and knowing that General Junot was assembling his army 20 miles to the

Major General Arthur Wellesley.

north, forbade Sir Arthur to advance south to Lisbon. However, while awaiting the landing of the reinforcing brigades, Wellesley received word of the approach of General Junot to Vimeiro Hill on 21 August. The resulting French attacks were poorly coordinated, with the British general showing at this early stage his appreciation of good defensive ground. The hard-fought Battle of Vimeiro was a comprehensive defeat for the French, with Junot capitulating. During the fighting Sir Hew Dalrymple had arrived but allowed Wellesley to complete his victory. The resulting Convention of Cintra gave the French far more generous terms than they could have ever hoped for, in which Portugal was to be evacuated by the French and the defeated army returned to France by the Royal Navy, along with its guns and 'private property', which in reality was the loot it had accumulated in the normal manner of a French army of the day. At home in Britain, news of the Convention of Cintra caused an outcry of protest and resulted in an official inquiry, with both Dalrymple and Burrard being found culpable. Wellesley, however, who had opposed the agreement, was exonerated.

On his arrival Sir John Moore took command of the army, now numbering some 25,000, and marched in October 1808 to support the disparate Spanish armies who, after a series of successes such as at Baylen, had driven the French back across the River Ebro. Moore's army entered Spain via Almeida and Ciudad Rodrigo and would head east, planning to join the Spanish around Valladolid. In

Lieutenant General Sir John Moore.

the meantime, with news of the Convention of Cintra and Baylen, Napoleon resolved to address the situation in the peninsula in person and, gathering troops from garrisons across Europe, sent them marching west. These included three army corps and cavalry from Germany plus, of course, the Imperial Guard. Altogether Napoleon would raise the number of French troops under his command in Iberia to almost 200,000.

Captain Marbot, then on the staff of Marshal Lannes, illustrates the immediate revival of French military fortunes:

> This army of recruits, which Moncey had not dared to lead against the enemy, were set in motion by Lannes on the day of his arrival, and marched against the enemy with ardour. We came up with him on the following day, the 23rd, in front of Tudela, and after three hours' fighting the conquerors of Baylen were driven in, beaten, completely routed, and fled headlong towards Saragossa, leaving thousands of dead on the field. We captured a great many men, several colours, and all the artillery; a complete victory.

However, in the aftermath of the battle Marbot had what he described as 'one of the most terrible experiences of my military career.' He was selected to carry

Captain Marbot as a colonel, later in the war.

dispatches through hostile country to the emperor and experienced at first-hand the effectiveness of the guerrillas that did so much to paralyse French command in the peninsula.

Meanwhile, Napoleon had reached Madrid on 1 December and summoned the rebellious city the following day, but was twice rejected. To demonstrate French power, he attacked an outlying position on a dominating hill to the east. After further negotiation, the city surrendered and the French marched in on the 4th. Once in Madrid, Napoleon started to receive information regarding the advance of Moore's army who were, via four routes, converging on the city of Salamanca. Dispatches captured and handed to the British during December indicated that initially Napoleon believed that the British were marching back to Portugal, whereas Moore was actually marching north onto the plains of León. Napoleon, with more accurate information coming into his headquarters, decided that the British were the next threat to be removed.

Word arriving at Moore's headquarters that Napoleon, at the head of his army, had successfully crossed the Sierra de Guadarrama in full winter conditions precipitated the dreadful retreat to Corunna. The advance guards of the armies clashed east of the River Elsa and the British fell back across the bridge at Castro Gonzalo, but with Moore deciding not to offer battle, the discipline of his army, less the rearguards, started to crack.

Napoleon's army crossing the Sierra de Guadarrama.

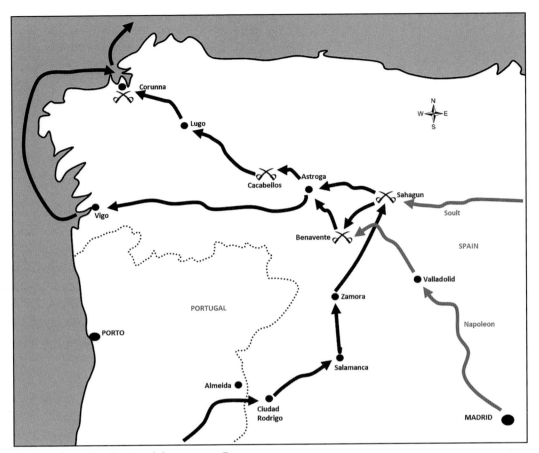

Advance into Spain and the retreat to Corunna.

Napoleon, however, having pursued the British as far as Astorga, received news that the Austrians were going to open hostilities. He promptly handed over the pursuit to Soult, clearly believing that it was only a matter of time before the British were destroyed and he returned to the affairs of state. In doing so it is widely believed that he missed an opportunity to inflict a decisive defeat on the British.

The retreat in front of Soult's force from the frozen plains of León over the snow-covered mountains, down into Galicia and on to Corunna was an epic of British military history. The army, despite all its disciplinary problems, came together in the defensive Battle of Corunna to administer a final check to the French as the army slipped away courtesy of the Royal Navy. All that remained of the British presence in the peninsula was General Cradock and 16,000 men in Lisbon.

Soult reorganized his army and prepared to invade northern Portugal. Eventually, with La Romana's Spanish army withdrawing east and his army defeating Portuguese forces in various engagements, the marshal occupied Oporto at the end of March 1809.

The death of Sir John Moore at Corunna.

The British Return

Having been exonerated by the inquiry, Wellington maintained a correspondence with Secretary of State for War Lord Castlereagh. On 7 March 1809, he wrote stating that 'I have always been of the opinion that Portugal might be defended whatever might be the result of the contest in Spain; and in the meantime, the measures for the defence of Portugal would be highly useful to the Spaniards in their contest with the French.'

He went on to say that he would need an army of 20,000 British soldiers including 4,000 cavalry, a reconstituted Portuguese army[2] and the Spaniards contributing by keeping large elements of the French armies fixed elsewhere in the peninsula. Based on this and with Austria occupying Napoleon's attention on the Danube, Castlereagh cajoled the Cabinet into agreeing to send a new expeditionary force with Sir Arthur Wellesley at its head, with the specific aim of defending Portugal.[3]

Meanwhile, with northern Portugal occupied, General Cradock marched his force north from Lisbon towards Oporto as soon as the season allowed. Wellesley, who arrived at Lisbon on 22 April 1809, joined the army at Coimbra on 2 May and set his first target, the liberation of Oporto. Arriving on the southern banks of the Douro opposite the city, he took Soult by surprise when the British slipped across the river and the marshal was forced to flee north, narrowly avoiding destruction of his army when Spanish commanders were slow to react and would not authorize the blowing of a bridge.[4]

Soult, the second member of Napoleon's marshalate defeated by Wellington in the peninsula.

Wellesley concluded his note to the Duke of Richmond 'I am now moving the army as fast as possible to the eastern frontier [of Portugal] by which a Corps of Victor has entered. I hope soon to be able to force them out also.'

Wellesley's Difficulties

At this early stage of the campaign Wellesley was already critical of the state of his army with discipline being a particular problem, writing 'The army behaved terribly ill. They are a rabble who cannot bear success any more than Sir John Moore's army could bear failure. I am endeavouring to tame them', and to Castlereagh: 'We are an excellent army on parade, an excellent one to fight but we are worse than an enemy in a country; and take my word for it, that either defeat or success would dissolve us.' These were prophetic words foreshadowing events in the aftermath of the sieges of Ciudad Rodrigo and Badajoz.

Another perennial problem in 1809 was supplying the army. Not only for the sake of discipline was Wellesley insistent that looting would not be tolerated, but also for good supportive relations among the allied peoples across whose lands and livelihoods the British campaigned. Solving this problem was exacerbated by the army being perennially short of cash with which to purchase food and pay the soldiers who, often months in arrears, despite flogging and hangings regularly resorted to theft. It became even more difficult to persuade merchants to accept Treasury promissory notes in return for supplies. Even when such supplies were available, moving them to the army was another constant problem. The roads in Portugal and generally across the peninsula were described as 'execrable' and unusable for long periods from autumn through to spring. In addition, there was also a transport shortage in the form of bullock carts and mules. On 22 May 1809 Wellesley wrote: 'I cannot be certain of the subsistence of this army, unless the Portuguese Governor will let us have 300 or 400 good mules, with saddles and drivers. It is ridiculous that in Portugal that number cannot be found.'

Clearly Sir Arthur had much work to do to keep his army in hand and forge the weapon that would eventually see the French driven out of the Iberian Peninsula. Provost staff and developing a reasonably effective commissariat to reduce looting were early tasks but lack of money in his military chest was a perennial difficulty.

The Talavera Campaign

Having seen off Soult, another marshal, Claude Victor, was approaching Castelo Branco with his corps marching along the River Tagus and was only 70 miles from Madrid. In addition, King Joseph and Marshal Jourdan were within supporting distance. The British, numbering 21,000, marched east along the Tagus to join General Cuesta's Spanish army near Almaraz but the allies missed an opportunity to deal the French a severe blow against Victor's exposed corps. Nonetheless, Sir Arthur Wellesley crossed the border from Portugal into Spain on 2 July with the aim of co-operating with Spanish generals Cuesta and Venegas in an attack on Madrid, which was now King Joseph Bonaparte's capital. The king and Marshal Jourdan, however, had plans for a counter-offensive with the aim of a renewed invasion of Portugal by Marshal Soult's corps.

On 20 July 1809, Wellesley joined General Cuesta and advanced to attack Marshal Victor's corps near Talavera and came into contact with French cavalry vedettes and infantry outposts two days later. Victor, in the face of pressure, withdrew and Cuesta followed him for some 40 miles east. At Torrijos, however, the Spanish were confronted by Joseph Bonaparte's army of 46,000 men, in front of which Cuesta promptly withdrew to link up with Wellesley at Talavera.

On the evening of 26 July, the allied armies were positioned on the north bank of the River Tagus at Talavera. The Spanish were located around the city and on the ground to the north. Further beyond Talavera a ridge of high ground became Wellesley's main position stretching as far north as the dominating Cerro de Medellin. It was a classic Wellingtonian defensive position.

Victor attacked the Cerro de Medellin during the evening of 27 July, just before dark, with General Ruffin's division and reached the crest of the key feature taking the British by surprise, causing consternation and some confusion;

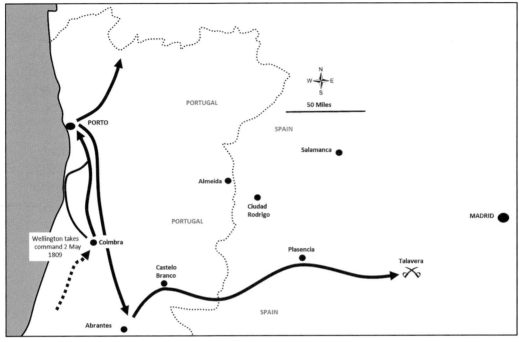

Wellesley's 1809 campaign.

The Battle of Talavera, 27–28 July 1809.

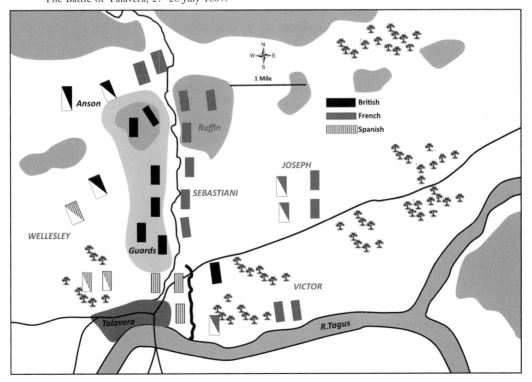

that is before General Hill deployed a reserve brigade to counter-attack and drive the French from the Cerro de Medellin.

The following day, Marshal Victor again ordered Ruffin's division on to the Cerro de Medellin, with fire from a grand battery of some fifty artillery pieces in support. The British were, however, expecting the attack and were lying down below the crest line and therefore less vulnerable to the French artillery. As the French infantry reached the top of the hill, the British battalions stood up, volleyed and charged, driving Ruffin's men down the hill and across the stream at its base.

A pause in the battle followed while Joseph Bonaparte held a council of war and Victor, keen for a victory, pressed for a resumption of the attack. Consequently, columns attacked the ridge at its lowest point only to be driven back down the slope after some bitter fighting. The British followed too far and were in trouble as the French turned to renew their attack in what was a dangerous moment in the battle. Wellesley brought up reserves, behind which the infantry was able to reform, and the counter-attack was defeated. At the same time yet another attack on the Cerro de Medellin was seen off, along with an attempt to outflank the British to the right.

Sensing a turn in fortunes, Wellesley launched his cavalry but a hidden gully brought them to a halt as the leading troopers plunged headlong into it. After this the French assaults waned and Joseph's army withdrew during the night, abandoning several artillery pieces.

These few words cannot do justice to what was undoubtedly one of Wellesley's most hard-won battles. Although the French losses were in excess of 7,000 and the British just over 5,000, the latter were from a much smaller force than the overall French number. Consequently, when Wellesley realized that Marshal Soult, with some 30,000 men, was manoeuvring to cut his army off from Portugal, he was forced to order a precipitate withdrawal back across the border.

When news of the victory reached home Sir Arthur Wellesley was promptly ennobled as Viscount Wellington of Talavera; 'Wellington' being a title suggested by his brother in order to avoid confusion with the existing title of Lord Wellesley.

Notes

1. J.W. Fortescue, *The British Army and the Peninsular War*, Vol. 1 (Leonaur edition, 2016).
2. Marshal William Beresford was busy reforming the Portuguese army based at the Royal Palace of Maffra outside Lisbon. Part of the palace is still the Portuguese Infantry School.
3. Elizabeth Longford, *Wellington: 'The Years of the Sword'* (Weidenfeld & Nicolson, 1969).
4. Wellesley to the Duke of Richmond, 22 May 1809.

Chapter Three

Preparations for the 1810 Invasion of Portugal

In August 1809 the news of Napoleon's victory at Wagram over the Austrians, the collapse of the Fifth Coalition and the inept and disastrous British Expedition Force to Walcheren reached the army in the peninsula. They correctly feared that it would be their turn next as Napoleon, unopposed elsewhere in Europe, would be able to turn the might of France to crushing and finally ejecting the British from the peninsula.

The emperor at first planned to lead the campaign, which would begin in December 1809. There were, however, domestic considerations for Napoleon and France that needed to be addressed that both diverted the emperor and delayed the invasion of Portugal by six months. At home, in order to create a dynasty Napoleon needed an heir but the Empress Joséphine, his wife of fourteen years, had been unable to provide him with a child. Consequently, Joséphine agreed to a divorce which took place on 10 January 1810 and is described as a 'grand but solemn social occasion' during which the couple bizarrely read statements of devotion to each other! The divorce freed Napoleon, who could no longer be regarded as a 'Corsican upstart' in the palaces and courts of Europe, to re-marry. The Treaty of Schönbrunn signed in October 1809, though harshly imposed on Austria, proclaimed a mutual friendship. To cement the 'alliance' Napoleon was to marry a 'political chattel': the 19-year-old Marie Louise, Archduchess of Austria, and a great-niece of Marie Antoinette. The marriage took place during March 1810, but Napoleon needed to win over his new empress and get on with the business of having an heir to his throne.

Marie Louise, Napoleon's second wife.

In Europe, at the zenith of his power, Napoleon as de facto leader of the continent also had political imperatives to address: his Continental System, designed to exclude British trade, needed advancing; relations with the Papacy required nurturing; and the Code Napoleon settling into annexed and subjugated territories. Wellington, however, wrote of this wider European situation in early April 1810: 'Recent transactions in Holland show that it is all hollow within, and that it is so inconsistent with the wishes, the interests, and even the existence of civilised society, that he cannot trust even his brothers to carry it into existence.'

All this meant that Napoleon would remain in Paris and hand over the task of dealing with the British in the peninsula ('driving the leopard into the sea') to his brother King Joseph and André Masséna, former smuggler[1] but now newly-ennobled as the 1st Prince d'Essling.

Ney's First 'Siege' of Ciudad Rodrigo

In the autumn of 1809 Jourdan had been replaced by Marshal Soult as King Joseph's military commander and was promptly dispatched to Andalucía to bring that wealthy province into Napoleonic Spain. On the back of a string of successes in what was undoubtedly a bleak time for the Spanish, Soult ordered Marshal Ney's weak VI Corps to march from Salamanca and summoned Ciudad Rodrigo, the belief at this stage clearly being that the Spanish would be demoralized and surrender the city without the necessity of a siege.

Ney assembled the 12,000 men of his corps from its widely-spread cantonments and marched the 60 miles from Salamanca, starting on 8 February 1810. They left with ten days' rations in their knapsacks and on mules, with just forty cartridges per man in their cartouche boxes, arriving on the plains before Ciudad Rodrigo on 11 February. The following day Ney, having sent the governor a letter under a flag of truce, formally summoned the fortress with the words: 'All the fortresses of Andalucía have opened their gates to his Catholic Majesty ... You are reasonable Monsieur le Governor to realise that nothing can delay these results in the future. It is in this context that I beseech you to give me assurances in response to my letter.'

The aging but fiery Spanish garrison commander of Irish ancestry, General Herrasti, roundly rejected Ney's terms with these words: 'I have sworn to defend this place for the legitimate sovereign, Don Fernando VII, until the last drop of my blood: this I am determined to do along with the entire garrison and the inhabitants. This is the only proposition I am able to make to you.'

With no easy resolution Ney rode around the city with his chief engineer *Chef de Bataillon* Couche on a reconnaissance. Lacking, however, either the manpower or resources for a formal siege and only having the normal complement of field artillery, he had to content himself with siting a handful of guns and howitzers on the Greater Teson and opening fire to underline the French threat.

General Andrés Pérez de Herrasti.

Don Julián Sánchez or *El Charro* ('The Cowboy').

The Spanish artillery replied engaging both enemy guns and infantry, while the mounted guerrillas (one of the better-organized and equipped bands that fluctuated between 60 and 600 men) under Don Julián Sánchez took on Ney's cavalry. That night the French howitzers fired up to 100 shells on the town, starting a number of blazes, while their infantry pressed forward to be met by Spanish musket-fire from the walls.

The following morning an embarrassed Ney, realizing that Spanish determination outfaced his resources, withdrew back towards Salamanca having suffered some casualties, believed by the Spanish to have been 'significant'.

The result of this precipitate winter foray was for the French to consume valuable food, lose equally scarce mules and the goodwill of the soldiers of VI Corps, who had taken part in a manifestly hopeless venture in poor weather conditions. The exercise had also revealed the parlous state of Ney's corps, which clearly needed reinforcement before it could take to the field with any hope of success. For the Spanish, however, Ney's appearance before the walls had been a call to arms. If anyone had doubted that war would once again come to Ciudad Rodrigo, these doubts had been well and truly dispelled. Preparations to hold the city against what would surely be a more determined French attempt were soon under way.

Preparations for the 1810 French Invasion of Portugal

On 16 April 1810 the aging, unhealthy and reluctant Marshal Masséna was appointed to command the Army of Portugal, replacing General Junot. The marshal was suffering from a partial loss of sight due to a hunting accident with Napoleon and a respiratory problem resulting from a fall from his horse during the Battle of Wagram around Lobau Island the previous year. Masséna, however, politely nicknamed 'the Spoilt Child of Victory', had a record of successful independent commands which many of the younger or more junior marshalate simply did not. No matter how reluctant, he was the man for the job as far as Napoleon was concerned and the emperor bulldozed aside all of Masséna's arguments.

According to Captain Marbot, then a middle-ranking aide-de-camp (ADC) on Masséna's staff, another reason was that he justifiably feared that his subordinates Marshals Ney and Junot would resent him being placed in command over them and would be reluctant to follow his orders. Junot had, of course, been the former commander of the Army of Portugal. This concern was not unfounded or without precedent: Napoleon, like most dictators, aimed to divide and rule and thus he kept his marshalate competing with each other and did little to address the issue of co-operation. Nor, of course, did he like them to be too independently

André Masséna,
1st Duc de Rivoli and
Prince d'Essling.

successful. The emperor, however, having promised his best commander the required numbers and that he would be 'lacking nothing in supplies', Masséna, still in need of rest and recovery from the fall from his horse during the 1809 campaign, eventually agreed to one last campaign. However, Marbot wrote:

> Although the Minister of War had assured the Marshal that everything was ready for the coming campaign in the peninsula, it was nothing of the kind, and the commander-in-chief had to stay a fortnight in Valladolid looking after the departure of the troops and the transport of stores and ammunition.

The number of troops that Napoleon had considered necessary when he was thinking of leading the campaign had also reduced from a reinforcement of 100,000 men under the emperor himself to less than 50,000 additional troops.

Marbot considered that this was largely the emperor's overconfidence, which along with other sundry delays, many of which were the result of positively casual command, fatally undermined the 1810 French invasion of Portugal. There is, however, another view and that is that Napoleon wanted the campaign only to cross into Portugal once the harvest was in, otherwise the troops and subsequently the occupied people would starve. Whatever the reason, well into the Iberian campaign season Masséna eventually arrived at Salamanca on 15 May, accompanied by his young mistress, Henriette Lebreton, the wife of another officer, dressed fetchingly in hussar style, as an 'additional aide-de-camp'. Madame Lebreton's presence was a continual source of strain between Masséna and his senior subordinates, who disliked the marshal campaigning with his mistress.[2]

A portrait believed to be Henriette Leberton or 'Madame X'.

On his arrival Masséna made the situation clear to his headquarters staff: 'Gentlemen, I am here against my own wish: I begin to find myself too old and too weary for active service.'[3] Not only that, his senior subordinates were already chaffing, despite some fine words of loyalty, at having to answer not to Napoleon but to a senior marshal. In short, they were resentful and disloyal from the start: Marshal Ney (VI Corps, 30,000 men) and Masséna were old enemies; Junot (VIII Corps, 17,000 men) was 'furiously jealous' at being replaced as commander of the Army of Portugal; and Masséna disliked General Reynier (II Corps, 14,000 men).

Arriving in Valladolid Masséna, despite Napoleon's promises, found that planning was far from entirely in his hands. The emperor at their final interview in Paris had said 'You will lack nothing in resources . . . You will be absolute master, and you will make your own preparations to open the campaign' but on the contrary, Napoleon was attempting to direct the campaign from Paris. With, however, much of the country between the Pyrenees and Salamanca dominated by Spanish guerrillas, this proved to be from first to last impossible. Instructions from the emperor were typically out of date by the time he wrote them and even more so by the time they arrived at Masséna's headquarters, if indeed they reached their recipient at all.

In planning the 1810 invasion of Portugal, French options boiled down to three choices. Firstly, there was the central route from Spain into Portugal via the road to the south of the Serra da Estrella; the one that had been used by Junot during the 1807 invasion. The problem here was that the country across which the French armies traversed had been comprehensively stripped of food and resources. As an already poor region, after just two harvests it had yet to recover from the depredations of the passage of an army that lived off the country. A renewed advance on this route following Junot's experience was unattractive and would doubtless lead to near starvation of the Army of Portugal and was consequently rejected by Napoleon and Masséna.

In contrast to Ciudad Rodrigo and Almeida, the southerly route via Spanish-held Badajoz and the Portuguese fortress of Elvas would also require difficult sieges against two significant defended cities that dominated the roads in the area. In addition, the country around the River Guadiana was unhealthy and would inevitably weaken the invader's divisions. That left the northerly route between the River Douro and the Serra da Estrela, which not only had yet to be completely denuded of food but was only guarded by the second-rate Spanish fortress of Ciudad Rodrigo and its equally weak Portuguese twin of Almeida. It was argued that an army with a proper siege train would not take long to reduce these if working at pace. Once taken, even though the four roads passable to artillery that radiated from Almeida were terrible and through difficult country, this axis of advance offered the easiest and quickest route across the Spanish frontier into Portugal. This was despite Wellington ordering the destruction of one of the

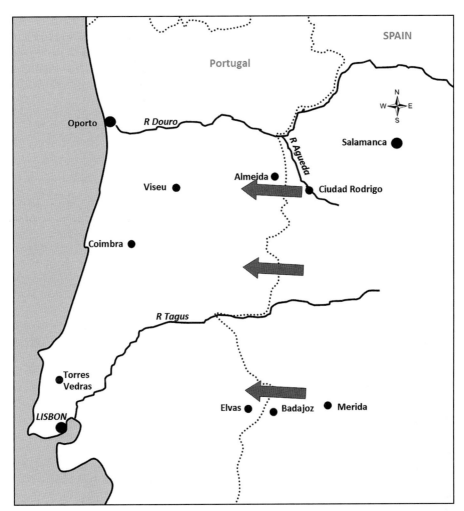

The invasion routes.

roads, the Estrada Nova (New Road), the denial of which was completed in February 1810.

Another factor in concentrating on the northern route was that Masséna with an army numbering 65,000 simply did not have enough men to launch an attack on a subsidiary axis, as Wellington feared. If the marshal had had the total of 100,000 promised by Napoleon, a corps of 30,000 south of the Tagus could have made all the difference between failure and success.

Despite the northern route's obvious attractions, the French, with some largely ineffective deception measures, did their best to keep Wellington having to cover all options for some time. These measures focused on the two potential southerly axes of advance, where General Reynier's II Corps was active on the approaches to Badajoz, where nearby he defeated General Pedro la Romana's army at La Roca. This development required the Spanish to be extracted by the arrival of General Sir Rowland Hill's 2nd Division.

General Pedro la Romana.

Spanish guerrilla.

As ever, Wellington was well-informed as to the location, numbers and movements of French troops and saw through the deception as the enemy assembled stores and men around Salamanca. Ciudad Rodrigo, the first obstacle on Masséna's northern road into Portugal, was transparently likely to be his first objective but the question of whether it would be bypassed and dealt with at leisure remained. Preparations for a siege of even a second-rate fortress and subsequently the relatively small fortress of Almeida were, however, obvious to the British exploring officers, to their numerous agents and the Spanish guerrillas. This was particularly so once the French siege train was on the move. As early as 23 March, Wellington noted: 'They are bringing a battering train into Spain from France, which looks like an intention to go regularly to work.'[4]

Well-informed and while still covering the southern routes with Marshal Beresford's Portuguese command, Viscount Wellington was able to start the process of concentrating the bulk of his force to oppose an invasion by Marshal Masséna on the northern route.

The French siege train of some fifty pieces of heavy artillery along with all the ammunition and equipment needed to move, serve and maintain the guns had earlier in the year been assembled at Burgos and Valladolid. During the second week of March it began to be moved painfully slowly across poor roads with a large escort to be concentrated at Salamanca. Wellington could be reasonably sure that the French would not open operations until it was in place and was able to keep his own army at rest and adjust his deployment base according to the stream of information coming in to his headquarters.

Another indicator to Wellington's agents of French intent was the establishing of magazines and the construction of a dozen very large ovens at Salamanca for the baking of bread to fill the haversacks of Masséna's invading army. The hard school of experience had shown that living off the land to the extent that French armies normally did in northern Europe did not work in the peninsula and that Masséna would have to at least supply a proportion of the Army of Portugal's

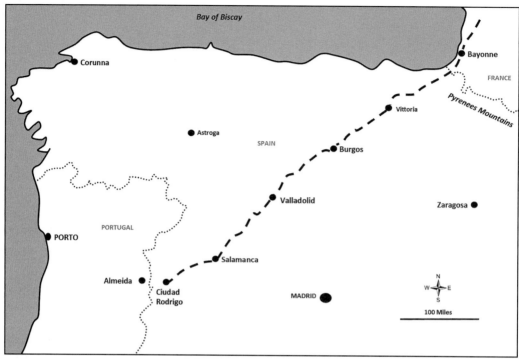

The Army of Portugal's lines of communication from France.

rations. To that end, according to French returns in May 1810, there was enough food to feed Ney's VI Corps for six weeks and the cavalry, artillery and their mounts for a month. This was quite generous for one of Napoleon's armies and would at least give the marshal's men a head start, allowing them to remain concentrated for longer and obviating the necessity of splitting up to forage from the outset.

While the full panoply of preparations for siege and invasion was being played out at Salamanca, General Junot's 12,000-strong VIII Corps was off to the northern flank to take over the besieging of the minor fortress of Astorga. In another underestimation of Spanish resolve when behind walls, General Loison's division, again lacking all but his normal field artillery, had failed to cow Astorga's garrison into submission. Initially Junot had no siege artillery either, so all he could do was properly invest the place and prepare for the arrival of eighteen heavy guns from Valladolid. It wasn't until 22 April 1810 that Astorga fell.

Meanwhile, Ney had pushed most of his two divisions forward towards Ciudad Rodrigo in a half-hearted attempt to blockade the city. All he achieved was to denude a vital piece of country of the remaining available food before the campaign had begun.

The month-long siege of Astorga and Junot's subsequent march south to Salamanca delayed the concentration of the Army of Portugal. Not only that, but Reynier's II Corps was still to the south. In consequence, according to Marbot: 'The marshal wasted three more weeks at Salamanca waiting for General

The Romano-medieval walls of Astorga at the site of the French breach.

The siege of Astorga.

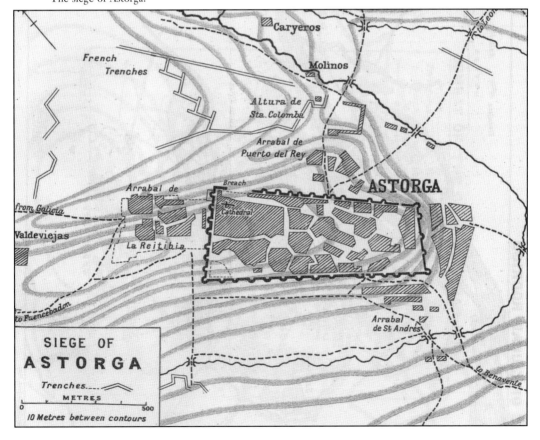

SIEGE OF
ASTORGA

Trenches
METRES
0   500
10 Metres between contours

Reynier's corps to be in position to the south. These delays, while hurtful to us, were all in favour of the English.'

What Marbot is alluding to here is that the sundry delays in beginning the campaign allowed Wellington time to develop the Lines of Torres Vedras, begun in the autumn of 1809. They started out as a defended embarkation point west of Lisbon and a single line of hilltop redoubts across the peninsula between the sea and the Douro north of Lisbon. In the additional time available, the engineers and gangs of Portuguese labourers developed the hills around Torres Vedras into a formidable double line of defences; all produced while shrouded by a highly-effective blanket of operational security. The existence of the lines was ultimately almost as much of a surprise to Wellington's own army as to the French.

In early May 1810, Ney's VI Corps started pushing its outposts forward towards the northern side of Ciudad Rodrigo. On 12 May a staff officer was sent to General Herrasti with a summons promising a safe conduct to the garrison and population in exchange for a prompt surrender and a change of loyalty to King Joseph. The reasonable words were, however, followed by the almost obligatory threat to the garrison:

> On the contrary, if you refuse all accommodation, His Excellency, whose arms have always been crowned with success ... will act with all the force at his disposal, and in a few days, he will reduce the fortress that you will be unable to defend and the garrison that you will be unable to save.

According to Herrasti, his loyal and bold response was 'Since the answer I have given previously is final, it should be understood that no more representatives will be admitted in the future under a flag of truce. Now we have to talk only with guns.'

After a protracted and unseasonably wet spring, it wasn't until the last week of May that Marshal Masséna was able to fully set his army in motion heading west towards Ciudad Rodrigo, the Portuguese border and its border fortifications. Instructions from Napoleon in Paris were 'that the invasion of Portugal must be conducted methodically and without haste, after preliminary capture of Ciudad Rodrigo and Almeida.'[5] Captain Marbot commented on the significance of Ciudad Rodrigo from the French perspective:

> The last Spanish town towards the Portuguese frontier is Ciudad Rodrigo, a fortress, if the strength of its works alone be considered, of the second class, but having great importance owing to its position between Spain and Portugal, in a district with few roads, and those very difficult for large guns and the apparatus of a siege train. It was, however, absolutely necessary that the French should get possession of the place. With this resolve, Masséna left Salamanca ... and caused Rodrigo to be invested by Ney's corps, while Junot covered the operations from the attacks of an Anglo/Portuguese army,

Marshal Ney, commander of VI Corps.

which was encamped a few leagues from us, near the Portuguese fortress of Almeida, under Lord Wellington.

Notes

1. Allegedly members of the marshalate referred to Masséna, behind his back of course, as the 'Old Smuggler'. Other nicknames were more flattering, such as 'Masséna of the flashing eyes' but this was no longer the case as remarked by several observers, nor would he be 'the Spoilt Child of Victory'.

2. Henriette Lebreton (née Renique), was born at Maubeuge on 23 April 1780 and died at Saint Amand-les-Eaux on 31 August 1836. She was allegedly married to an officer of the 27th Dragoons (a former adjutant of Masséna's), who she abandoned to accompany the marshal, a notorious womanizer, on campaign. Her family today insist that she was not married to this officer. Aged between 18 and 20 and a former ballet dancer, she was known to the army as 'Madame X' and *la poule à Masséna*, variously described as being dressed as a hussar or a dragoon officer, but as an additional ADC (he already had fourteen) she may well have been dressed in the specially-tailored white hussar-style uniform of Masséna's other ADCs. This, of course, added insult to injury as far as the aides were concerned.

3. Sir Charles Oman, *A History of the Peninsular War*, Vol. X (Clarendon Press).

4. Letter to Craufurd, Light Division.

5. J.W. Fortescue, *The British Army and the Peninsular War*, Vol. 3 (Leonaur edition, 2016).

Chapter Four

Barba del Puerco

The village with the unlikely name of Barba del Puerco (Beard of the Pig, now Puerto Seguro) was the scene of one of the highly-celebrated incidents in the history of the 95th Rifles. The action below the village in the so-called Valley of the Eagles, through which in wintertime the River Águeda thunders, took place in mid-March 1810 while Marshal Masséna's Army of Portugal was forming.

With Wellington's army in winter quarters, the Light Brigade, still at that stage a part of the 3rd Division, had in early January been deployed to the Portuguese frontier forward of its border fortresses Almeida and the nearby Spanish Real Fuerte de la Concepción (Fort Concepcion). While much of the army was more comfortably housed in Portuguese towns, life for Brigadier General Craufurd's light infantrymen was less comfortable. Captain Leach records that the division took up billets in the scattered villages of 'Figuera, Mata de Lobos (Wood of the Wolves), Escallion, Escaigo, etc.':

> Deep snow fell soon after we had taken up our new quarters, which rendered the otherwise miserable desolate villages forlorn. Coursing and shooting were our chief employments by day, and at night we either whiffed away cigars over some Douro wine, and speculated on the campaign which was soon expected to commence …
>
> To detail the manner in which we killed time every day during the dreary winter months, some weeks of which we were nearly snowed up in our hovels, and in the poorest villages in the Peninsula, would be nearly a repetition of what I have just stated.

Leach concludes his reminiscences of winter quarters in this part of the border area with observations on the local people who he thought were 'the most wretched, dirty, idle, ignorant, priest-ridden peasantry anywhere to be found.'

Forward some 5 miles across the large granite boulder-covered area occupied by Craufurd's battalions is the bridge at Barba del Puerco. It is a 100-yard-long Roman structure and was one of the few crossings of the Águeda north of Ciudad Rodrigo, in this case where the road from the French-held San Felices de los Gallegos descends steeply down into the Valley of the Eagles and up again towards the frontier. At this stage, the 1st King's German Legion (KGL) Hussars were under command of the Light Brigade who mounted a string of piquets and

Valley of the Eagles looking down on the River Águeda.

vedettes to keep watch on the river line, including at the bridge at Barba del Puerco.

The state of quiescence did not last and Barba del Puerco became possibly the most active point on the Light Brigade's long front during the late winter of 1809/10. When Ney's VI Corps moved forward to summon Ciudad Rodrigo, Marchand's division had been pushed forward to San Felices de los Gallegos and the Águeda as a covering force. On 16 February, a column of Macune's brigade marched down from San Felices to the bridge; however, they did not cross and withdrew the following day. This was probably all a part of Ney's demonstration of force and it was clear to Wellington that a new more active phase was developing in his northern area.

This impression was confirmed on 27 February when about 200 French troops chased a patrol of riflemen away from the bridge and beyond Barba del Puerco. The French remained in possession of the village and looted the place before Captain Creagh's company of the 1st 95th Rifles was dispatched to reconnoitre the village and ended up skirmishing with the French. He was joined by Captain Leach's company and another was sent forward in support. On the following day Leach, in sending patrols forward, found that the enemy had withdrawn from the

Captain Jonathan Leach, 1st Battalion, 95th Rifles.

Brigadier General Robert Craufurd when serving with the 60th North Americans.

village and he subsequently posted a piquet down in the valley where their French equivalent patrolled only yards away across the river.

It was the job of the piquets to observe, report and delay; not to get involved in a fight that would overwhelm them. Oman describes the chain of outposts established by Craufurd as 'trembling like a spider's web' at the first touch of a French boot, enabling prompt and appropriate action.

Brigadier Craufurd's brigade, now elevated to the status of a division,[1] was covering some 40 miles of front on the River Águeda and the smaller River Azaba with widely-scattered detachments. With a division totalling just 3,000 men, he was facing VI Corps now 30,000 strong and in addition he was also responsible for maintaining communication with Ciudad Rodrigo. Being the only part of Wellington's army in the north in contact with the enemy, this required a re-deployment of the Light Division, with the area between Ciudad Rodrigo and Almeida being the main effort.

Lieutenant Harry Smith of the 1st 95th describes one of the ways in which such a long frontage was covered:

At this period General Craufurd had officers at two or three of the most advanced vedettes where there were beacons, who had orders to watch the enemy with their telescopes, and, in case of any movement to report or fire the beacon. I was on this duty in a remote spot on the extreme left of our

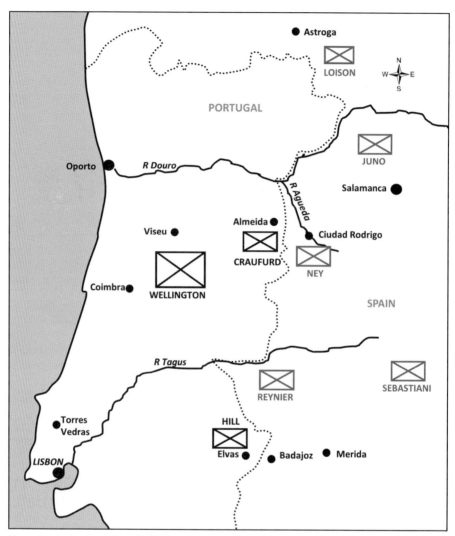

Opposing deployments in early 1810.

posts. The vedette was from the 1st Hussars [KGL] piquet. These men would often observe a patrol or body of enemy with the naked eye which was barely discernible through a telescope, so practised were they and watchful.

There were, however, only three bridges below Ciudad Rodrigo of which Barba del Puerco was one but the rivers were fordable at no less than fifteen points across the front of the Light Division and north to the Águeda's confluence with the Douro. Consequently, it was the duty of the KGL Hussars' patrols to monitor the depth of the Águeda every morning and inform Craufurd of the viability of the fords. With, however, the first half of 1810 being particularly wet it was not often that the Light Division had to stretch its resources to cover the more marginal or remote fords.

As a result of the increasing enemy activity on his long front, Craufurd withdrew the infantry piquet from Barba del Puerco and replaced it with a cavalry piquet and vedette down at the bridge. However, probably as a result of observation or intelligence,[2] he ordered the deployment of a strong force of riflemen to return to Barba del Puerco on 8 March. Before this could be put into effect, on 9 March Macune's brigade, supported by a couple of squadrons of cavalry, seized the bridge from the 1st KGL Hussars. The two French regiments, 6th Light and 69th Line, forced the German cavalry to withdraw southwards before themselves retiring to San Felices, again taking from Barba del Puerco all the food and goods of any worth. This operation has been characterized as a French reconnaissance in force.

By 13 March Craufurd had redeployed the 1st 95th Rifles. He dispatched one wing of four companies under Lieutenant Colonel Sidney Beckwith forward to Barba del Puerco, the other wing to Villar de Ciervo and the remaining two companies to Escalhão and Almofala (Leach's) to cover the fords. Consequently, where there had been a state of live and let live, there was now a strong presence and a properly-organized system of piquets. For the riflemen, this meant a regular turn of duty down onto the steep-sided gorge-like valley. While two companies rested in reserve, two were deployed. One was detached to piquet a ford to the south of the village and another was responsible for observing the French and

A KGL Hussars.

A fully-accoutred rifleman of the 95th in marching order.

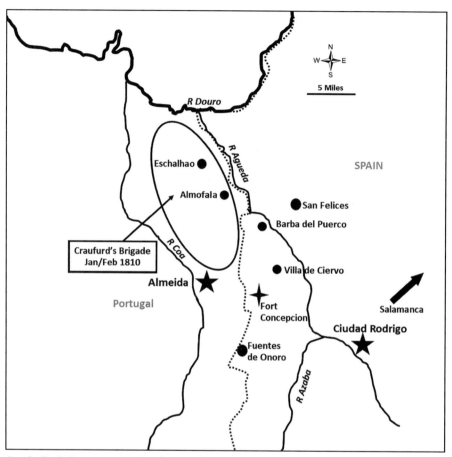

Craufurd's deployment on the border, March 1810.

confronting any incursion across the Águeda on the bridge at Barba del Puerco (Pass of San Felices).

A note in Lieutenant Simmons' book indicates that the Rifles were not entirely isolated, with a Spanish piquet of about fifty men to their right. For liaison purposes Captain O'Hare had posted a corporal and two riflemen with them.

For piquet duty, the regulations under which the Rifles operated[3] stated that 'The strength of the pickets [*sic*] must in great measure depend on the ground it is intended they should occupy, the distance or proximity of the enemy and the importance that may be attached to the post to which they are intended to give security.'

The strength of the company on duty at this point in the war was typically around sixty. Pairs of sentries would be deployed along the riverbank at likely crossing-points but when the river was high and unfordable a single pair guarded the bridge; according to Lieutenant Simmons they were hidden in rocks some 15 yards from the bridge. He noted 'we had to ... place our sentries in the different intricate pathways, and to post them in the dark in order to deceive our enemy and take them off before daylight.' Rifleman (later Bugler) Green is the most detailed authority on the deployment of elements of the outlying piquet further up the hill: 'a Corporal and six men were posted in the night about half way down the hill, and a sergeant and twelve men on top' of the steeply-rising ground of the Valley of the Eagles. A duty subaltern or piquet officer was responsible for visiting and relieving sentries throughout his period of duty and Simmons mentions an 'officers' tent'. Presumably this would have been pitched somewhere on the slope to minimize the distance between him, the sentries and elements of the outlying piquet. While the officers may have had the luxury of a tent in a static situation, the ordinary riflemen would typically build rudimentary shelters among the rocks where they could rest out of the worst of the weather, but they would be fully accoutred and ready for action at a moment's notice.

The inlying piquet, consisting of the remainder of the company (approximately forty men), was located in a small chapel on the eastern edge of the village several hundred yards behind the sergeant's part of the outlying piquet. Under its captain, most of this group would be unaccoutred, but with their weapons and equipment always at hand and the men ready to support the outlying piquet within minutes. Simmons recorded that:

> The French had a piquet of seventy men on the opposite side of the mountain on a level with ours. On this side we for some time were in the habit of looking at each other with only about half a mile in a direct line between us. They now and then tried to pick some of our men off, but their shots never took effect.

The fact that it takes a good twenty-five minutes to descend steeply on a rough track from the village to the bridge by day gives an indication of how unusually spread out the piquets were and that any engagement of an enemy force by the inlying piquet would have taken place about halfway up the hill.

Major Napier of the 52nd Light Infantry states that thanks to Craufurd's system, the other two companies in the village were expected to react quickly:

> ... seven minutes sufficed for the division to get under arms in the middle of the night, and a quarter of an hour, night or day, to bring it in order of battle to its alarm-posts, with baggage loaded and assembled at a convenient distance to the rear. And this not upon a concerted signal, nor as a trial, but on all occasions.

As proved to be the case at Barba del Puerco, this was no casual claim!

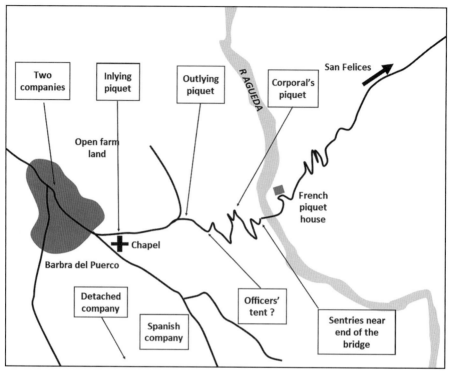

The deployment of Beckwith's wing of the 1st 95th Rifles at Barba del Puerco.

Barba del Puerco today, but despite its new name of Puerto Seguro, it feels that little has changed.

The fact that Craufurd's men with increasing French activity were now fully alert and were well and truly shaken out of the mentality of winter quarters is illustrated by an exchange recorded by Second Lieutenant Kincaid:

> The chief of the 1st German Hussars[4] meeting our commandant one morning: 'Well Colonel,' says our gallant German in broken English, 'how do you do?' 'Oh, tolerably well, thank you, considering that I am obliged to sleep with one eye open.' 'Mine Gott,' says the other, 'I never sleeps at all!'

During their time at Barba del Puerco the local priest or padre came under suspicion. Kincaid recorded that:

> The Padre of the village, it appeared, was a sort of vicar of Bray, who gave information to both sides so long as accounts remained pretty equally balanced between them, but when the advance of the French Army for the subjugation of Portugal became a matter of certainty, he immediately chose that which seemed to be strongest, and it was not ours.

He would be plied with grog[5] by the subalterns and 'he invariably fancied himself the only sober man of the party.' It is supposed that the lack of sober officers was reported to the French in San Felices to their ultimate ruin!

By 19 March General Ferey's brigade of Loison's division had taken over the French outposts on the river line and was tasked to attack on a miserable night with two battalions each of the 66th and 82nd Line regiments along with a detachment of the Hanoverian Legion. The water thundering down the gorge of the Águeda covered their approach down the steep and rough track to the bridge.[6] To help, there was no moon and the added cover of rain. Consequently, they moved unheard down the zigzag track to the bridge and no doubt wearing their dark-coloured greatcoats to hide the white of their breeches and the front of their tunics helped. In a letter from Ney to General Junot the marshal explained that the mission of this 2,000-strong force was 'to disperse the enemy's advanced posts on the Águeda and push on as far as possible to Almeida.' It was during this period that Ney hoped Masséna would ignore instructions from Paris and bypass Ciudad Rodrigo, attack the lesser fortress of Almeida and press on with the invasion of Portugal. A successful advance would be a way of demonstrating that it was possible, if not actually forcing the point.

Meanwhile, across the valley to the British piquet all seemed to be routine and quiet. One of the other subaltern officers, Lieutenant Simmons, was out checking the sentries:

> I crawled over the bridge to the French side to see if I could see their sentries or observe if any of them were coming near the bridge, but saw nothing and returned up the mountain to the tent pitched for the convenience of the officers for lying in between the hours of going their rounds.

In 1810 General Claude Ferey commanded a brigade. He was killed at Salamanca two years later at the head of a division.

The duty officer visiting the sentries would be checking that the regulations for piquets were being observed. They state that piquet officers

> must also forbid, under pain of severe punishment, to strike fire, or smoke tobacco at night: nor are they on any account to be permitted, during cold or rainy weather, to wear caps which cover the ears, as they must necessarily

prevent them from hearing, and in such weather, above all the utmost vigilance is required.

Rifleman Green was on sentry duty up in the village at the colonel and adjutant's lodgings and recorded that

> The Adjutant came out and asked me the time of night.
>
> I said, 'It's about 10, sir.'
>
> He said, 'The Colonel and me sleep in this lower room; if any alarm is made tap at this window.'
>
> When I was relieved I gave this additional order to the man who took my post. I went to the Piquet House [the chapel], put my rifle in a certain place, lay down with the men, and dropped asleep.

Captain O'Hare's company was on duty but he was reported as feeling unwell and as no attack seemed likely he went to bed at about 2100 hours, leaving Lieutenant Mercer in charge of the piquet at the officers' tent. Given that O'Hare was on the scene within less than fifteen minutes of the action beginning and followed shortly after by Beckwith and the two resting companies, the action cannot have been too far down the slope.

Down on the hillside, one of the officers was continually out on patrol. Simmons recalled that 'The other lieutenant returned and pronounced all quiet. At twelve o'clock we heard several shots fired.'

Whether by *ruse de guerre* or simply by dashing across the long, 4-yard-wide bridge, the French infantry led by the 82nd Line overwhelmed the two sentries, Riflemen Moor and McCann, but not before they fired the warning shot. The French bayoneted one and took the other prisoner.

The chapel where O'Hare and the inlying piquet were based.

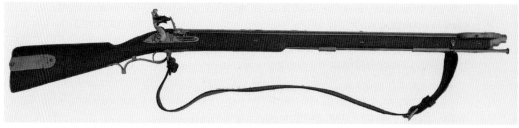

The Short Infantry Rifle (*aka* the Baker Rifle), designed by master gunsmith Ezekiel Baker.

In periods of rain and damp, sentries on duty for an hour or more found it difficult to keep the powder in the pan of the Short Infantry Rifle[7] dry, let alone the main charge. In such circumstances locks were often covered by wrapping oiled cloths around them which, of course, took time to remove. These practical difficulties could also explain the single warning shot fired by the sentries before being overwhelmed.

According to Lieutenant Cooke of the 43rd Light Infantry, it was ascertained from a prisoner that to maintain security the 'French general kept it quite a secret and let his men go to bed in their usual way. Between ten and eleven he had the whole men turned out and marched with some of his horsemen as quick as possible across the bridge.'

Once across the bridge the 82nd headed up the equally steep track and precipitate rocky slope on the western (Light Division) side of the gorge and were quickly upon the corporal's part of the outlying piquet and scattered it. Simmons reported that with 'the enemy being so numerous, they could not impede their progress.' Shortly afterwards the French ran into Sergeant Betts' men heading downhill. The sergeant was shot through the mouth and his men were in danger of being outflanked to left and right and they too were overwhelmed.

Hearing the firing below, Lieutenant Cowan was dispatched from the officers' tent to fetch Captain O'Hare. Simmons continued:

> We directly fell in the remainder of the company and marched towards the bridge. We soon met a man coming with information that the French were passing the bridge in great force. We marched forward and found them forming in line, with drums beating and yelling furiously. They fired to the amount of five hundred rounds, the balls whistling over our heads. Our gallant Commander [at this stage Lieutenant Mercer] ordered us not to let the men fire until we came within fifteen yards of them. The French fired another volley. We still moved on as silent as possible, fired, and gave them an English huzza. The men opposed to us were a little staggered.

Rifleman Green was in the chapel with the inlying piquet: 'I was awoken by the officers with the words "Be quick men, and load as you go to the brow of the hill."' He arrived at the scene of the fighting where the Rifles were almost firing muzzle-to-muzzle with the French grenadiers. Green describes how 'three of these big ugly fellows … came within ten yards' of him and his partner:

> The moon shone very bright, so that we could see them; they were spent out climbing up the rocks … I had got my ball in my rifle, but had not time to return the ramrod, so both ball and ramrod went through one of them. My comrade fired, and the ball struck another in the breast. I threw my rifle down, as it was no use to me without a ramrod, and retired about twenty yards. A sergeant of ours lay on his back, a musket ball having passed through his belly.
>
> I said, 'Sergeant Bradley, are you wounded?' He was groaning, poor fellow, and I said 'Lend me your rifle, I have fired my ramrod away with the ball!' I had not time to return it, as the Frenchman had his firelock at his shoulder, and probably in another moment I might have been killed or wounded! The sergeant bid me take his rifle, and said: 'It is of no use to me, they have done me, I am dying!'
>
> I left him and, running to join my comrade, I saw our officer stretched on his back, his sword in one hand and his spy-glass in the other. I said, 'Mr Mercer, are you wounded?' but his spirit had fled.

Simmons wrote in his account:

> In a moment, after the arrival of the main body of the piquet, the French were literally scrambling up the rocky ground within ten yards of us. We commenced firing at each other very spiritedly.
>
> We again loaded and came breast to breast. Lieutenant Mercer called, 'Simmons', and rushed on towards a stone several had got behind, while he drove others in front. Our men were shooting them in every direction, when an unlucky ball passed through poor Mercer's head just as he was saying, 'Our brave fellows fight like Britons.'

A rifleman shoved the muzzle of his rifle into a French officer's face and blew his brains out, shouting 'Revenge for Mr Mercer'; however, he was promptly hit by several musket balls.

Simmons continued:

> Their drums beat the charge, and the French attempted to dislodge us without effect.
>
> Several were now falling and the moon for a few minutes shone brightly then disappeared, and again at intervals let us see each other. We profited by this circumstance, as their belts were white and over their greatcoats, so that where they crossed on the breast, combined with the glare of the

Captain Peter O'Hare leading his company in action at Barba del Puerco. (*Christa Hook*)

breast-plate, gave a grand mark for our rifles. Our men being in dark dress, and from their small number, obliged to keep close together, the ground being exceedingly rugged, were all in favourable circumstances.

Simmons concludes by saying that slowly falling back towards the 'top of the pass' they fought like this at close quarters 'for half an hour against fearful odds'.

Captain O'Hare, who rejoined the company when his men were already very hard-pressed, was heard shouting: 'We shall never retire. Here we will stand. They shall not pass but over my body.' Such was the action until support from the rest of the wing sleeping in Barba del Puerco arrived.

Meanwhile, at the Spanish piquet to the right, the Rifles' corporal was under pressure from a Spanish captain to leave and rejoin his own company. When he refused to do so, 'the noble Castilian and his men started off' rather than assist O'Hare's company. Colonel Cox, the garrison commander of Almeida, recorded that the Spanish troops 'behaved shamefully; they all ran away except the Captain and four men without firing a shot.'

Hearing the sounds of battle from below, Colonel Beckwith and the two companies billeted in the village stood to arms, buckling on their accoutrements over their shirts. Within minutes Beckwith himself led his men, numbering about 120, out of Barba del Puerco and down the track to the brow of the valley. Beckwith was wearing his dressing-gown and a red nightcap, sword in hand! His aim would have been to add weight to O'Hare's company, which was fixed in battle at close

The French view across the bridge to the steep hillside beyond and the track defended by the 95th Rifles' piquets.

quarters in the face of a superior force as it struggled to hold the enemy or to cover O'Hare as he fell back towards the village.

Beckwith and his supports arrived in time to stem the French advance, which on the steep rocky ground had not been speedy or on a wide front. If they had been able to break out and deploy on the less steeply rising farmland between the brow of the hill and the village, the outcome may have been different. The speed with which the two companies were under arms was crucial. In the event the volume of fire from the reinforcing riflemen checked the French and started to push them back down into the valley.

Armed only with his sword, Colonel Beckwith was seen successfully throwing a rock at a Frenchman who was aiming at him. A young officer later explained: 'Our swords[8] were soon fixed and giving the war cheer we closed on the foe sending them helter-skelter down the pass and into the gorge and as fast as their legs would carry them.'

During the engagement, a small party of the French managed to outflank the Rifles among the rocks, but Lieutenant Stewart and a section of riflemen were dispatched to cover this threat. Stewart recalled that at one stage he was fighting three Frenchmen at the same time until a rifleman came to his assistance. One was shot and the others turned and headed back down into the valley.

With the 82nd's assault battalion falling back across the Águeda, the balance of the French force – said to number 1,500 men – remained on the far side of the river ineffectually firing at the riflemen. Simmons concluded: 'Eventually they retired to San Felice leaving a strong body of men in the piquet house just above their end of the bridge.'

At some point in the latter part of the action a young French soldier who had been taken prisoner was being questioned by Colonel Beckwith and had some-how retained his musket, which he fired. Fortunately the shot only grazed the colonel's head but according to Simmons there was no angry response from Beckwith:

> A rifleman was going to blow his brains out, when the Colonel stopped him, saying, 'Let him alone; I dare say the boy has a mother. Knock the thing out of his hand, that he may do no more mischief with it, and give him a kick on the bottom and send him to the rear.'

The lad, over breakfast in the colonel's billet, said it was an accident and he hadn't realized that his finger was on the trigger!

With the French falling back, Green recalled that the Rifles 'took about fifty prisoners and killed about sixty men'. He went on to say that they 'were then posted in chain order and remained so until daylight'; that is to say deployed in a scattered line of pairs across the front.

The following morning, they buried the dead: 'We had killed one officer, one sergeant, one corporal and ten rank and file; wounded, one sergeant, one corporal and six rank and file.' Sad to say, all but one of the wounded subsequently died. 'We buried the officer, sergeant and ten men in one grave.'

Colonel Cox, who rode over from Almeida the following morning, recorded that the troops from the Spanish piquet who had departed when the firing broke out 'as soon as the French retired they were all present to pillage the wounded, and would have gloriously put them to death if they had not been prevented by our soldiers.'

After the action Colonel Cox reported: 'The bodies of two officers and seven men have been taken prisoner, and three have been taken who were not wounded of the French. The total of French casualties was approximately forty and the British seventeen.' No doubt to help make light of Ferey's failure Ney estimated the 95th's casualties at 120, way above the generally agreed figure.

As word of the French attempt to force the Águeda reached the Light Division's headquarters at Villar de Ciervo, General Craufurd, believing that Ferey's attack was only the first act in a concerted French drive on Almeida, stood his division to arms. A company of the 43rd and at least two of the 52nd were sent

Lieutenant Colonel Sidney Beckwith commanding the 1st Battalion, 95th Rifles in 1810.

An officer of the 43rd Monmouthshire Light Infantry.

to reinforce Beckwith's wing of the 95th Rifles. Lieutenant Cooke was in the company of the 43rd:

> The company which I was in were ordered to march to support the 95th regiment. We were about 7 or 8 miles distant from them. On our arrival there all was quiet; they were expected to make an attempt in the night. It was nearly as light as day, therefore at early morning two officers and myself went down to see what was going on. Our curiosity tempted us to go to the bottom of the bank, and then to cross the bridge. Immediately we returned they commenced firing upon us. We were not more than three hundred yards from their sentries. Their balls came very near but they did no damage. The same day the French general and several of his officers were reconnoitring the river and all the places around, and from that circumstance we expected them to make another attack, but I am sorry to say they did not.
>
> In the evening, the General ordered four more companies to come to the bridge. We had there between eight and nine hundred men and very ready to meet them, but they knew better than to try us a second time.
>
> The next day our company was ordered back to its old quarters.

The position at Barba del Puerco was, however, ultimately considered to be too exposed and that any further French move could be countered from nearby Villar de Ciervo.

The attack across the Águeda at Barba del Puerco was indeed an isolated event and matters resumed the normal pattern of life in the outposts for the remainder of the month. With the heavy rain persisting into April it made 'outpost work simple, as the number of points to be observed went down from fifteen to four.'[9]

The action at Barba del Puerco where little over 200 riflemen saw off nearly ten times their number became a much talked-of event among the rest of the army, few of whom were in contact with the enemy.

Notes

1. Although styled a 'division', Craufurd's command remained in reality at brigade strength and it would take some time for additional British and Portuguese units to be permanently added to bring it up to anything like divisional strength.
2. Captain Shaw-Kennedy was responsible for questioning deserters who came through the Light Division's lines. Consequently Craufurd, with additional information coming in from Wellington, was well-informed of the make-up of the VI Corps' opposite and its movements.
3. Regulations for the Exercise of Riflemen and Light Infantrymen and Instructions for their Conduct in the Field, originally written by Dundas but revised and republished throughout the wars. Now available in print from the Naval & Military Press.
4. Lieutenant Colonel von Arentschildt in conversation with Lieutenant Colonel Sidney Beckwith.
5. Rum, water and, when available, lemon or lime juice. Rum was issued to units of Wellington's army.
6. Kincaid describes this force as '600 chosen grenadiers'. It was common practice for the French to group their grenadier and *voltigeur* (light) companies into elite battalions. In this case French records state that attack was led by the *82ème Ligne*, so the four elite companies from the two battalions of the regiment may well have been the spearhead of the attack. French companies in a six-company organization as opposed to the British ten-company equivalent were theoretically larger.
7. Only those Short Infantry Rifles made by Ezekiel Baker should be correctly known as the 'Baker Rifle'.
8. A sword bayonet to make up for the length of the Short Infantry Rifle; not to be confused with a proper sword.
9. Sir Charles Oman, *History of the Peninsular War*, Vol. III (Greenhill Books reprint, 1996).

Chapter Five

The French Investment of Ciudad Rodrigo

Wellington had been puzzled by the French manoeuvres during the spring of 1810, commenting to General Craufurd at his Light Division's headquarters: 'I don't know whether the state of tranquillity in which affairs have been for some time is advantageous to the French but I know that it is highly so for us.' Time had been gained not only to incorporate the reinforcements that the government was increasingly willing to send to the peninsula after Talavera but to improve the standard of training in the re-formed Portuguese army. The British had been brought up to a respectable 35,000, while the Portuguese represented almost another 30,000 men, many of whom were now being incorporated into British divisions. These numbers, however, were still far below the combined totals of the 350,000 French troops in Spain, many of which – if they could or indeed would co-operate – could be massed against Wellington.

On 25 April, the final elements of the now-reinforced French VI Corps, numbering 36,000, marched from Salamanca. Wellington learned of Ney's move two days later and immediately started to concentrate his divisions around Almeida. At this stage, he had not heard of the surrender of Astorga and the consequent release of Junot's VIII Corps, therefore at this early stage in the campaign he hoped 'to attempt the relief of Ciudad Rodrigo if ... expedient.'

Finally, following a protracted period of unseasonably heavy rain during May, which made the roads very difficult and slow, on the 30th of the month Ney's VI Corps was once more before Ciudad Rodrigo. Marshal Junot's corps was deployed as a corps of observation, not only to keep an eye on the British on the borders of Portugal but to cover other routes against possible intervention by Spanish armies.

The Defenders of Ciudad Rodrigo

General Herrasti,[1] the governor and garrison commander, had in theory around 8,000 men with which to defend the city, but only about a quarter were regular soldiers. In 1808 as the insurrection against the French began, Ciudad Rodrigo's Junta of Defence began work to repair the city walls and had by the end of May 1810 not only turned the convents and suburbs into outworks but had raised significant local troops. All men aged between 17 and 40 were required to serve in the city's defence. They were organized into six companies of militia and three locally-raised battalions of Cazadores (light infantry), alongside regular troops from the regiments of Avila, Minorca and the provinces of León and Valladolid. In addition, there were about 800 artillerymen and a company of engineers, but by the time of the siege the theoretical figure had been much reduced by sickness, desertion, etc. Herrasti claims that the true figure was as low as 5,500. This total also includes up to 800 mounted guerrillas of Don Julián Sánchez's band, of whom 200 were mounted lancers.[2]

By the time the French appeared, Ciudad Rodrigo was well-supplied with food and 'an abundance of [gun] powder'. There was also a determination among both the defenders and population to emulate the Saragossans who had successfully resisted the assaults of the French in a brutal siege during 1808–1809. The junta being resident in Ciudad helped, but even so there were the so-called *Afrancesados* or French sympathizers, who were by 1810 keeping their views to themselves if they valued their lives. This was especially so as false rumours were circulating that the garrison and population of Astorga had been put to the sword!

Determined though the city was, General Herrasti was not trusted by Wellington and his officers. Relations were poor between Herrasti and Colonel Cox, commander of the fortress at Almeida, and Wellington himself; after the Talavera campaign he had a thoroughly jaundiced view of Spanish commanders. When Herrasti appealed for British help to drive the first French away Wellington commented:

> If the force near Ciudad Rodrigo is only 4,000 men, and the Governor wishes to remove them, he is surely able to effect that operation himself. Why are the English to undertake it? If he is not able to effect that object, I am sure it will answer no purpose for us to relieve him, when we shall be more seriously pressed.

In a later letter to the governor that was slipped through the investing French troops, Wellington concluded by saying that his army was in a position to help 'if circumstances should permit me to do so', but he ended by cautioning Herrasti that 'the protection of that place is not the only object entrusted to me.'

The French Investment of Ciudad Rodrigo

Ney's corps arrived around the city but the siege artillery was lagging behind, requiring eighteen mules to move each of the forty-three guns through the mud-churned roads. It took six and a half days to cover the 40 miles from San Muñoz. Not only that, according to Masséna's senior staff officer Jean Pelet the French had only one-third of the draft animals required to move the siege train and all the equipment in the normal manner. The French engineers' tools necessary for the siege had been similarly delayed in north-west Spain and replacements of dubious quality were procured or manufactured locally. Ney's situation at

Chef de Bataillon (Major)
Jean Pelet.

Ciudad Rodrigo was not helped by Junot's refusal to release VIII Corps' carts, as directed by Masséna, to move all that was required for VI Corps' siege forward from Salamanca.

During this period Don Julián Sánchez's guerrillas successfully and regularly descended on French outposts and poorly-protected convoys on the route from Salamanca via San Muñoz to Rodrigo. This was aided by the terrain, which was for much of the distance at the time a wilderness of scrub and forest.

Pelet described the ground conditions at the time of the investment following the protracted and unseasonably heavy rain during May: 'The army corps [VI] suffered to an exceptional degree during the entire siege, and from the very beginning water gushed out everywhere, even on the highest ground. Soldiers were in the mud and exposed to almost continual rain and extreme variations in heat and cold.'

He also recounted that the bread supplied was a quarter-ration, that the surrounding country had already been stripped bare of food and that without grain the horses surviving solely on green forage were deteriorating, as was saddlery in the continual rain. It is fair to say that the siege got off to a slow start in difficult military and weather conditions.

On 1 June with his troops still arriving and deploying north-east of the 120-yard-wide River Águeda, Ney with the siege artillery commander and Couche his engineer officer conducted a reconnaissance of the environs of Ciudad Rodrigo. With only one viable ford and with the river running deep and fast, it was obvious that to enable his troops to cross to the southern bank and fully invest the city, a bridge was needed. The marshal promptly ordered VI Corps' engineers to build a bridge half a mile above the city and on 5 June a second below the city. When Marshal Masséna arrived from his headquarters, which from early June was at Salamanca, to carry out a reconnaissance and to inspect Ney's deployment, he found 'This bridge, not yet finished, was on trestles and all the wood needed for its construction had to be carried from Salamanca.'[3] Wellington, being informed of the construction, hoped that the Águeda, which could rise in spate at any time, would carry away the bridges[4] but they withstood the force of the waters along with the passage of troops and artillery.

The bridges and their bridgehead defences were finally completed on 7 June after a considerable round-the-clock logistic effort and the labour of up to 600 men at a time. As the bridges were finished, French troops, with caution now that those to the south had the river at their back, were finally able to begin properly investing Ciudad Rodrigo.

French operations, if not interfered with by the British were, however, certainly not uncontested. General Herrasti dispatched a sally on 1 June when French skirmishers began to push forward to within 70 yards of the city walls at dawn. The 300 Spanish infantry and 120 mounted men were soon confronted by General Loison's *tirailleurs* (sharpshooters) and cavalry who together drove them back to the city. Later the same day a second stronger sally of 300 horsemen and 1,000 infantry were again outside the city walls, but Loison once again drove them back, pursuing the Spanish to their walls.

The action on 1 June was typical of those around Ciudad Rodrigo, with sallies that followed growing in scale during the period of the investments. The Spanish aim, if not to hold ground, was to drive the French off key terrain north of the River Águeda, make their hold on the Teson tenuous and put off the day that siege operations could begin. As more French troops crossed the Águeda, operations along the River Azaba against Wellington's screen provided by the Light Division and the 1st King's German Legion Hussars gained tempo. Neither Herrasti, who regularly dispatched sallies towards the bridging sites, nor Craufurd were passive onlookers in early June (see Chapter 6).

Lieutenant Jonathan Leach of the 1st Battalion, 95th Rifles recalled:

We were stationed so close to the outposts of the French as to render it necessary for the soldiers to sleep fully accoutred, and the officers conse-

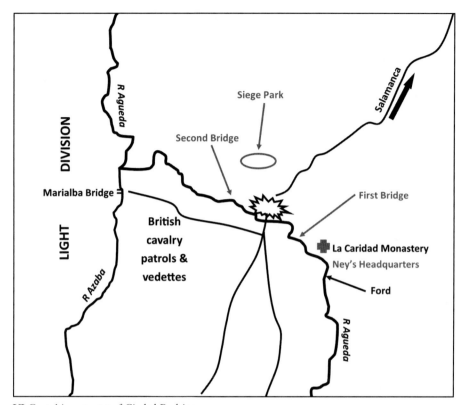

VI Corps' investment of Ciudad Rodrigo.

quently with their clothes on, ready to get under arms in an instant; and we were, as a matter of course, always under arms one hour before break of day. In short, the French cavalry were eternally in motion, in large bodies, towards our chain of posts, and we as often under arms waiting for them.

The armies had been well and truly shaken out of their state of live-and-let-live that had existed for much of the time between the opposing outposts during the winter of 1809/1810.

On the night of 9 June, the convent of Santa Cruz to the west of the city was attacked by the French, because in Spanish hands it would be able to enfilade the trenches that were to be dug on the Teson features. The men selected were 100 members of the *chasseurs de siège*, who were sharpshooters chosen from the *voltigeur* companies of VI Corps' infantry regiments. Their primary role was to snipe at the Spanish gunners from foxholes at the foot of the glacis slope. In this *coup de main* attack on Santa Cruz they would be supported by other grenadier and *voltigeur* companies, forming an elite battalion.

A re-enactor's impression of a classic French *voltigeur*.

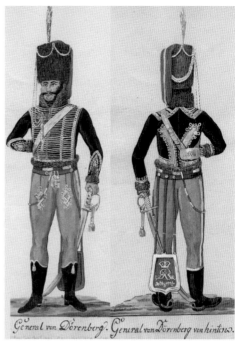

General von Dörenberg. General von Dörenberg von hinten.

A well-dressed representation of Sánchez's cavalry (*left*) and officers of the 1st KGL (*right*). The campaign reality would have been very different.

Emerging from behind the Greater Teson and initially taking the Spanish by surprise, the force under the command of Captain François broke down the gates with axes. After a stiff fight amid the various buildings, the Spanish abandoned the place leaving twenty-one dead and wounded, while the French suffered five casualties. The following morning the Spanish heavy guns on the walls some 150 yards away battered the convent building, making it untenable for the French, and the Spanish duly reoccupied it.

Meanwhile, to protect the brigades deployed around Ciudad Rodrigo from Herrasti's sallies a number of posts were established. Up on the Greater Teson three flèches (parapets with two faces) were dug and a further two were established on the low ground towards the Santa Cruz Monastery to the west of the city.

Complete investment of Ciudad Rodrigo was achieved between 11 and 13 June when contact between the city and the Light Division's outposts and cavalry patrols, provided by the Hussars of the King's German Legion, was severed. Ney, however, remained cautious; understandably so with his force split astride the Águeda, the Light Division only a few miles away and Wellington assembling his army over the Portuguese border.

As preparations for the siege proper reached their climax, Junot's VIII Corps marched to support Ney. This of course exacerbated the supply problems with two under-resourced corps around Ciudad Rodrigo competing for scant transport, food and fodder. While Ney concentrated on the siege, General Junot continued to cover the operation.

Throughout this period Ney predictably advocated the launching of an attack on the British outposts forward of the bridge over the Azaba at Marialba. The emperor's instructions were, however, explicit: Masséna was to be methodical in taking Rodrigo first and would not contemplate ignoring instructions from Paris.

To the British the slowness of the French in opening the siege and confining action against them to bickering on the Azaba during these opening stages of the campaign had surprised almost everyone. Wellington wrote to a number of

The French works during the investment.

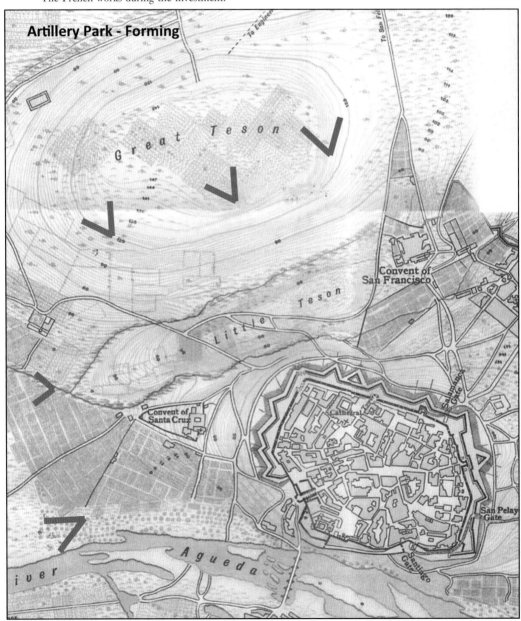

The Nuestra Señora de la Caridad monastery 3 miles south-east of Ciudad Rodrigo on the banks of the Águeda was Marshal Ney's headquarters during the 1810 siege.

correspondents and stated that 'This is not the way in which they have conquered Europe.'[5]

Other than amazement at the slow pace of the French investment, Wellington's reaction now that he was certain as to the focus of French operations and that Rodrigo was not going to be bypassed as Ney was advocating was to move his headquarters forward from Viseu to Alverca. More importantly he ordered Brigadier General Craufurd to maintain his outposts well forward, almost dangerously so, on the River Azaba so as to be as close to the besieged city as possible in order to spot any opportunity to relieve Ciudad Rodrigo.

Finally, after two weeks before Ciudad Rodrigo, with the weather beginning to show signs of improving, the first picks and shovels rang on the rocky ground of the Greater Teson and in some dummy trenches east of the city. With the engineers having traced out the first parallel and the communication trenches in advance, the French finally broke ground to begin the siege proper on the night of 15 June 1810.

Notes

1. His full name was Don Andrés Perez de Herrasti.
2. Jean Jacques Pelet, *The French Campaign in Portugal 1819–1811* (University of Minnesota, 1973).
3. Ibid.
4. Ibid.
5. Ibid.

Chapter Six

The Light Division as Corps of Observation

Excelling in outpost work in January 1810, it had fallen to what shortly became the Light Division under Brigadier General Robert Craufurd to provide the army's corps of observation while it remained in winter quarters in central and northern Portugal. The Light Division was deployed forward between the River Côa and the line of the rivers Águeda and Azaba. The general situation and the action at Barba del Puerco has already been covered but as spring arrived and the investment of Ciudad Rodrigo developed, the focus of operations was further south on the Azaba as Marshal Ney's VI Corps and subsequently Marshal Junot's VIII Corps sought to cut communication between Wellington's army and the beleaguered city of Ciudad Rodrigo.

Wellington, in a letter to Craufurd in March 1810, makes plain both his intent and the degree of trust he had in the Light Division and its commander:

> Since we took up the position which we now occupy, our outposts have come in contact with those of the French; and although there is some distance between the two, still the arrangement of our outposts must be made on a better principle, and the whole of them must be in the hands of one person, who must be yourself. I propose, therefore, as soon as the weather will allow of an alteration of the disposition of the advanced corps, that your Division, with the Hussars[1] which will be put under your orders, should occupy the whole line of the outposts, and, with this, the Portuguese corps shall be brought up to the front as soon as the state of the weather will allow them to march.

These Portuguese were two battalions of Caçadores[2] from the newly re-formed army who were to become a part of the Light Division. Wellington continued:

> I am desirous of being able to assemble the army upon the Côa, if it should be necessary; at the same time, I am perfectly aware that if the enemy should collect in any large numbers in Estremadura, we should be too forward for our communications with General Hill even here, and much more so upon the Côa. But till they will collect in Estremadura, and till we shall see more clearly than I can at present what reinforcements they have received, and

A Portuguese Caçadore. Battalions were distinguished by different facing colours to their collars and cuffs.

A French dragoon.

what military object they have in view, and particularly in the existing disposition of the army, I am averse to withdrawing from a position so favourable as the Côa affords, to enable us to collect our army and prevent the execution of any design upon Ciudad Rodrigo.

As we have seen, relations between Napoleon's marshals is best characterized as a jealous competition that the emperor himself did little to address, but all was not comradeship in Wellington's army either and in his instructions to Craufurd he in effect places two senior officers under the direction of a brigadier who in the circumstance held a more important command: 'I intend that the Divisions of General Cole and General Picton should support you on the Côa without waiting for orders from me, if it should be necessary; and they shall be directed accordingly.' The difference was that few of Wellington's divisional commanders were given much independence and scope to vent their rivalries and dislikes to the detriment of the campaign, though Picton's conduct during the combat on the Côa later in the year is questionable.

Brigadier General Craufurd's aide-de-camp, Captain Shaw-Kennedy, explains the aim of operations between the rivers Côa and Águeda/Azaba:

The objects to be gained by the Light Division holding as long as possible the whole of the country on the left bank of the Águeda up to the bridges

Captain Shaw-Kennedy.

and fords over that river were to encourage the governor of Ciudad Rodrigo to make a stout defence, to keep open the communication with Almeida as long as possible, and to command the resources of the country. These were objects of great importance, as delay in taking these towns was a formidable obstruction to the French army, from its obliging them to undertake the operation against Portugal at a late season of the year; and was of immense value to Lord Wellington in allowing time to bring greater maturity to his defensive preparations.

Even though the Portuguese infantry enhanced his numbers, Craufurd was greatly outnumbered and in an exposed position even with the addition of the 16th Light Dragoons and Captain Ross's Horse Artillery troop of six pieces.

Captain George Napier[3] of the 52nd Light Infantry described the essence of Craufurd's remarkable ability in outpost work:

> The moment his division arrived at its ground ... he never moved from his horse till he had made himself master of every part of his post, formed his plan for its defence if necessary, and explained all his arrangements to the

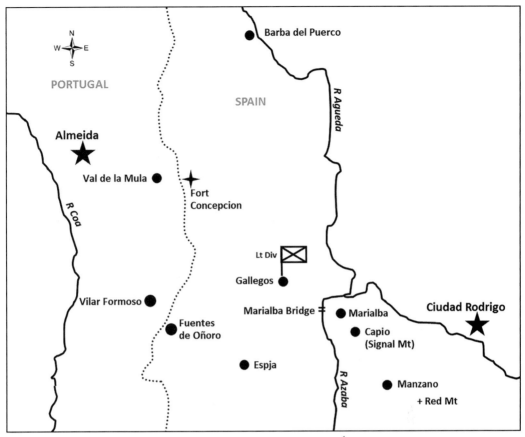

The Light Division's area of operations between the Côa and the Águeda/Azaba.

staff officers and the field officers of each regiment, so that if his orders were strictly obeyed a surprise was impossible.

He was seldom deceived in the strength of the enemy's outposts, for he reconnoitred them with the eye of one who knew his business well.

In his headquarters well forward in Gallegos, Craufurd was only too aware of his potentially difficult position and the need to make his deployment based on plans to get his division back across the River Côa. Consequently, his deployment was based on this calculation. The skill of the 1st Hussars of the King's German Legion in outpost work and the fact that he could speak to them in their own language meant that there would be no misunderstandings, plus the fact they were, of course, far more mobile than the infantry. Consequently, Craufurd elected to deploy the cavalry astride the line of the Águeda and the Azaba. However, other than the companies of the Rifles at Barba del Puerco and Villar de Ciervo, until withdrawn as a part of the previously mentioned reorganization, he posted most of the Light Division's infantry 'upon the *calculation* of the time that would be required to retire the infantry to the Côa, after he received information from the cavalry posts of the enemy's advance'. This meant that the main bodies were deployed so as not to get fixed by the superior number of French cavalry and overwhelmed, but that is not to say that smaller piquets of infantry and their patrols were not forward. The British battalions took it in turn to take part in duties on the outpost line. Captain George Napier recalled an early incident when few French troops were on the banks of the Azaba stream during one of his deployments forward of Gallegos:

> One day I was on picket [*sic*] at a ford and a staff coming down the road on the opposite bank towards the ford. I called out across the river, which was narrow, to desire them to go back, and at the same time drew my men up and told the French general that I would fire at him if he persisted in coming down to the ford. They seemed to hold my threat in perfect contempt and still moved down; upon which I fired and shot one of their horse. This had the desired effect and they wheeled about and went back at the trot. The general … was Marshal Ney who rode a white horse; and as I was not aware at the time that it was he, I made my men do all they could to shoot him; as it is always a good thing to shoot the enemy's general, as it must make a great confusion in his army.[4]

A rotation of troops across the Light Division was established by the end of April at about the time when French numbers were increasing. This rotation included

The River Azaba.

the Portuguese Caçadores but they were not employed on outpost duty on their own. The billets for the battalion providing the outposts were Gallegos and Espeja, each for one wing (half-battalion) and Vale de la Mula and Vilar Formoso for the other, with the reserve, more often than not at this stage the Caçadores, astride the Côa. Writing on 30 April 1810, Lieutenant Simmons of the 1st 95th Rifles describes one of these rotations during the protracted period of poor weather:

> This day I marched 4 leagues [12 miles] under a continuous torrent of rain. I am now under tolerable shelter, sitting drying my trousers over a fire of wood upon the ground, and am in a very ill-humour, having burnt the leather which encircles the bottoms. I have my jacket off and a blanket round me until my jacket and shirt are dried. I am so much accustomed to get wet I think little about it. For some time, the French had been stationed about 8 leagues from us, but lately they made a move and menaced Ciudad Rodrigo.

For some time, there was little serious activity on the Águeda and Azaba. George Napier was there again:

> Another day, being on picket at the same place, where opposite to us the enemy had now also a picket, some of the French soldiers asked my leave to come across and get tobacco from our men, as they had none, and could not get any, in consequence of the siege. I allowed two of them to come, who immediately stripped off their clothes and swam across (for I would not let them try the ford), got the tobacco, told us all the news from France, and returned quite happy.

In notes written for his sons who were due to join the army, Napier wrote of this incident:

> Now this was all wrong, because, when a man is placed in charge of a post, he should never permit his enemy to come within reach of being able to observe what he is about, the strength of his party, or the nature of his defences. The safest plan is to keep him at a distance, and to allow of no familiarity or intercourse between your men and the enemy's.

Patrols of the 1st KGL Hussars had until the end of May skirmished on an almost daily basis with French dragoons on the left bank of the Águeda, sometimes in close proximity to Ciudad Rodrigo. Once, however, VI Corps was present in strength and the second pontoon bridge had been built over the Águeda near the Ford of Loro, the Hussars found operations altogether more difficult. On 5/6 June Marshal Ney sent across Marchand's division and half of Mermet's, plus Lamotte's brigade of light cavalry to complete the investment of the city. This changed the balance of force on the line of the River Azaba, as had been expected by Craufurd. Of this period, Captain Leach commented that once again

> We were stationed so close to the outposts of the French as to render it necessary for the soldiers to sleep fully accoutred, and officers, consequently, with their clothes on, ready to get under arms in an instant; and we were, as a matter of course, always under arms an hour before break of day.

During 5 June, the French launched three columns along roads west and south-west of Ciudad Rodrigo. They pushed KGL cavalry patrols back to Marialba and on towards Gallegos, where reinforcements from the 16th Light Dragoons and the Caçadores were required to restore the situation. In the centre, a strong French column of a brigade of dragoons supported by an infantry battalion and four guns threatened. They advanced on Carpio and to the south, driving back a troop-sized vedette, a further group of French advanced 2 miles beyond El Manzano. This was a reconnaissance in force and Ciudad Rodrigo was now increasingly isolated from Wellington's army, but British cavalry patrols remained within 5 miles and in sight of the city from high ground forward of the Azaba.

The following day, however, with diversionary action by the Spanish in Rodrigo, along with assistance from a large body of British cavalry and Julián

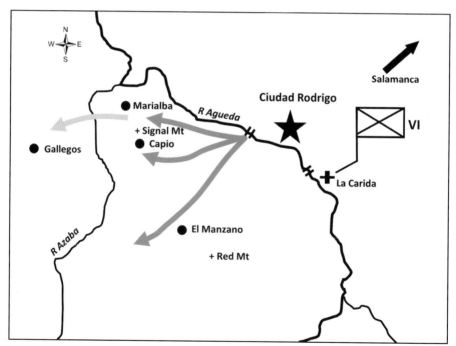

Action east of the Azaba on 5 June.

Sánchez's guerrillas, a convoy of 100 mules laden with grain slipped through the Santa Maria suburb, across the old bridge and into the city. This, of course, demonstrates that the French investment of the fortress was still less than watertight and was a boost to Spanish morale.

Simmons recorded in his diary later in the month, once the siege proper had begun:

> June 19th: The Light Division assembled at Gallegos, being the nearest point toward Rodrigo, and as the enemy's fire is increasing daily [at this stage against Herrasti's sallies] before the besieged town, our General has concentrated his Division so that we may be ready to fight or retire according to circumstances. From the frequent alarms we receive, one body or other of Frenchmen are continually falling in and moving, we are becoming very active, and can move off with all our baggage in a quarter of an hour at any time.

In the early hours of 25 June, the French bombardment with heavy guns finally began and General Junot's VIII Corps fully took over coverage of the river line, with far greater numbers. This allowed Ney to concentrate on the siege of Ciudad Rodrigo and would prevent Wellington from intervening. The French were now strong enough to hold back British probing towards the city and the mounting pressure on the vedettes and piquets is evident in the diary of Captain Cocks of the 16th Light Dragoons whose regiment by now shared duties with the KGL Hussars:

> 1 July: This morning no cavalry were in sight except a regiment or two out foraging. Three enemy guns were to the right and the chasseurs in the same position as yesterday. They continued quiet all day except for some occasional firing from the advanced vedettes; we were very jealous whenever the enemy appeared to be trying the ford … [so far, so normal].
>
> 2 July: The enemy brought down a regiment of cavalry this morning and encamped them with their right on Marialba; this makes our situation very ticklish, it appears superior to our three squadrons and is not 400 yards from our vedettes.
>
> 3 July: Four squadrons of the enemy came down this day and reconnoitred Carpio ford. At sunset, they made an attempt to carry off some cars [waggons] we had thrown across the Marialba bridge.

Possibly as a result of this French activity, Brigadier Craufurd assembled the Light Division on the heights behind Gallegos. Lieutenant Simmons was with the 95th Rifles' outposts:

> We still occupied Gallegos by day, but every evening General Crawford [*sic*] marched his infantry to a wood on some heights behind the village, towards

the river Dos Casas, where we bivouacked, and returned soon after daybreak to the village. This, I presume, was a precautionary measure, fearing the enemy might attempt a night attack on the village, which their extreme proximity rendered probable.

Captain Leach believed, correctly, that this deployment forward on the 3rd may have been misinterpreted:

> From some commanding ground in the French lines, the return of our division from the heights to the village could plainly be perceived; and possibly being deceived on that point, mistaking us for reinforcements sent across the Côa to join General Crawford [*sic*], Masséna ordered General Junot to cross the Azaba at Marialba Bridge on the 4th July; with him was supposed about fifteen thousand men.

At the beginning of July, with the siege of Ciudad Rodrigo nearing its climax, both Wellington and Masséna were at the front and it is probable that the presence of the British commander, who needed to gauge how long the fortress would hold out, was interpreted as a possible reinforcement of the Light Division and a further sign of an intent to intervene in the siege. Also with the British cavalry vedettes still in positions of observation within 6 miles of the city, Junot decided on action to drive them back, test the strength of the Light Division and British intent.[5] With his corps very hungry, the sight of the ripe crops in the fields on the open slopes running up to Gallegos may have been a temptation as well.

The French force consisted of Lorges' 2,500-strong cavalry division, detached from VI to VIII Corps for the duration of the siege, elements of Sainte Croix's dragoon division and a brigade of infantry. The action began on the morning of 4 July, with shots from the KGL Hussars' piquets on the high ground at Marialba. Clearly outnumbered, with enemy cavalry fanning out across the plain and pushing the single KGL squadron back, Craufurd stood the Light Division to arms on a scrub-covered ridge between Gallegos and Almeida.

The 95th Rifles had piquets forward in Gallegos but Captain Leach, his company and the rest of the battalion were already under arms back on the ridge from where they could see the Hussars who, under pressure, were withdrawing across the Azaba. The French orders were that 'General Sainte-Croix or others such as you deem advisable' were to 'with 600–800 cavalry and artillery, if you believe necessary, with orders to overthrow all principal English posts in order to know the exact location of the British Army and the line they hold.'

On his part of the front, Captain Cocks, commanding one of the two 16th Light Dragoon squadrons deployed that day, was faced by the rapid advance of 200 enemy horsemen across the Azaba. He was nearly taken by surprise and wrote: 'I mounted my men as they came upon us at a gallop, and I had some difficulty in getting away.'

The Azaba bridge at Marialba.

Leach recorded that the KGL a little further north were not surprised at the Marialba bridge and fell back on Gallegos and the Light Division drawn up on the ridge beyond. They

> retired slowly and in excellent order, keeping up a continued skirmish. Captain Krauchenberg of the 1st German Hussars, an officer of the highest merit, distinguished himself on this occasion. Forming his squadron on some eligible ground near a small narrow bridge over a rivulet which runs through Gallegos, he waited until as many of the French dragoons had crossed as he thought proper to permit, when he instantly charged and put them into confusion, killing and wounding many of them, and bringing some prisoners with him to the heights.

Captain Cocks, having extricated himself, was sent to support the KGL Hussars and adds a little more information to events around Gallegos:

> About half a mile in rear of Gallegos is a marshy brook, crossed by a narrow bridge, and behind this Krokenburgh [sic] made a rally with the skirmishers and dashed several times very gallantly at the advance of the enemy as they attempted to cross. Three French officers, a serjeant and some men were sabred and one dragoon taken with his horse. The enemy might have been stopped here longer had he not turned our right.

Brigadier General Craufurd had summoned the remainder of the Light Division including Captain Ross's troop of horse artillery[6] and deployed them in line

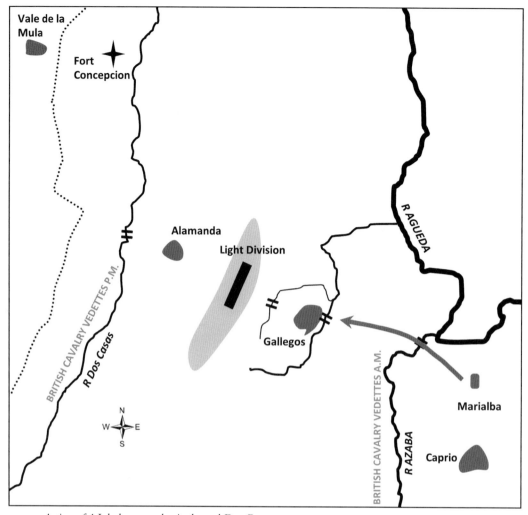

Action of 4 July between the Azaba and Dos Casas.

across the Gallegos-Alamenda road but sent a section of guns forward to support the cavalry. Captain Cocks commented: 'Our artillery served with considerable effect and did execution in their crowded columns. We had two 6-pounders under Lt Macdonald of Capt Ross's troop of Horse Artillery.'

Having advanced 2 miles from Marialba, French progress slowed but continued through Gallegos. Lieutenant Simmons, in Captain O'Hare's company, wrote:

> Our Horse Artillery fired shrapnel and round shot at the enemy's columns of cavalry as they approached us, and the 3rd Caçadores fired a volley as soon as they perceived the French, without doing any mischief. This sort of thing was excusable, being young soldiers. We are in hope that time may accustom them to judge their distance better.

Captain Hew Dalrymple Ross, RHA.

The history of the KGL provides more detail of the action in Gallegos:

> . . . a party of dismounted men, under Cornet Cordemann, maintaining a small bridge in front, while two other parties of hussars under George von der Decken and Schaumann observed two fords on the flanks. One of these fords [to the right] was at length passed by the enemy in considerable force, while the hussars were at the same time hard-pressed in the village. Captain Krauchenberg therefore ordered the guns to the rear with directions to unlimber on the other side of the town at a bridge which led from Gallegos to Almeida, and from whence the retreat of his squadron could be protected. This movement was well executed by Lieutenant Macdonald; and Krauchenberg, as soon as he saw the guns were nearly in position, led his squadron off at the gallop to gain the bridge.

Outnumbered and in constant danger of being enveloped, Brigadier General Craufurd decided it was time to retire towards the frontier and across the Dos Casas stream covered by the Hussars and Light Dragoons. Captain Cocks was again among them:

> Almost a mile further to the rear, as the enemy began to press us very hard again, we met the infantry and Elder's Caçadores pouring a running fire into

him; this completely checked him. The enemy's artillery hardly ever got into action … The Hussars behaved particularly well. It would be unfair not to bear unqualified testimony to their courage, zeal and knowledge of their duty.

In this same action Simmons

saw a Light Dragoon attack a French Horse Grenadier [most probably a dragoon] and trounce him handsomely. The man's helmet was nearly all brass, with large bars across in various ways; he had literally cut through this and also the man's head most severely and brought him in a prisoner. Our General sent the cap home as a present to some of his friends to show with what strength the Englishman had dealt his blows upon the Frenchman's head.

While the bulk of the Light Division manoeuvred back via the bridge over the Dos Casas beyond Almeida the cavalry and the 95th were still in action. Simmons records that he

was much amused by the dexterity displayed by a body of French Dragoons [their elite company] who passed through Almeida and dismounted, leaving their horses in line under the charge of some of their men. They then trotted off in their big jack boots and large hairy caps as light infantry to skirmish with us. As we had got the high ground across the river and they could

Officer of the 16th Light Dragoons.   A French elite company dragoon.

The bridge where the section of guns unlimbered with a view of the Alamenda Road and the high ground where the Light Division was deployed.

neither check nor impede our progress, they returned to their horses and became dragoons again.

Captain Leach summed up the withdrawal:

> This movement was covered by some cavalry and our battalion, who skirmished with the advance of the French until we had passed the river, which was effected with a very trifling loss on our part. Two hundred riflemen and some cavalry were left on the heights of Fort Conception [*sic*] as a picket [*sic*], the remainder being placed in a position near the Portuguese village of Vale de la Mula, behind the rivulet called Turon, which is the boundary of the two countries.

This simple summary cannot do justice to the skill with which Craufurd and his men manoeuvred in the face of enemy cavalry who were constantly attempting to outflank them. This model withdrawal took them back a further 3 miles to the next defensible line: the ridge on the border between Portugal and Spain on which Fort Concepcion stands. The French did not follow but retired to establish their piquets on the Azaba. They had established that the Light Division had not been reinforced, nor did there appear to be any intent by the British to attempt to raise the siege.

Meanwhile, the Light Division established its own new outpost line with piquets deployed on the ridge while the remainder of the battalions took up positions in the low ground to the west. The main body of the 1st 95th Rifles occupied Vale de la Mula but sent forward two companies to assist the engineers in their preparations to slight the fortress walls. According to Lieutenant Cooke of the 43rd 'we were in a continual state of alarm ... Our pickets [*sic*] were very frequently having little skirmishes with the enemy but of no great consequence.'

The Light Division now numbered 4,000 infantry and, with the addition of the 14th Light Dragoons who had been sent to join them, had 1,200 cavalry but remained in contact with advanced elements of the Army of Portugal numbering some 65,000 French troops.

Casualties in what was a fighting withdrawal were remarkably light, mainly because the French infantry lagged behind the cavalry and their artillery being similarly slow had little opportunity to engage. Even so, many within the Light Division wondered at the lack of the usual drive among the French, while those outside the division were already commenting that Craufurd's deployment was too far forward.

Back at Ciudad Rodrigo, the bombardment continued.

Notes

1. 1st King's German Legion Hussars.
2. Portuguese light infantry, dressed in distinctive brown uniforms, which eventually resembled the pattern of those of the 95th Rifles.
3. As was the case with many of the Light Division officers quoted in this book, George Napier was promoted between the 1810 and 1812 sieges. His rank at the time of the respective siege is used.
4. Wellington disagreed, later saying 'Generals have better things to do than shoot at each other.'
5. Some commentators say that it was Masséna who ordered the advance but the marshal's senior ADC, Jean Pelet, makes it clear that he was dispatched to find out what was going on.
6. 'A' (Ross's) troop's 5 × light 6-pounders and 1 × 5.5in howitzer.

Chapter Seven

The 1810 French Siege of Ciudad Rodrigo

With the Spanish garrison so active, the plan for breaking ground on 15 June within 500 yards of the enemy was complex and involved a large number of troops, provided by all of VI Corps' divisions. They contributed both guard force and labourers to the operation and to the deception plan. To occupy and deceive the Spanish, a false parallel was started to the east of the city and noisy attacks launched on the Santa Marina suburb down on the Águeda and on the convent of Santo Domingo. The usual outposts were to be pushed forward but behind them and fifty paces in front of the labourers digging the trench, nine companies of grenadiers were deployed in a firing line in a prone position. To support them another five companies were deployed just behind the crest of the Greater Teson. Further behind and to the flanks, battalions stood to arms ready to protect the whole force from sallies or from British attack while the corps was breaking ground.

Some 2,300 men were detailed to form seven labour gangs led by engineer officers who, when orders were given at 2200 hours, started their men digging along 510 yards of the first parallel plus the communication trenches where they crossed the crest of the Greater Teson onto the forward slope. By dawn at 0330 hours the trench was 4.5ft wide and had reached a depth of 2.5ft, with the spoil forming a parapet several feet high on both sides.

As it grew light the Spanish realized what had happened and opened a heavy bombardment on the parallel but the trench was deep enough to shelter the labourers and casualties were remarkably light. The labourers and the guard force were soon replaced by another twelve-hour shift, which under continuing fire deepened the parallel and opened the communication trenches down to the artillery and engineer parks.

Chef de Bataillon Constantin furnished us with details of the progress:

The first five nights were spent perfecting the parallel and the communication trenches. They were ten feet wide at the bottom, three feet deep, and had four-foot parapets with two banquettes [fire-steps]. On 18 June, the parallel was extended on the left by a 120-yard reverse after the enemy attempted a sortie to seize it. General Eblé located and determined the

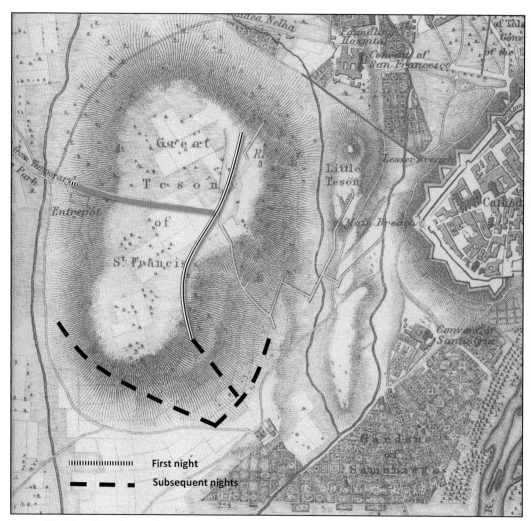

The French break ground.

emplacement for the batteries on the 17th and the work was completed only during the night of the 19th to the 20th. At first there were six in number.

The conditions under which the 600-man shifts of French infantry laboured during June 1817 are furnished by *Chef de Bataillon* Pelet. He is the prime source for details of the siege from the French perspective and provides information on an unexpected problem for troops digging in on a hilltop in the Spanish summer: 'The rains continued and we encountered a few springs of water that obstructed our works considerably because the lower part of the parallel filled with water and delayed our progress.'

Worse still, Masséna reported to Berthier in Paris that the drainage arrangements that they made were inadequate and on the western part of the Greater Teson work had to be abandoned. Things improved when the trenches were

General Jean Baptiste Eblé, commander of the siege train.

widened and a fire-step dug for the musketeers but the bottom of the trench remained in some cases little more than a stream, while in others it became a slough of mud churned by the continual passage of feet. Meanwhile, on the eastern end of the parallel where nature was not on the side of the French, parts of the parallels were effectively abandoned. The conditions oscillated between cold and wet and, when the clouds lifted, hot and sweaty. Rarely, though, did the mud in the trenches and the roads dry out more than superficially.

The period of bad weather noticed in Europe around 1810 is traditionally referred to as the 'Little Ice Age' but recent scholarship has attributed the unusual worldwide weather conditions to a possible volcanic eruption in Indonesia during 1809 that threw up a layer of dust into the atmosphere, reducing the power of the sun for several years. Whatever the reason, the wet spring had a significant impact on the Iberian Peninsula and continued to slow French siege operations at Ciudad Rodrigo.

The weather simply added to the supply difficulties in what was already an ad hoc logistic system. Pelet, during a visit to the troops on the banks of the River Águeda while Ney's men were breaking ground, records:

We slept with General Marchand's division. The conversation there was only about the lack of food. The shortage was so severe that we could not obtain bread, forage, or lodging for our escort of five dragoons. According to several officers, abandoning the siege was the only way to relieve this misery.

For an army that was used to living off the land to a great extent, this was a remarkable admission of problems to a senior officer and further illustrates the difficulties, particularly for VI Corps, who remained concentrated around Ciudad Rodrigo. In the peninsula Masséna's army was fighting with one hand tied behind its back, unable to conduct the usual style of French Napoleonic warfare.

Until the arrival of the siege guns and the opening of the bombardment, the French could only rely on a handful of field guns to answer the well-protected fire of the Spanish fortress artillery. Inevitably, while the Spanish behind their wall suffered few casualties, Ney's troops labouring in the parallels suffered a steady stream of injuries that further sapped morale and this, compounded with all their other sundry difficulties, meant that the men were miserable.

As has already been recorded, the business of getting the guns to Ciudad Rodrigo over terrible roads was protracted. In the event, they arrived in the artillery park to the north of the Teson in small groups and only then after General Eblé had appealed for road-making parties from VI and VIII Corps. However, progress continued to be slow with the 24-pounders being stranded at San Muñoz for some time and another forty ammunition caissons being stuck in mud up to their axles with even double teams unable to move them. Also badly delayed

Looking down on the Águeda and the old bridge from the city walls.

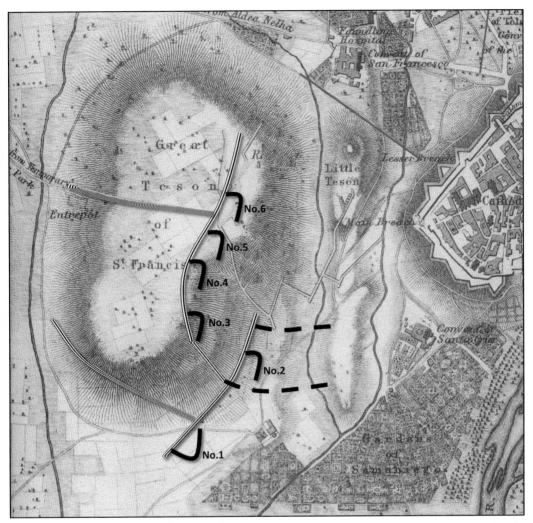

The first stage of the French siege works.

was General Eblé's engineer siege train containing many of the tools, material and wood necessary for preparing the battery's gun platforms on which the guns would be mounted. Nonetheless, six batteries had been prepared by 21 June.

With the investment becoming ever tighter and *voltigeurs* being posted to within 150 yards or a long musket-shot of the walls, at the foot of the glacis slope General Herrasti ordered Don Julián Sánchez to break out of the city and join the British. In a subsequent report to Lord Liverpool, Wellington recorded:

> Don Julián Sánchez, who commands a party [of guerrillas], which has been attached to the Garrison for some time quitted it with his party of men without loss, on the night of the 22nd, and brought me a letter from the Governor, in which he states his determination and that of the garrison to hold out to the last.

At midnight on 23/24 June the Santa Cruz convent was again attacked as fire from its cannon was causing significant casualties around Batteries 1 and 2. This time it was on a greater scale and included a diversionary attack on the San Francisco convent. Some 300 grenadiers of the 82nd Line under the command of *Chef de Bataillon* Rocherond formed up in the sap running down from the parallel, while two columns both numbering approximately 120 *chasseurs de siège* and engineers formed up in the cover of trees and bushes on the banks of the Águeda. They were to attack the convent's front and rear gates.

With the moon hidden by clouds, the three columns advanced towards the convent. The sappers blew in the barricaded gates and the French infantry stormed into the courtyard. The elements of the 3rd Battalion, Avila Regiment were driven back to the main convent building after hand-to-hand fighting. Again, the engineers blew open the doorway and the Spanish were forced to withdraw their men – now reduced to about 100 – to the upper floors. As they climbed the staircase, the stairs were broken up behind them in order to impede the French. Captain François in leading his chasseurs up the remains of the stairs 'with sabre in one hand and a torch in the other' was shot dead and his men driven back. Similarly leading from the front, Captain Meltzen was shot twice and mortally wounded. The French fell back, stalemate set in and a firefight in the convent went on for over two and a half hours. The attack of the grenadiers on the northern face had failed to break in over the convent walls and consequently the French chasseurs and engineers in the cloister had insufficient numbers to overwhelm the brave men of the Avila Regiment.

The attack had failed, the Spanish were still in possession of Santa Cruz and having suffered heavy casualties, the French fell back to the parallels under a

The attack on the Santa Cruz convent.

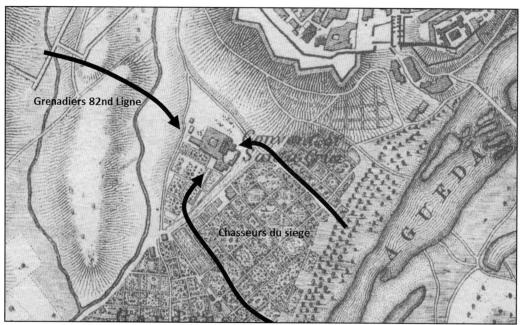

French engineer in siege armour.   The uniforms of typical Spanish soldiers.

blistering fire from the Spanish musketeers. In order to facilitate further assaults engineers were, however, ordered forward again with 100lb charges of gunpowder to blow two substantial holes in the cloister wall on its northern side. The total French casualties in the attack were fifteen dead and fifty-three wounded and General Herrasti was well pleased with the success of the Avila Regiment and wrote in his diary: 'The night was full of glory for us, and they paid dearly for the single barbaric satisfaction they gained in burning some buildings at the convent of Santa Cruz.'

Yet the night was not entirely unsuccessful for the French, with approach trenches being dug towards Santa Cruz and up onto the Lesser Teson under cover of the fighting around the convent. The diggers were, however, eventually forced back into cover when, being illuminated by the light of the burning convent buildings, enemy fire forced them out of the forward trenches.

With the supply situation having been improved as much as was possible in Spain, Masséna finally moved his headquarters from Salamanca to the monastery at La Caridad. Marshal Ney in turn moved his headquarters closer to the siege, taking up residence in a rudimentary hut built in the engineer park.

The Bombardment

With the arrival of forty-six heavy guns the labour-intensive process of mounting them in the six batteries that had been prepared for them and bringing forward the necessary quantities of ammunition could begin. Finally, months after blockading Ciudad Rodrigo, three weeks after the beginning of the invest-ment and ten days after breaking ground, it was agreed that the bombardment would begin on either 26 or 27 June 1810. Marshal Ney, however, had other ideas and Pelet furnishes us with another example of disloyalty and naked ambition in the Army of Portugal. Despite the agreement on the opening of the bombard-ment, Ney brought it forward to 0400 hours on 24 June 1810 without Masséna's authority. Pelet recorded:

> The Prince [Masséna] was warned at midnight by General Eblé that the bombardment was to begin at four o'clock in the morning in spite of what had been previously agreed upon and announced. The Prince immediately called General Fririon and I and sent us to the Marshal [Ney] with all speed. We had hardly arrived when the Prince himself came, complaining vigor-ously about the haste and the disastrous effects it might have. Despite the explanations I was convinced, and it was later confirmed, that the Marshal did not expect the Prince there that day; he hoped to overwhelm the fortress at the outset and have it fall at the first fire. The Marshal wanted to capture it before our arrival and get the credit alone. Nevertheless, as I have indicated, all the arrangements had been made to commence fire. The Prince did not give contradictory orders, and he went to the camp to see its effects.

As feared by Masséna, despite its impressive noise the rushed bombardment did not bring about the collapse of Spanish morale that Ney had hoped for; certainly not in the stern figure of General Herrasti. Pelet continued:

> At dawn, every battery opened fire at the same time with all forty-six of their guns. At first the city appeared disconcerted. Initially it replied with rather sporadic and uncertain fire; later there was a more intense fire from a number of guns which were superior to ours and of a larger calibre. Soon guns were firing vigorously from both sides and the noise was terrible. Those who had never before seen a siege believed that everything would be destroyed. Nevertheless, there was little result on either side. In our camp, the first day resulted in a few accidents occasioned by our haste in opening fire. A small powder magazine for the batteries, not sufficiently covered, had exploded, resulting in the loss of a few men.

Although Pelet makes light of the French losses, by the end of the 25th the Spanish had silenced Battery No. 6. An exploding shell had ignited a magazine located between Batteries 5 and 6 detonating almost 900lb of gunpowder, which flattened the two batteries' protective parapets, killing twelve artillerymen and wounding forty-two. Similarly, the labourers in the trenches and their guard suffered heavy losses from the Spanish garrison in Santa Cruz and by the heavy

The view from the walls to the Greater Teson and the advancing French trenches, with cannon mounted on the faussebraye.

fire from the fortress's batteries. This produced another 21 dead and 162 wounded to add to the tally for 25 June 1810.

While the Spanish soldiers on the city walls suffered from enemy fire, the main effect of the French bombardment was felt by the people of Ciudad Rodrigo. Almost 600 high-explosive shells were fired by French howitzers and mortars, which set fire to buildings in both the suburbs and city, killing 150 and wounding 500 and not unnaturally causing dismay and panic among the population.

On the night of 25 June Santa Cruz was again attacked at 2300 hours. This time not only were there the holes that had been blown in the northern wall the previous night, but the convent had been softened up by artillery during the day. With the chasseurs having suffered heavy casualties in the two previous attacks, the task was handed over to a better-organized assault by the 300 grenadiers who had failed so significantly to break into the convent the previous evening. This, the third attack, was a success, with the convent's garrison withdrawing to the main fortress. Half the grenadiers remained in the by now largely burned-out shell of the building constructing barricades that would give them some protection from Spanish fire that was now at a range of just over 150 yards.

Shortly after the bombardment had begun Masséna headed west to inspect the outposts facing the British Light Division and to look at the ground to the west of the Águeda on which he might have to fight. Pelet recorded that:

We carefully studied the terrain that might be our battlefield if the enemy decided to disturb the siege by marching directly towards us. It consisted

A portrait of an ageing
Marshal André Masséna.

of great plateaus, slightly inclined, rather exposed, and well adapted to
manoeuvres. The front of the Azaba could be defended with advantage but
the enemy would not fail to advance towards our left.

With the French having carried out their reconnaissance and estimate and made
provisional plans, if Wellington had consequently marched to the relief of
Ciudad Rodrigo he would not, as a habitual part of his art of war, be fighting the
enemy on good defensive ground of his own choosing. In short, the risk of having
to accept battle on French terms was a major factor in Wellington's decision not
to relieve Ciudad Rodrigo. He was, after all, commanding 'England's last army'
and was constantly being beseeched 'not to lose it'.

However, all was not well with the siege. The sundry difficulties in gathering
and assembling the myriad of siege necessities at Ciudad Rodrigo, plus Ney's
precipitate start to the bombardment and of course the ground conditions under
which the French gunners and engineers laboured all played their part in slowing
the pace of operations. It was argued by some that it would be better to suspend
the bombardment until all the resources were in place in the engineer and artillery parks, but this would be an unacceptable admission of failure, be a boost to

the garrison's morale and it was feared even invite attack by Wellington. Masséna wrote to General Eblé: 'Everything depends on this siege being conducted with the greatest vigour. It is important to the health of the army that it be ended as soon as possible.[1] Do not neglect the art of siege warfare in making the fortress of Rodrigo fall into our hands.'

Masséna, with some direct orders, was finally able to concentrate the resources of VIII Corps so jealously guarded by General Junot to assist his rival marshal with the siege. His artillerymen were dispatched to join Ney's, along with his ammunition caissons and much of his transport, while additional men were set to work to improve the road from Salamanca via San Muñoz. To assemble all that was required would take time but at least the French had recognized the determination of the Spanish defence.

With the siege still making slow progress, on 29 June Wellington wrote in a dispatch: 'Ciudad Rodrigo is making a capital defence, and I only regret that the enemy have collected such a force that it is impossible for me to attempt the relief of the place.' Not only would the ground be of French choosing if they attempted to break the siege, but with Junot's troops now around the city, the British would be outnumbered.

The view over the buildings on the Lesser Teson to the Greater Teson from the centre of the northern city walls.

Wellington's views on intervening in the siege can be summarized as follows: if the French were equal to the siege, then he would not be equal to its relief as he could not take on a superior force in open country with fewer cavalry and the River Côa behind him.[2] On the lack of attempt to relieve Ciudad Rodrigo, Captain Marbot stated that: 'The French, unable to believe that the English would have come so near the place just to see it captured under their eyes, expected a battle. None took place.'

Following the difficulties of the previous days, shortly after dawn on 27 June General Eblé again ordered all forty-six guns of his siege artillery into action, joining the howitzers and mortars that had between them fired up to seventy shells into the city during the short hours of mid-summer darkness. With the batteries repaired and reorganized to concentrate on creating a breach rather than counter-battery, masonry was soon falling from the wall and faussebraye but, largely unmolested, the Spanish gunners were able to strike back, dismounting several French cannon. Meanwhile, the approach trenches were being dug with particular progress being made at night.

During the early afternoon of 28 June, the breach was tentatively declared practicable but there was some discussion about the relative lack of damage to the counterscarp of the outer moat. With Ney keen to press on, an aide-de-camp was sent with a speculative letter to summons the fortress. It began with the customary pleasantries:

> His Highness the Prince of Essling ... has ordered me to make this last summons. I am pleased to render justice to your fine defence and to the courage that the troops of your garrison have shown but these efforts, always recognised by the French Army, will destroy you if you continue your defence much longer.

The marshal could not resist drawing attention to Herrasti's 'perfidious allies': 'If you hoped to be aided by the English, you are deceived. How could you fail to realize that this had been their intention, under no condition would they have permitted Ciudad Rodrigo to be reduced to such a deplorable condition?' He concluded with the equally usual threat: 'You have a choice between honourable capitulation and the terrible vengeance of a victorious army.'[3]

The Junta duly rejected the summons after protracted discussion, with Herrasti's view prevailing; i.e. that the breach was not yet practicable. The French aide-de-camp returned with apparently deliberately-planted information, gained in conversation with Spanish officers while the Junta deliberated. He reported that morale was low, supplies were running out and that British reticence was further undermining the defenders' morale. He told the marshal that Rodrigo could only hold out for four or five days and this welcome news spread around VI Corps like wildfire as it appeared that there would be an early relief of their suffering. The hopelessly over-optimistic promises of the French artillery commanders that had begun with their belief that the enemy guns would be dismounted within three hours of opening fire had undermined the French soldiers' confidence from the start. Then French optimism that the fortress would capitulate when the breach became practicable, fuelled by reports from faint-hearted deserters and shocked prisoners of war, had come to nought. Now when this opinion coming from officers inside the city meant that the siege showed no signs of ending in the expected time frame, French morale again dipped sharply.

With Ney rebuffed, his weary gunners, engineers and infantry bent to their labours once again and the siege continued. French vengeance was terrible as shot and shell targeted the city and cathedral, as well as the walls. Herrasti, however, noted that in the circumstances the determination of the people of the city to resist was remarkable. Overnight the garrison fought fires and struggled to repair the breach but to no avail, as the following day it was again pounded open but French progress on reducing the counterscarps was slow. What was needed was enfilading fire from a flank but cannon in the fortified suburb of San Francisco prevented the siting of additional batteries. The fortified convent that dominated that quarter would have to be taken. Pelet recorded that 'Our firing continued with some success, and the Prince ordered it to be increased. We fired vigorously and by salvos. I visited the entire trench network. It was not very safe anywhere, but the enemy appeared to be demoralized ... They fired occasionally from a few guns or howitzers.'

There was, however, a looming problem and that was ammunition supply. What was becoming a protracted siege at the end of a very long line of communication was, in the prevailing weather conditions and with guerrilla activity, becoming tenuous with just 600 rounds left for the 16- and 24-pounder guns. A re-supply was on the way but until it arrived the tempo of the siege would be reduced.

New Batteries

In a fraught meeting with Ney and his divisional commanders, Masséna replaced VI Corps' artillery and engineer officers with his own officers in order to give the siege a new momentum, but this was at the cost of a further deterioration in relations between the two marshals. Pelet recalled in his account of the siege: 'Henceforth it became necessary to entreat the Prince to maintain as much moderation as firmness in his relations with the Marshal, for under the circumstances he truly had reason to complain about him. Disagreement was apparent on every occasion.'

Masséna's artillery commander Colonel Valazé toured the siege works and confirmed the worst fears that more time would be necessary to construct additional batteries to properly breach the walls. This of course meant constructing them on the Lesser Teson, which would, of course, be enfiladed by fire from the

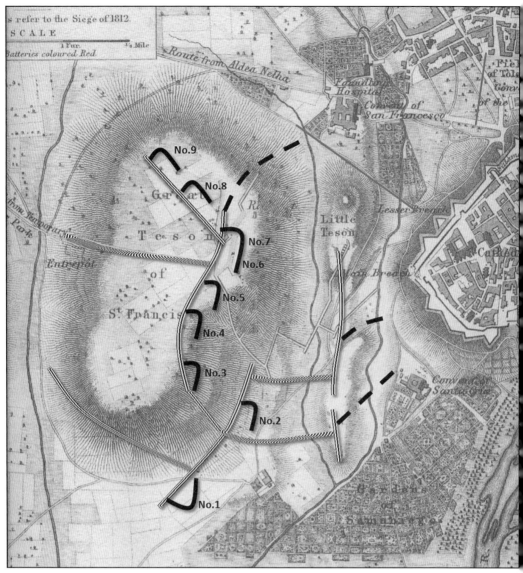

The second group of batteries.

San Francisco convent which, containing two cannon and a pair of howitzers, could engage the trenches on the Teson. Pelet commented that the fire from San Francisco was particularly effective because of poor tracing (laying-out) of the parallels by the engineers. Although far more experienced in siege-craft than their British enemy, the French engineers clearly made their own mistakes.

The reasons for the slow progress of the siege so far were not only the French difficulties and the weather, but above all the stout resolve of the Spanish garrison from General Herrasti downwards. Sallies were mounted as a regular feature of Spanish resistance and proved to be a consistent brake on progress.

In early July Masséna wrote to Marshal Berthier in Paris that he would enlarge the breach and reduce the counterscarp and that 'I will make another summons and if they refuse a capitulation, I will take it by force and put the garrison to the sword without sparing the inhabitants who are the most stubborn.'

As a first step in redirecting the siege, additional batteries were constructed: No. 7 to batter San Francisco and Nos 8 and 9 with 12-pounders and howitzers to subdue the suburb. With the latter batteries established and in action against San Francisco, General Simon was ordered to attack the convent during the night of 1 July. His methodology was a combination of subtlety and dash. At 2100 hours the force of 600 men was ready and waiting for the moment to attack. With broken cloud above, they only had to wait for a cloud to obscure the moon and forward to the palisade went a small party of volunteer chasseurs from the Légion du Midi armed only with their short sabre-briquets. Climbing the palisade, they took the Spanish sentries by surprise, killing three of them before they could raise the alarm. With an entry point into the San Francisco defences secured, the first of three columns of 200 men, who had equally successfully moved up under cover of darkness, took on another Spanish sentry post before they could fire their muskets and alert the other defenders. Those that escaped were pursued and bayoneted.

The Spanish were now alert and defenders in both the convent and up on the walls fired muskets at the fleeting French targets, who moved quickly to take San Francisco from the flank and rear. After a short but determined fight, the Spanish were driven out. However, the second column had not been so lucky. After breaking into the convent, they found themselves in a maze of outbuildings and it took them some time to find their way into the main part of the convent and join the first column. A third column followed across the palisade and secured the Foundling Hospital.

Meanwhile, 150 labourers had been waiting to dig a communication trench from Battery No. 7 on the Greater Teson down to the convent and extended the second parallel eastwards, as well as beginning to dig a second approach down from the Lesser Teson. Altogether it was a successful night, with General Simon capturing San Francisco with just a handful of casualties.

The business of digging and battering continued apace with gabion baskets being brought forward to protect the men digging in the approaches and the second parallel. Going was, however, difficult up on the Lesser Teson with its rocky soil. Consequently, much labour was required to move spoil from further back in order to create a parapet rather than hack into the rock only a foot or so below the surface.

During the night of 2 July Ney's troops launched an attack from San Francisco across the suburb to seize the Santa Clara convent. They successfully cleared the area and extended a trench, despite the Spanish being alert and having moved additional cannon to cover the suburbs, with which they raked the area with canister fire.

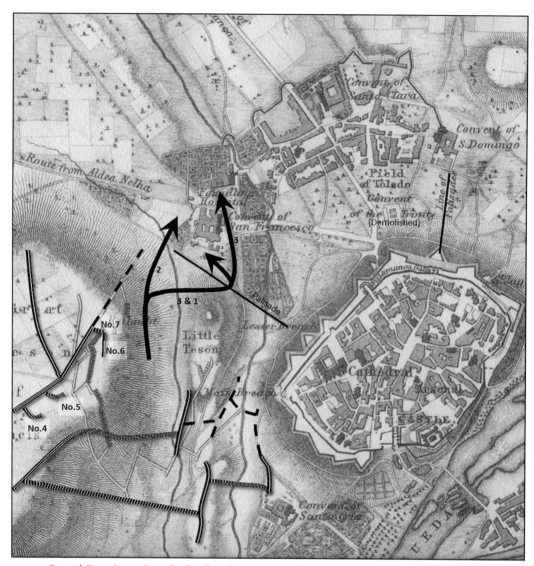

General Simon's attack on the San Francisco convent and entrenching on the night of 1 July 1810.

Elsewhere work was continuing apace, with new batteries sited by General Eblé now both closer to the walls and effective, while the engineers and their trenches were creeping up the glacis slope towards the breach and the counterscarp. Here they started to tunnel in order to place mines, totalling 800lb of powder, to reduce the vertical drop into the moat. The French were not, however, having things entirely their own way. Though reduced in quantity, fire from the walls of Rodrigo was still effective and causing a steady stream of casualties to both men and guns.

Twenty-four days after the French broke ground Masséna, in response to favourable progress reports, ordered a last push to take the fortress. Ammunition that had been husbanded for this final effort and all available guns were brought into action against the breach, its approaches, enemy cannon and the defenders. The British, even though they had been pushed back towards the border, could hear the renewed intensity of the bombardment and realized that the siege was reaching its climax with 1,689 shot and shell being fired at the defences, along with 420 heavy shells falling on the walls and city during 9 July. That night the mines were blown, demolishing a section of the counterscarp and further reducing the depth of the moat with a ramp of rubble. The breach itself was two piles of rubble demolished by gunfire on the north-west corner of the fortress. The time for the storming of Ciudad Rodrigo had come.

The finished French siege works.

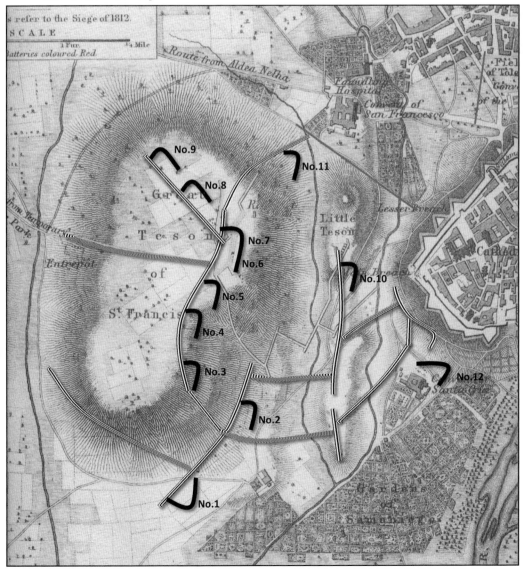

The Surrender of Ciudad Rodrigo

A disruptive fire was maintained on the breach during the night in order to impede Spanish repairs and retrenchment and at dawn on 10 July all forty-six pieces of artillery resumed their bombardment:

> Shells were falling with great rapidity and excellent marksmanship. On every side arose thick clouds of dust and smoke, pierced by the flames of the fires. The wreckage of buildings and walls was tumbling down with great noise, and several of the small magazines exploded periodically with tremendous detonations. The city seemed overwhelmed by fire.

The Spanish flag, however, remained stubbornly flying and in an indication that he had not expected the fortress to stand, Masséna dispatched Pelet to the San Francisco convent where from its battered tower he and the siege directors were able to inspect the top of the breach with their telescopes. It seemed that the enemy had made some effort to barricade the breach but under fire by night and heavy bombardment all morning they had been able to achieve little.

Meanwhile, General Loison was preparing to storm the city. The forlorn hope consisted of fifty engineers wearing their trench armour. The 100-strong storming party would follow under the command of Major Delomme. They were made up of three companies of grenadiers, volunteers from across the division, and were to be followed by the remnants of the *chasseurs de siège* and 150 infantrymen as labourers with digging tools. The forlorn hope's task was to secure the top of the breach, while the stormers would clear the ramparts and occupy adjacent houses. The *chasseurs de siège* were to expand the lodgement, while the surviving engineers and the labourers were to enlarge and reduce the steepness of the breach.

A second column was to follow up through the breach. Two companies of *voltigeurs* were to be left as a reserve just inside the breach, while the other five would turn left and make their way along the ramparts to the Puerta del Conde, spiking guns as they went. Once at the gate, a distance of 300 yards from the breach, they would open or blow it down to admit a force that was assembling under cover of the San Francisco suburbs who would in turn secure other key points in the city and break open gates to let in further troops. A total of five battalions was deemed to be sufficient to crush the resistance, based on information supplied by Spanish deserters.

With the assault troops ready, the guns finally started to fall silent in the mid-afternoon and the red flag, the signal to begin the storm, was waiting at the foot of a flagpole on the Lesser Teson, ready. Pelet recalled:

> All the army talked only about burning the whole city and massacring the entire garrison … Everybody seemed to be revolted at the proposition of a new summons. Everything was ready for the assault and everyone wanted the

The battered remains of the one-time San Francisco convent and prison.

violence and fury. The Prince grasped the horror of sacking the city and decided to do everything in his power to prevent it ... The Prince ordered that the city should be summoned at four o'clock for the third time, and if it had not lowered its flag after a quarter of an hour, then the signal for the assault would be given.

Meanwhile, Pelet was ordered to take three infantrymen to the foot of the breach and sent them off upwards to prove the route. Even though death seemed a certainty, there were said to be 100 volunteers. Marshal Ney's stirring words of 'You will be killed, but you will die as honourable men' worked on the besiegers, despite their previously low morale:

> The commanders of the engineers and the artillery came along. Those three grenadiers were superb, marching like heroes, and proudly announcing to everybody that they were going to open the path to glory. They were electrifying, and they electrified me. I could feel that I too was a grenadier and a volunteer, marching at their front. Arriving on the counterscarp, they went quietly up the two breaches. In a few seconds, they were at the summit firing their guns on the fleeing garrison; they shouted '*Vive l'Empereur!*'

several times and reloaded their weapons. It was necessary to call them and order them to come down; since they had not received a single shot, they wanted to begin firing again. Their names were Thirion, corporal of the 50th Grenadiers, and Bombois and Billeret, carabineers of the 6th Leger. Thirion was the most excited; coming down, he offered me some brandy to drink. I drank – it was from a brave man.

 We had only taken a few steps in the trenches when we heard, with rapture, shouts of peace.

Herrasti's view was that by 10 July 'Our fire and resistance was exhausted, we no longer had any hope of aid, and the enemy had reduced the breach to a state such that the assault could be delivered.' It is said that the two distinct ramps of rubble that made up the breach were wide enough for sixty men to advance up in line. Pelet continued that this was

 peace from the same voices who had demanded an assault only minutes earlier. I climbed on the parapet of the trench and saw the white flag beside the breach. I ran to announce this news to the Prince, since he was on Teson where he could not see the flag very well. Others arrived ahead of me, but I presented my three heroes. The Prince gave them his purse, but they

French infantryman.

Cross of the Légion d'honneur instigated by Napoleon.

refused, saying, 'My Prince, we did not do this for money but for honour and country.' This was an ingenious way of asking for the Cross [Légion d'honneur]. It was promised to them, and they received it.

Meanwhile, the Marshal had already gone to the breach where he conducted negotiations in his own name and according to his own fancy. He secured the entrance to the ramparts with a few companies ... Later I was told that Governor Herrasti presented himself to the Marshal in the breach. The Marshal put his hat back on after greeting him and the Spaniard replaced his hat also, retaining much of his dignity. The governor was fifty-five years old, with a good face and bearing. I think he was responsible for raising the first piece of cloth he could find while the clergy of the Junta were still protesting from deep within their caves. The Prince went to the breach and returned with the Marshal. I went into the fortress to take a look. It was dreadful. We entered by the breach. Everything adjoining it had been crushed, pounded, and destroyed. The ruins and devastation extended to the middle of the city. At every step, one could see collapsed or burned houses. We went all along the ramparts; our posts were already established.

Sometime later Pelet was ordered back to the city where 'everything was in great confusion. It was already midnight. We did not have time to take all the necessary measures to maintain order in the midst of so much confusion. Obviously, those who had planned the arrangements for the assault did not think of police measures.'

Even though it had been promised that the city would not be sacked, the result was increasing disorder. Pelet believed that by waiting till the last moment when the storm was imminent, Herrasti had made a mistake: the troops keyed-up for the assault could not be restrained:

When I entered the city, I realized there was no way of imposing any restraint except with sabre thrusts. A few other officers and I struck right and left at the pillagers, no matter who they were. My eyes were impervious to distinctions of rank, and if I recognized anybody I only hit harder. I complained vigorously to the post commanders. Little by little they were able to call in their men and send them on patrol. If the disorder did not stop completely, at least word spread that it was not allowed or tolerated; thus, it took place secretly in a few isolated corners.

Masséna entered the town the following day and ordered an inventory of captured arms and equipment to be made. It totalled 118 bronze guns of a variety of calibres, along with 82,477 shot and shell and 147,100lb of powder (much of which proved to be of dubious quality) and 7,255 stand of small arms, with almost a million cartridges. While, however, the 269 waggons and vehicles may also be seen as a boon, there were no draught animals to move them. All in all, Masséna's

One of the many fine old buildings such as this off the Plaza Mayor would have been looted.

ammunition problems had been greatly reduced with the capture of the powder, shot and shell, while Spanish-calibre lead ball could easily be recast to fit the French Charleville musket. The food found in the fortress was sufficient to stave off hunger but only for a very short time; however, coin and valuables seized would help to buy some food and assist in paying to put the fortress into a state of defence.

During the seventy-two-day siege, Spanish losses are estimated at 2,000 soldiers and civilians, including those killed in the disorder after the storm. Some 4,000 men were taken prisoner and sent to France. French casualties were lighter, being 180 killed and somewhat over 1,000 wounded. Herrasti expressed his feelings in a letter to the Spanish Minister for War on 30 July: 'The valour, the fortitude and the sacrifices of the garrison and the inhabitants deserve a better fate. They have had the misfortune of not being supported by the arms of our allies after defending themselves during such a long siege with firmness and vigour.'

While one can sympathize with Herrasti's bitterness, one cannot fault Wellington's calculation that he would recklessly imperil his army and fail in any attempt to relieve Ciudad Rodrigo.

The memorial to General Herrasti in the square that bears his name between the cathedral and the breach.

Conclusion

Masséna had a far from free hand in the conduct of the siege and indeed the campaign as a whole. He was ordered to be methodical and not just to bypass Ciudad Rodrigo, which ultimately bought Wellington two and a half months extra to complete the integration of re-formed Portuguese regiments into his Peninsular Army and to extend the construction of the Lines of Torres Vedras into a state of

Napoleon tried to conduct the campaign from a distance throughout.

almost impregnability by the end of 1810. Masséna had, however, faced some very real difficulties: the climate was against him in 1810 in what should have progressed with the season from cool to hot and dry, but with the weather against him the already difficult roads of Spain were rendered almost impassable. The slow tempo of logistics and Ney's early foray to Ciudad Rodrigo both exacerbated the food supply situation, which was already inadequate. In short, Masséna's already poor situation was made impossible by bad relations with his subordinate marshals and by Napoleon's insistence on trying to conduct the campaign across 850 miles of mountainous and guerrilla-infested country.

Notes

1. During protracted siege operations, outbreaks of disease were always a threat, as during Henry V's siege of Harfleur in 1415.
2. Julian Rathbone, *Wellington's War: His Peninsular Dispatches* (Michael Joseph, 1984).
3. Archives du Masséna. A copy sent to Berthier.

Chapter Eight

The Affair at Villar de Puerco

Following the action on 4 July that had seen the Light Division driven back beyond Gallegos and the River Dos Casas, the French had retired back across the Azaba/Águeda and as a result the intervening 5 miles became no man's land for a period. This was fertile country for renewed outpost actions, the mobility of which contrasts strongly with the static nature of the last days of the 1810 French siege of Ciudad Rodrigo. Much of the activity centred around protecting the hungry French foraging parties who were gathering in the crops which had finally, with the last ten days of sun, started to ripen.

In addition, during the first week of July 1810 General of Brigade Godert, commanding 3rd Brigade of Clausel's 1st Division in Junot's VIII Corps, had regularly dispatched a force of cavalry and infantry into the area of no man's land to ensure that the British were not going to mount a last-ditch effort to relieve Ciudad Rodrigo. Lieutenant Simmons explains: 'The enemy had a piquet of cavalry and infantry in advance of Villar de Ciervo but withdrew them after dark and reoccupied the post at daylight.'

To reach Villar de Ciervo the French marched before dawn via the villages of Villar de Puerco and Barquilla. This habitual intrusion into what Brigadier General Craufurd clearly believed was his territory required a response from him. Therefore, on the night of 10/11 July he planned to deploy, under cover of darkness, what was in effect an area ambush with a substantial and well-supported force of cavalry and riflemen.

During 10 July, the same day Rodrigo had fallen, General Craufurd gave orders for the operation to the various elements of his force assembled along the border from Fort Concepcion southwards, the forward element of which would be six squadrons of cavalry (three of the 14th Light Dragoons, two of the 16th and Captain Krauchenberg's squadron of the KGL Hussars). They would be supported by nine companies of infantry (seven from the 95th Rifles and two from the 52nd) and a pair of guns. In addition, covering the northern flank, was Captain Gruben's KGL Squadron and several miles further back companies of the 43rd, the 3rd Caçadores, plus the rest of Ross's troop of horse artillery were all in support. The remainder of Craufurd's troops were deployed in routine piquets, vedettes and patrols across the rest of the division's front.

Mounted gunners of the
Royal Horse Artillery.

At 2300 hours, Craufurd's force started to advance east across the Dos Casas, taking up positions as shown on the map opposite around Villar de Puerco (now renamed Villar de Argañán). Rifleman Costello recorded that:

> We soon guessed that some secret enterprise was about to be undertaken, as strict orders were issued to keep the men from talking, and to make them refrain from lighting their pipes, lest our approach should be noticed by the enemy. Even the wheels of two of Captain Ross's guns that accompanied us were muffled round with hay bands to prevent their creaking.

In addition, patrols were sent further forward to watch the roads from the east and the flanks for the approach of the enemy.

Captain Cocks of the 16th Light Dragoons recalled the deployment:

> We moved off soon after 11 pm and, crossing the ford, circled by Alamanda in order to get beyond Villar de Puerco. Ciudad Rodrigo preserved a dead silence and it became more and more apparent that it had surrendered. Had

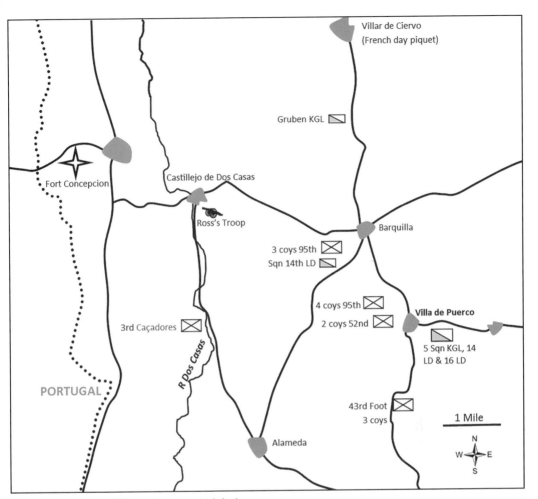

The action at Villar de Puerco: initial deployment.

this been foreseen it is probable that we would never have attempted what we were about, but as it was we were far too engaged to give it up.

We reached Villar de Puerco and formed in close column of squadrons beyond it a little before daybreak.

There is little detail of positions taken up by the units in the various accounts but reconciling those that do give some details and the line of the roads and surrounding ground does provide a probable deployment, which is shown in the map above.

The country to the west and south of Villar de Puerco was difficult and not ideal for cavalry. There were wooded and scrub areas, defiles and walled fields scattered across the area but in front there was a substantial open field, referred to in some accounts as a 'plain', suitable for manoeuvre.

As dawn broke on 11 July, the French column that was to occupy Villar de Ciervo that day and observe British activity to the east set out at about 0230 hours.

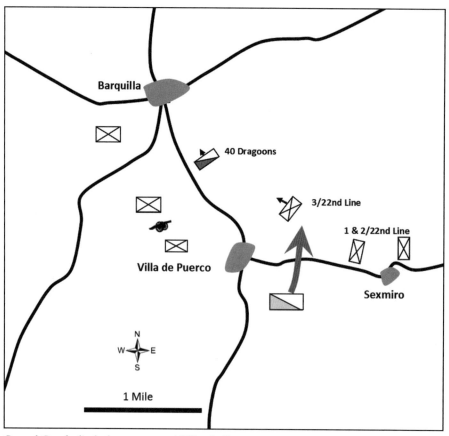

General Craufurd's deployment around Villar de Puerco.

It was commanded by Colonel Armand of the 22nd Regiment of the Line. His advance guard consisted of a half-squadron of dragoons numbering between thirty and forty mounted men, and his 3rd Battalion, commanded by Captain Gouache, which was about 300 strong. The infantry advance guard had probably left the road from Sexmiro to Villar de Puerco to give the latter place a wide berth and to cut off the corner. The other two battalions of the 22nd followed some distance behind.

The ambush force had been in place for about an hour before General Craufurd went down alone to the road at Villar de Puerco and seeing only a small group of enemy dragoons already having passed and heading north to Barquilla, he ordered the cavalry into action. The detail of what followed is provided by letters written by Captain Cocks to General Sir Stapleton Cotton, commander of the light cavalry.

A pair of British light dragoons. Such patrols would operate in front and to the flanks of advancing columns.

First to move were the KGL Hussars with Captain Ashworth's squadron of the 16th Light Dragoons under command. Moving out of the defile into the open area was difficult and time-consuming due to low stone walls that had to be navigated in single file. Once beyond this obstacle, Krauchenberg or a 'staff officer' (accounts differ) ordered Ashworth forward and to deploy his squadron in line to attack alongside the KGL. Meanwhile, two of Craufurd's staff officers, Major Campbell (Major of Brigade) and Captain Shaw-Kennedy, rode on ahead to find the enemy dragoons who had in the meantime moved on towards Barquilla. In doing so they spotted the bayonets of the leading French infantry out on the plain. They had not been spotted earlier because of the cover provided by tall 'Indian corn' (a variety of maize), which was the predominant crop in the open area. Cocks wrote: 'The Hussars endeavoured to form to the front and charge, as did the 1st Squadron (Ashworth's) of the 16th.'

Captain Gouache had, however, seen the threat posed by the cavalry and immediately broke into the life-saving drill of forming square. Once so formed, the French infantry were ordered to lie down to make it difficult for the cavalry to

Villar de Puerco and the surrounding ground.

bear down on them accurately. Captain Brotherton's squadron with Colonel Talbot at its head charged the enemy square. Brotherton wrote:

> It was lying down, concealed in some high-standing corn, and only rose up when my squadron came within pistol-shot of it, and was beautifully steady. We charged it most gallantly, but they fired a deadly volley into us, and half my men fell killed or wounded. Colonel Talbot, who commanded the Regiment, had put himself at the head of the squadron along with me. Poor fellow, he fell pierced by eight balls, literally on the enemy's bayonets. The moment the square had fired into and so sadly crippled us, it moved off to join its support close by, and we were so shattered as not to be able to follow.

Cocks recalls:

> They got a heavy volley, which knocked down thirteen or fourteen men and nearly as many horses. They then wheeled to the left, and made at the cavalry. The 3rd Squadron (Bellis's) followed their example.
>
> The sun was directly in our eyes, and from that circumstance and the dust we could see nothing, and, except the two squadrons who had charged, no one knew whence the volley had proceeded. Then three squadrons rode at the cavalry, and took nearly forty with their horses. Very few got away.

A miniature portrait of an unknown officer of the light dragoons.

A portrayal of the
16th Light Dragoons'
uniform in 1810.

What had happened was that deployed in line of two squadrons, only a relatively few cavalrymen were directly in line with the compact ranks of the French square made up of just 300 infantrymen. Although Bellis's squadron (16th LD), which followed up did not face the same concentrated fire of the first French musket volley, their horses would not press home the attack against the defensive hedge of bayonets presented by the square and the squadron flowed around it to the right.

Steady squares were very seldom broken by cavalry alone and in this case the sangfroid of Captain Gouache and his men was remarkable. Craufurd, however, expecting that a small isolated group of infantry should nonetheless be overthrown, ordered Captain Thomas Brotherton's squadron, the 14th, to renew the attack. Cocks wrote that:

> The [enemy] fire was independent [i.e. not easily discernible infantry volleys], and no one of this squadron could tell whether it proceeded from infantry or cavalry. When, therefore, the order was passed down to move on the cavalry, it was obeyed with alacrity and without surprise ...

Neither Colonel Talbot nor Captain Brotherton saw them [the enemy] and they were obliged to ask the General where they were.

It is impossible to do justice to the intrepidity of this body of men [the French square]. They stood the second charge as well as the first, knocked down some by a running fire, and bayoneted others … When he saw the enemy had formed an oblong, he endeavoured to bring his right flank forward and charge the upper face of the square. He moved on like a lion, had his horse killed close to the enemy, and fell himself fighting sabre in hand in the middle of the square.

Meanwhile, the three companies of the 43rd positioned to the rear of the cavalry, along with the 95th and the pair of guns concealed behind the ridge, were ordered into action. Rifleman Costello was among them:

At length, the cold grey of the morning appeared faintly in the east, when the commands were given with scarce a pause between to 'fall in', 'double', and 'extend' [deploy into a skirmish line]. This was accomplished in a moment, and forward we ran through the corn field up to an eminence, looking down from which we beheld a gallant skirmish on the plain beneath. The 14th Dragoons were in the act of charging a body of French infantry, who had, however, thrown themselves into square. The cavalry cheered forward in gallant style, but the French, veteran-like, stood firm to meet the onset pouring in, at the same time, a close running fire that emptied many saddles.

A pair of riflemen of the 95th.

Lieutenant-Colonel Talbot, who headed the charge, fell almost immediately, together with the quartermaster and from sixteen to eighteen privates.

Sir Stapleton Cotton, in a letter to General Cole, described the final phase of the cavalry action: 'The 5th Squadron (14th LD) under Colonel Arentschildt, was then advancing to support Talbot, but upon seeing a squadron of the 1st Hussars in the distance approaching, and taking them for the enemy, he halted the 14th.'

This was Captain Gruben's squadron that had been posted to the north of Barquilla heading south to join the action. Some commented that Craufurd had clearly forgotten that he had deployed this squadron, but in still less than daylight caution was correct as misidentification is endemic in warfare and it is unlikely that Arentschildt would have fared any better than Talbot.

Rifleman Costello continued:

After an unavailing attempt to shake the square, the cavalry was obliged to retire – a movement which the enemy on their part immediately imitated. An attempt was made to annoy them with our guns, but in consequence of their smallness, being but light field-pieces, our shots were attended with very little effect.

He should perhaps have also added that the Riflemen, of which he was one, sent down to the plain amid the tall Indian corn also had little impact on the French.

Captain Gouache had managed to maintain his square throughout the cavalry attacks and now still in that formation, march back to the west off the plain into cover, with Cocks commenting that 'In the dust and confusion that ensued the enemy got off through the corn into the woods.'

Craufurd on his reconnaissance had only seen the small party of enemy cavalry and had clearly not thought it necessary to deploy his infantry, but in acting precipitately he missed the main prize: the destruction of an entire French infantry regiment. If he had waited and used a combination of cavalry, artillery and infantry the French could have been fixed by the cavalry and destroyed by the infantry and artillery.

There was of course blame, criticism and praise, the latter only for Captain Gouache and his French infantrymen, as in Costello's words they 'veteran-like, stood firm to meet the onset pouring in, at the same time, a close running fire that emptied many saddles.' Major George Napier of the 52nd heaped praise on Captain Gouache:

... this small intrepid band made good its retreat and escaped, after having behaved most gallantly and withstood the charges of several hundreds of our dragoons. The officer commanding had proved himself as skilful as he was brave, and every man who witnessed his conduct was delighted to see him escape.

French infantry in a Spanish village street.

Gouache's remarkable action, without the loss of a single infantryman, against a superior force earned acclamation from both Masséna and Wellington, along with promotion to major, while his sergeant major received the coveted cross of the Légion d'honneur.[1]

Craufurd's impetuous handling of the affair at Villar de Puerco, however, was the focus of criticism from within his own division, as well as from those jealous detractors elsewhere in the army. George Napier wrote:

> The fault was not in our cavalry, but in General Craufurd, who, upon seeing that the first charge of the dragoons made no impression, should have instantly sent a party of infantry, who would have settled the affair at once and saved the life of a gallant young officer of great promise, as well as the lives of the poor soldiers who fell, a useless sacrifice to his obstinacy.

Another staff officer wrote 'That six hundred British Dragoons should have been baffled by two hundred French infantry, was a circumstance for which no one can account.' Even though he inflated the British numbers and reduced the French by a hundred, there is no denying that an army growing in size, skill and confidence expected better than this.

One of the most pernicious was a rumour circulated that the 16th Light Dragoons had failed in their duty and not taken part in the cavalry attack and

Brigadier General
Robert Craufurd.

that Craufurd had tried to blame the escape of the French infantry on them. Wellington personally had to scotch these falsehoods, but felt constrained to give General Craufurd clearer instructions as to the future conduct of outpost duties. The whole affair without a doubt left Craufurd feeling that he had much to prove. Costello commented that 'for some days after, I thought he wore a troubled look, as though he took our failure to heart.'

Note

1. We will see the 3rd Division doing the same only on a much larger scale at El Bodón in September 1811.

Chapter Nine

The Peninsular War, 1810–1811

This chapter outlines events in the Peninsular War between the conclusion of the French siege in mid-July 1810 and the preliminary moves to the British 1812 siege. This is necessary to provide context for the British siege.

Following the fall of Ciudad Rodrigo, the French rapidly repaired the walls of the fortress, filled in trenches and batteries and the important parts of the city began to be rebuilt. The city was, of course, now with the imminent invasion of Portugal, an important place for the French to hold, being a refuge on their line of communication against guerrillas and the surviving Spanish armies.

On 12 July, while not ruling out an attack by Wellington, Marshal Masséna ordered Marshal Ney's VI Corps forward to take over the northern section of the Azaba front from that river's confluence with the Águeda 4 miles south to Aldeanueva. Marshal Junot's VIII Corps continued the front in a southerly direction. Both corps had a growing number of patrols, piquets and vedettes pushed forward towards the British positions on the Dos Casas stream. As pressure mounted with the number of French troops operating against the Light Division increasing, Brigadier General Craufurd prepared to withdraw across the frontier back into Portugal. He was, however, not going to move his division as far back as Wellington arguably intended, i.e. to positions beyond the River Côa, leaving just patrols forward of that river. Craufurd wanted the whole of his division to remain forward in support of Almeida, which would surely be the next French objective, for as long as possible.

Meanwhile, to ensure that it would be of no advantage to the French, the small Fort Concepcion was prepared for demolition. By 20 July 1810 the British and Portuguese infantry had been pulled back and according to Lieutenant Simmons of the 95th Rifles they were back across the Rio Turenos [*sic*], which marked the border, and were 'upon the high road to Vale de la Mula, upon a plain, the cavalry piquets upon the Dos Casas and a few men with the Engineer officer left in Fort Concepcion ready to blow it up at any moment.'

Captain Brotherton of the 14th Light Dragoons wrote:

> The blowing up and complete destruction of this important and beautiful little star fort which guarded the frontier of Spain was an operation of great delicacy, and of most critical and precarious execution, for Colonel [captain

Lieutenant George Simmons,
1st Battalion, 95th Rifles.

at the time] Burgoyne, the talented officer of Engineers selected for the task, had positive orders not to blow it up till the very last moment (that is, till the advance of the enemy), so that we might make use of it till the last moment, but not leave a vestige of it for the enemy's use. These instructions were carried into effect with extraordinary precision and most thoroughly.

I had some little share in the execution of this critical operation. I happened to be on piquet in front of the fort on the night it took place, or rather the morning, at daybreak. As it was a matter of great importance to Masséna to preserve the fort, if possible, and prevent its destruction, which he knew was planned, he thought he would best obtain this object by a sudden and rapid advance on our piquets, driving them back at a gallop, and arriving on the glacis of the fort as soon as we did, when, he thought, the officer of Engineers would hesitate to blow it up for fear of destroying our people. The match was always kept ready in the fort for instantaneous explosion. Knowing the state of the case, I had only just time to exclaim to an officer

The entrance to a restored Fort Concepcion, which is today a hotel and well worth a stay.

close to me, named Wainman, who was beautifully mounted on a thorough-bred horse, to go at speed to Burgoyne and apprise him that we were being driven back most rapidly, and that we had no time to lose. He arrived at the fort only just in time to enable Burgoyne to explode his mine.

Lieutenant Simmons recalled the detonation:

July 21st: At daylight Fort Conception [sic] exploded and made a tremendous noise. I was lying under a tree in a sound sleep. I sprang up, thinking the French army had got into the camp, and seized my sword, which hung upon a bough of the tree, and proceeded to our alarm post. I found the same effect produced by the noise upon the whole of us, and the only feeling we had was to sell our lives at as dear a rate as possible. When the cause was known, and that the enemy had not driven in our outposts, we fell out and took our breakfast.

Captain Brotherton's squadron of 14th Light Dragoons were not as lucky as the 95th. They had been providing vedettes to prevent the French occupying the fortress and were too close when the charges were blown. Both men and horses were killed and injured by flying masonry.

All four bastions were breached by the explosions, along with three of the demi-lunes and other important features of the fort and outlying battery.

Combat on the Côa

During the following two days, it became apparent that French forces were massing on the border. Craufurd maintained his division on the right bank despite the obvious danger and Wellington's cautioning, even though he had the River Côa behind him. To make matters worse there was only a single bridge,

Officer of the 14th Light Dragoons. A new uniform was authorized in 1812 and adopted over the following year.

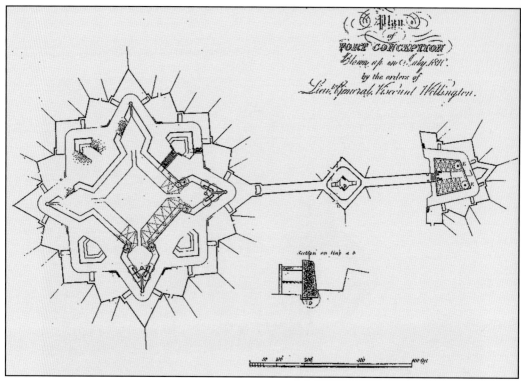

((Plan of FORT CONCEPTION Blown up on 21 July 1811 by the orders of Lieut. General Viscount Wellington.))

Section on line a b

Fort Concepcion, 1810.

and a couple of fords across the river and its gorge. As recently as 22 July 'the Peer' had written to Craufurd that he was 'not desirous of engaging in an affair beyond the Côa.'

Before dawn on 24 July, covered by torrential rain which had rendered the Côa fords impassable, Marshal Ney set the divisions of Ferey and Loison in motion across the frontier in the third French invasion of Portugal. Some 24,000 French troops faced the 4,000-strong Light Division deployed on a 2-mile-long ridge to the south-east of the fortress of Almeida whose guns seemed to provide a secure left flank. With the enemy approaching, Craufurd had plenty of time to withdraw behind a screen of skirmishers and across the river; instead he chose to delay his move by standing and fighting. Not for the first time and certainly not the last, a commander's personal agenda stood in the way of sound military sense and ignoring the calculation based on the respective movement times of infantry, cavalry, artillery and baggage that had served him so well during the spring of 1810.

Several hours after dawn, the British cavalry were driven in and the French infantry 'advanced at pace' and Craufurd's five battalions came under attack from thirteen battalions of Loison's division. This first attack was, however, beaten off by the infantry's disciplined volley fire. At this point, despite artillery fire from the fortress, the French 3rd Hussars charged the Light Division's left flank, in the process overwhelming a company of the 95th strung out in skirmish order. Thus,

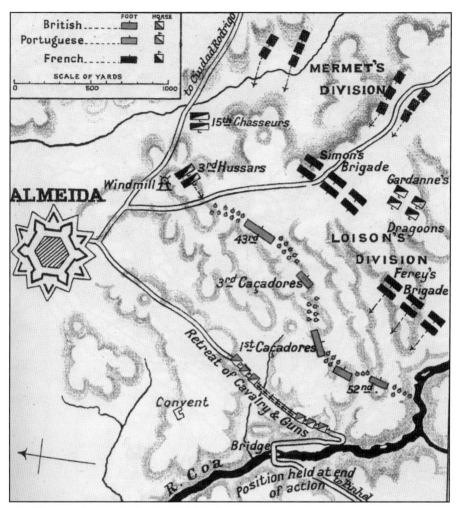

The Côa: Oman's map showing the initial deployment.

almost immediately Craufurd's position was compromised and in danger of being rolled up. A withdrawal was ordered by an unnerved Craufurd but with a single narrow bridge and with the division's baggage, artillery, its sundry vehicles, plus cavalry to be got across this was to be no easy task, especially as Craufurd's 4,000 men were already in close contact with 6,000 Frenchmen, with many more coming up behind them.

As the French repeatedly attacked, the 1st Caçadores followed the artillery and the cavalry down to the bridge in what was described as 'an accelerated pace', leaving the 3rd Caçadores and three British battalions to withdraw, locked in

The distinctive grey and red, black fur-trimmed uniform of the 3rd French Hussars.

Valley of the River Coa and its bridge.

Fortifications of Almeida

The ground on which the combat on the Côa was fought.

contact with the enemy in one of the most difficult phases of war. Once off the original ridge the country became more difficult for both armies. It dropped away to the River Côa and was broken by narrow valleys, vineyards, watercourses and stone walls. Fortuitously, this reduced use of the French cavalry to skirmishing and rounding up individuals who had become detached from their companies. For the British, on one occasion the 43rd Light Infantry found that they had withdrawn into a high stone-walled enclosure, which offered cover but there was no easy way out. Once it was time to withdraw again, the battalion struggled to climb the wall and get through small gaps they had made. Lesser troops, with the enemy pressing them hard, could have lost all cohesion and been destroyed.

The crisis, however, came at the bridge where the 1st Caçadores and the last guns and caissons were crossing under pressure to escape and clear the way for the infantry. Inevitably on the tight steep turn onto the bridge a caisson became stuck. With the French closing in, Craufurd struggled to deploy Ross's guns and the Caçadores, the latter into the rocks on the home bank.

Every regiment had its own distinctive uniform. In this case the 43rd (Monmouthshire) Light Infantry had their own lace, buttons in pairs trimmed by square-ended lace and white facing on the collar.

Meanwhile, on the far bank, having fought their way back well over a mile the battalions were beginning to become disordered as a result of enemy pressure and the ground, with on the left the 43rd and 95th's companies becoming intermingled. The situation became beyond the more senior commanders' ability to orchestrate and the 52nd up on a rocky knoll covering the right flank became isolated. Major McLeod, commanding the 43rd, realized this and 'immediately turned his horse round, called to the troops to follow, and taking off his cap, rode with a shout towards the enemy.' His men 'ran up the hill, exposed to a desperate fire, as the enemy had a strong wall to fire over'. The French, 'astonished at this unexpected movement', were forced back and the 52nd and a wing of the 43rd were given a breathing space to withdraw across the bridge and deploy onto the rocks beyond.

General Loison was determined to follow up success and ordered General of Brigade Ferey to rush the bridge. Colonel Jean Pierre Béchaud's 66th Line charged across it only to wither away under the fire of the 43rd, the Caçadores and the Rifles. Marshal Ney arrived and ordered the attack to be resumed with cries of '*Vive l'Empereur!*' echoing off the rocky walls of the valley and with the shouts mingling with musket fire and rifle shots, the French charged again. Captain Harry Smith of the 95th wrote: 'The bridge was literally piled with their dead and they made breastworks of the bodies.'

The Côa bridge and the slopes down which the infantry battalions made the final withdrawal.

Criticism was again heaped on General Craufurd from all quarters and brought into question his continuing command of the Light Division. From the British perspective, indeed that of his own soldiers as well, it was regarded as unnecessary and costly to get back across the river and the perception was only made worse by a further withdrawal from the Côa that night. The way was now open for the French to besiege Almeida.

The Siege of Almeida

Marshals Masséna and Ney lost no time in carrying out a reconnaissance of Almeida, but under instructions from Paris to be orderly and not to head deep into Portugal; until the harvest was in, the pace of tempo of French operations remained slow. The supply of food and the lacklustre campaign had in turn a continuing impact on the morale of French troops. The undernourished men were falling out in large numbers and the hospitals filling, despite efforts to harvest barely ripe crops.

The situation in the siege train was hardly any better. In addition to the general shortages, it was inadequately manned, lacked sufficient draught animals and having fired off a prodigious amount of ammunition at Ciudad Rodrigo during the protracted siege, it was lacking in that department as well. The powder and shot captured at Ciudad proved to be of poor quality but helped. Nonetheless, Masséna and General Eblé were requesting resupply from across Spain and back as far as France. All this plus a lack of co-operation among commanders across Spain meant that preparing for the next siege was a slow business. All Masséna could do was to blockade the place.

Meanwhile, the Light Division and the rest of Wellington's army had withdrawn 15 miles to strong defensive positions. The French in following found that

An aerial photo of the defences of Almeida and the compact town within.

while the British had gone, the Ordenanças (militia) and ordinary Portuguese people were resisting their invasion. In addition, Wellington made a 'Proclamation to the People of Portugal' in which he required them 'to render the enemy's advance into their country as difficult as possible, by removing out of his way everything that is valuable, or can contribute to his subsistence, or frustrate his progress.'

There was still precious little food to be had, which put further pressure on the extending lines of communication back via Ciudad Rodrigo. This force under General Ferey became the corps of observation for the siege of Almeida, again to prevent intervention by the British.

Meanwhile, Simon's brigade had started the process of investing Almeida and its commander delivered a letter from General Loison to Colonel Cox demanding the surrender of the fortress. His answer was to open fire on the French piquets surrounding the town, which drove Simon's infantry back beyond the range of the fortress's guns. As General Herrasti had done, Colonel Cox sent out regular sallies to keep the French at a distance.

The fortress of Almeida was, though smaller than Ciudad Rodrigo, if anything stronger with its defences in good repair having been strengthened under the direction of British engineer officers and artificers during the preceding months. The garrison, however, consisted of two weak, poorly-equipped and indifferent Portuguese regiments that had defied attempts to improve them, as had happened in the case of those regiments attached to Wellington's field force.

Masséna had been hoping to break ground on 9 August, but due to shortages and delays in the arrival of stores and the siege train this eventually took place on 15 August, by which time he had concentrated the resources of both VI and VIII Corps for what he hoped would be a short siege. Delays in starting the siege of Almeida had effectively bought Wellington a further month.

Initially the first parallel was dug at a range of 500 yards to the south of the city, in front of the San Pedro bastion. When it arrived the French siege train not only consisted of the original guns but also the pick of those heavier pieces captured at Ciudad Rodrigo. Consequently, work proceeded apace with the trench extending around to the west and east of the fortress with eleven batteries in place. Fire was opened at 0600 hours on 26 August with immediate effect against Portuguese batteries and the town, which was soon blazing in several quarters. Nonetheless, Colonel Cox was confident that the fortress would stand.

That confidence was shattered by a stroke of luck for the French. A shell fell by the entrance of the main magazine in the under-croft of the old castle that evening. The main door to the magazine was open to permit a powder re-supply party to leave. The sole survivor of the resulting explosion explained that a French shell landed in the castle courtyard, ignited a trail of powder from a leaking barrel and caused a flashback into the entrance of the magazine. A barrel just inside the door exploded and in turn set off the main powder store. The resulting

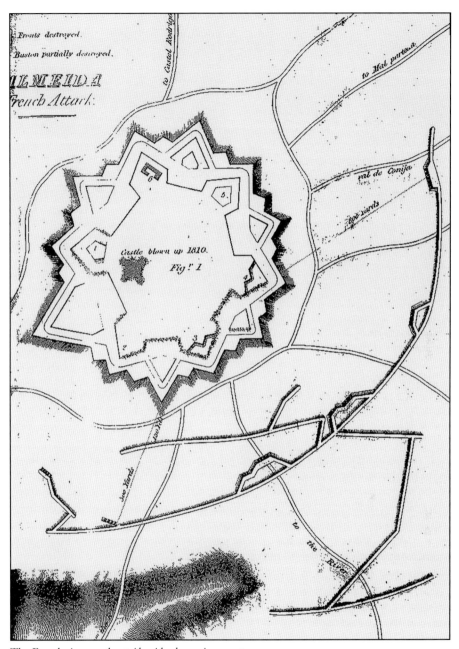

The French siege works at Almeida shown in a contemporary map.

The main gate of Almeida.

explosion devastated the castle, the adjacent cathedral and removed the roofs of virtually every house in the town. The garrison lost about 600 men killed in a flash, including over half the gunners. Stone blocks and shot were hurled around and it is recorded that even French infantry and engineers in the trenches were killed and wounded by the explosion.

This single lucky shot effectively ended the siege but Colonel Cox was determined to resist long enough for Wellington to relieve Almeida. The detonation of the magazine had, however, totally undermined Portuguese morale, including that of some of the officers. Cox attempted to bluff the French officers during a parley but some of the Portuguese informed the French as to the full extent of what had happened and the state of the garrison. Major Barreiros, a Portuguese gunner officer who was sent to negotiate with the French, deserted and informed Masséna that the troops in Almeida would offer no further resistance.

Masséna turned down all of Cox's entreaties and at 1900 hours on 27 August the French resumed bombarding the fortress. A Portuguese delegation of officers insisted that Cox surrender and that if he did not they would open the gates to the French. Colonel Cox no longer had any option but to surrender. On the morning of 28 August, the garrison marched out of the remains of the town. Under the terms of the surrender Masséna allowed the Ordenanças to return to their homes having given their parole, but the regular Portuguese troops were given a choice of being taken to France as prisoners or to join the French army. Most who had seemingly 'turned coat' rather than be a prisoner, however, deserted the French and re-joined their own army over subsequent days.

Invasion

With the fall of Ciudad Rodrigo there were once again delays to French operations occasioned by logistics, guerrillas and insubordination. Rations once again were a particular problem with the country stripped bare in accordance with Wellington's wishes. As a result a further six days were spent bringing up bread and biscuit. Masséna's army had also shrunk to less than 45,000 men due to casualties, sickness and the need to garrison both Ciudad Rodrigo and Almeida. Consequently, this meant that he had to call forward Reynier's II Corps, which while this enabled him to advance from the encampments around Almeida into Portugal on 15 September, with 65,000 men he feared for the safety of his lines of communication which were now denuded of a significant number of men. The French siege train was left at Almeida as there was no envisaged task for it nor, of course, were there draught animals to move it.

Masséna marched into the valley of the River Mondego where his intentions became clear with his army heading for Coimbra, avoiding Wellington's chosen point of resistance at Ponte de Murcella. Without even vaguely reliable maps, the marshal eventually diverted from a good road onto what soon became apparent was a dreadful one, on flawed advice from renegade Portuguese officers who thereby inadvertently aided their country.

As his troops fell back steadily deeper into Portugal, Wellington was under increasing pressure to act. His strategy in a country where 'small armies were defeated and large ones starved' was to draw the French deep into the denuded country and retire behind the prepared defences of Torres Vedras, but of course he could not annunciate this. As a result, he was being urged from all quarters to use his army to fight. Wellington could only respond to this political pressure if he could do so without risking his army, and by taking the Viseu-Coimbra route Masséna presented him with the opportunity to make a stand on the 10-mile-long, 1,600ft-high Buçaco Ridge that stood across the path of the French army.

The Battle of Buçaco

The position that Wellington took up was based on a walled convent at the point where the road to Coimbra crosses the ridge. There was a rough track along the crest of the ridge which rose 1,000ft from the east and had a minor road crossing it further south. Wellington as usual deployed his troops out of sight of the French on the reverse slope. On the evening of 25 September, however, Ney's advance guard identified the presence of allied troops and the marshal's assumption based on the previous pattern of Wellington's operations was that they were only rear-guard and that they would be set in motion again by a frontal attack. The allies had in fact deployed 50,000 men and 60 guns behind the crest of the ridge.

The following day Masséna joined Ney, agreed that this was just a rear-guard and ordered an assault the next morning, which in the first instance was to be carried out by Reynier's corps on the axis of the Ameal to Sardeirinha [*sic*] track. Masséna, unaware of the extent of Wellington's dispositions, assumed that Reynier would turn the British right flank and once this was achieved Ney's corps would advance up the road to Buçaco convent at the northern end of the ridge.

At dawn on 27 September 1810 the valley was shrouded with mist which delayed the initial French advance and further hampered their situational awareness. Heudelet's division advanced at 0600 hours, up the southern road onto the crest where unexpectedly they were met and fired on by the 74th Foot and two Portuguese battalions, supported by a dozen guns. The resulting exchanges of volley fire lasted most of the battle with neither side being willing to retire. Reynier's second division reached the top a little further to the north, being greeted by the fire of the 88th Connaught Rangers who had seen the French column climbing the hill and redeployed to meet it, along with several companies of the 45th Foot. Together they launched a determined attack and drove the French down the hill. Brigadier General Foy in renewing the attack was more successful, reaching the brow of the ridge and remained there until counter-attacked by a brigade of the 5th Division.

Ney, shrouded in mist back in the valley and hearing the sound of battle further south on the ridge, believed that Reynier's II Corps must have taken the feature and ordered his VI Corps to advance up the main road. Loison's division moved in column with its left on the road, but as they reached the crest he ran into the Light Division. The 43rd and 52nd Foot climbed out of their concealed position in a sunken road, formed, volleyed into the head of the column at a range of just 25 yards and charged with the bayonet, driving the French back down the hillside amid 'carnage'. Ney's second division, advancing alongside Loisin's, was halted in a similar manner by Pack's Portuguese brigade.

With the failure of his assault, Masséna halted the attack and sent cavalry to make a reconnaissance of routes to the north where they found a road that turned the ridge to the British left. Wellington's army remained on the ridge overnight but, finding that they were being outflanked, withdrew towards Coimbra having inflicted a significant reverse on Masséna's Army of Portugal.

What turned a French reverse at Buçaco into a serious matter was the effect on morale of Masséna's already suffering men and, perhaps even more importantly, the impact of the defeat on his commanders and their confidence. Finding the allies occupying another set of hills when they reached the lines of Torres Vedras on 10 October, most feared to take them on.

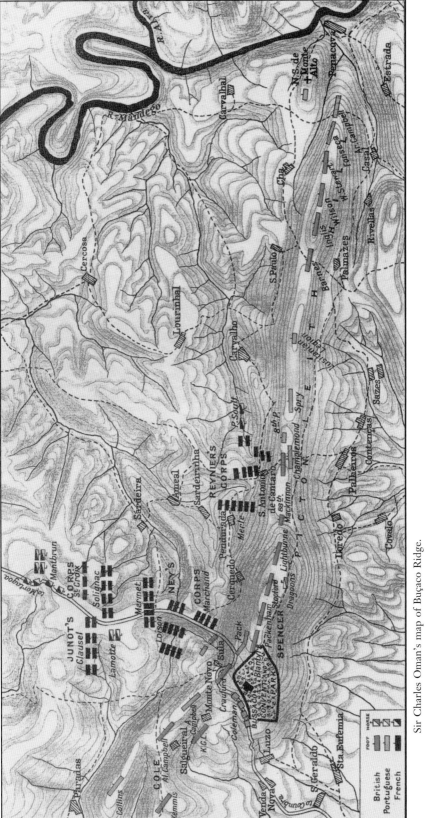

Sir Charles Oman's map of Buçaco Ridge.

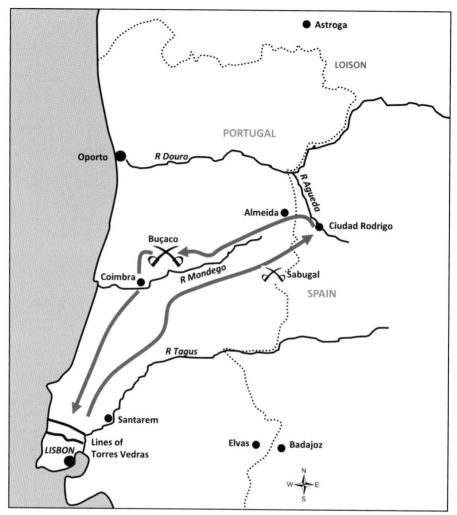

The third French invasion of Portugal.

The Lines of Torres Vedras

Wellington had issued instructions to his engineers for the construction of the Lines of Torres Vedras across the Lisbon peninsula in late 1809. He had to convince the government that he would not lose the army; therefore the first element of the lines was the defended embarkation point just west of Lisbon. Further north was a line across the hills of Sintra and some outworks principally around Torres Vedras. The lines were not a set of continuous fortifications but a series of mutually-supporting redoubts sited on commanding hills that abounded in the area; the design of each was based on its own tactical requirements. Where, however, the ground dictated, the slopes between redoubts was steepened to create an obstacle to cavalry and artillery. Work with forced but paid Portuguese labour had progressed well and above all in secret. Wellington was forced to keep the vast expenditure on the lines from his own government as Napoleon's greatest source of intelligence on British activities in the peninsula was the tittle-tattle of government leaking into society and from there into the press.

So successful were the engineers in their construction work and so slow were the French in invading Portugal that the outworks around Torres Vedras became the basis of a second forward line of redoubts. Both lines were about 25 miles long and, by the time the French arrived in front of them, totalled some 125 individual redoubts of varying size.

Arriving in front of the lines in October 1810 they were a nasty surprise to the French, so successful had the operational security surrounding their construction been. Masséna, on being briefed on the lines, expostulated 'Did Wellington create the hills?' His commanders, however, following their defeat in attempting to storm Buçaco Ridge, were reluctant to take on the British army in another prepared hilltop defensive position and, as a consequence, no attack on the lines was made. The preparation time afforded to Wellington from the investment of Ciudad Rodrigo onwards had been crucial.

Masséna was faced with an impasse and after a month before the lines withdrew to country around Santarem where foraging for his hungry army was likely to be more successful. Wellington had been warned by the Portuguese Regency that the population, rather than fully carry out his scorched-earth policy that had been agreed, would attempt to hide food and valuables, but a French army now static and used to living off the land were equal to finding the most carefully-hidden cache of Portuguese grain. This prevented the French from total starvation but even so, they were wracked with hunger and disease, hoping for supplies and reinforcements, neither of which in winter conditions was forthcoming. Eventually Masséna, with his army in a parlous state and no assistance coming from Madrid or other French commanders such as Marshal Soult, was forced to accept the inevitable and started to withdraw back to Spain.

Pursuit to the Frontier

When Masséna marched from Santarem during the first week of March 1811, he had not intended to retire to Spain. He hoped that by moving north into the Mondego valley he would find sufficient food to maintain his army long enough for promised reinforcements to reach him. The River Mondego, however, was an obstacle that could prevent him from reaching an area that had hitherto not been devastated by the passage of armies. In the event, such was the state of his army that, with only 6,000 Ordenanças holding the line of the Mondego the French failed to make a serious attempt to cross the river and Masséna abandoned his original plan and began his retreat to the Spanish frontier.

As the Army of Portugal turned east and began its march back to Spain, Wellington was caught out by Masséna's move with his divisions too widely scattered, and Marshal Ney conducted a skilful clean break, both of which prevented the British attacking the withdrawing French early in their retreat. When eventually sufficient allied troops had caught up, with a foretaste of the retreat from Moscow, Ney proved to be the master of the rear-guard, with Ney twice extricating his corps just in time when the British outflanked him.

On one occasion with Ney continuing to delay the British for as long as possible, the French command narrowly avoided disaster. Under pressure from the 3rd Division, Ney was forced to abandon a position and withdraw 5 miles east post-haste. This almost resulted in Masséna, who was dining with his staff, being captured by a patrol of KGL Hussars. Such was the state of relations that the marshal was convinced that Ney had deliberately attempted to have him taken prisoner.

Following a costly action by the Light Division at Casal Novo where General Erskine, who was commanding in the absence of Craufurd on leave, had incautiously attacked a French position in the fog that proved to be far stronger than expected, Wellington resumed his usual method of manoeuvring the French from a series of delaying positions. So it went on, with the French withdrawing via Guarda and Belmonte and Masséna's army re-crossing the Côa on 31 March, where instead of marching directly back to his magazines at Ciudad Rodrigo, the marshal allowed his troops a rest, not believing Wellington was at hand.

With the French spread out along the Côa, Wellington saw an opportunity to take on the enemy. His target was Reynier's II Corps, which was exposed on a flank at Sabugal but the attack on 3 April was again launched amid fog. Everything that could go wrong went wrong; nonetheless, Masséna was forced to abandon his last positions in Portugal and continue east into Spain. Wellington was now able to blockade Almeida.

The French withdrawal, though hurried along by Wellington's manoeuvring, was one of the more competent phases of what had been an ill-founded and badly-conducted campaign, with Napoleon sharing a large degree of the blame for the manner in which he created division among his marshalate and tried to conduct it from afar. There was, however, one last action before the curtain finally came down on Masséna and the third French invasion of Portugal.

Fuentes de Oñoro

Wellington's intention was to blockade Almeida and starve the fortress into submission, while Masséna felt that he had to intervene with his army that had been rejuvenated with reinforcements that he found waiting at Ciudad Rodrigo.

He also had Marshal Bessières and a small cavalry enhancement, giving him a total of 42,000 infantry, 4,500 cavalry and 38 guns.

Even though outnumbered with 34,000 infantry and 1,850 cavalry but with 48 guns, Wellington was determined to persevere with the blockade of Almeida. He deployed his troops into a reasonably strong position on the Dos Casas stream, which at that time of the year is a far from insignificant obstacle to the north, running through a ravine that prevented any meaningful large-scale attack on the left of the line. The allied right was, however, not as naturally strong; where the Dos Casas gorge ends the country is more open the further south one goes. The British line ended at Fuentes de Oñoro, beyond which there was very little to stop the French turning the allied line.

On 2 May the French marched from Ciudad Rodrigo, monitored by the Light Division and four regiments of light cavalry. The day was marked by numerous low-level skirmishes as the French advanced on Gallegos and Espeja. With the whole French army advancing, the outposts fell back to just in front of the main battle line and on the following morning they withdrew into the line at Fuentes de Oñoro alongside the main strength of the allied army. The village itself, being held by twenty-eight light companies detached from their parent battalions, supported the 2/83rd Foot.

Masséna recognized the natural strength of the allied left, and therefore concentrated opposite Fuentes de Oñoro where he would make a frontal assault during the afternoon of 3 May. Ten battalions of Ferey's division attacked the village, while II Corps was to make a diversionary attack on Wellington's left.

Only the attack on Fuentes de Oñoro itself made any progress, with Ferey's brigade capturing the lower part of the village before being ejected, but a renewed assault managed to force the British back to the upper part of the village. Wellington sent three fresh battalions to clear the village and by nightfall the French had been repulsed.

Such fighting as there was on the following day was again focused around Fuentes de Oñoro, where skirmishers exchanged fire across the Dos Casas. Masséna spent the day reconnoitring Wellington's position, and discerned the weakness of the allied right flank and planned to envelope it with three divisions and almost all of his cavalry. His plan was that three other divisions would attack Fuentes de Oñoro, while Reynier would continue to threaten the allied left. Wellington was, however, aware of the threat to his right and redeployed the 7th Division, and a cavalry screen was also put in place guarding the line from Fuentes de Oñoro to Nava de Aver.

On 5 May Masséna launched his attack on the British right, forced the 7th Division back and continued to attack Fuentes de Oñoro village. Wellington was consequently forced to form a new line with the 1st and 3rd divisions, along with Ashworth's Portuguese. This, however, did not prevent the 7th Division from being in great danger and it needed the British cavalry to go into action in

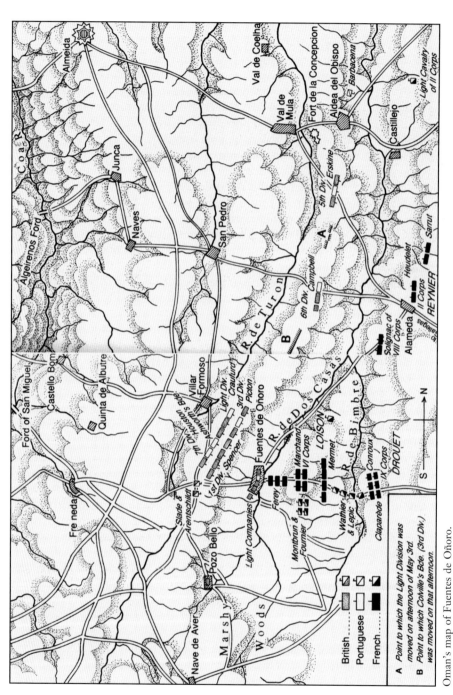

Oman's map of Fuentes de Oñoro.

British volley fire.

order to buy time for the arrival of the Light Division to come up in support of the 7th. Craufurd's men marched hard to reach the right and hold off the French to allow the 7th Division to withdraw. The Light Division then executed a masterful withdrawal of its own to Wellington's new defensive line.

With the French attack around the allied flank making progress, the attack on the village, launched two hours after dawn, drove the 71st and 79th Foot from most of the houses and farms but a spirited counter-attack by the 2/24th drove the French back to the river. The French tried again with eighteen elite grenadier companies and forced the British back to the immediate high ground, which the grenadiers were unable to capture nor were they able to reach the plateau beyond. The ebb and flow of battle continued with Masséna sending eight fresh battalions who finally ejected the defenders of Fuentes de Oñoro. The French were, however, in turn counter-attacked with the bayonet by Mackinnon's brigade and the French battalions fled.

The French retired across the rivers Águeda and Azaba, with the British following leaving behind the now-isolated fortress of Almeida, which was evacuated and blown by the garrison (see Chapter 4 for details of their escape via Barba del Puerco).

Retreat of the Almeida Garrison, May 1811

In the immediate aftermath of Masséna's failed attempt to relieve Almeida (the Battle of Fuentes de Oñoro, 3–5 May 1811), the 11,000 men of Reynier's II Corps withdrew via Barba del Puerco to San Felices, having sent their ammunition caissons and heavy baggage on an easier route. The subsequent presence of General Heudelet's division at San Felices was partly to facilitate the withdrawal of General Brennier's 1,400-strong Almeida garrison, which Masséna had ordered to be abandoned in a cyphered message that had been sneaked into the fortress.

General Campbell's 6th Division surrounded Almeida but it was only deployed in a loose blockade with its brigades and battalions being cantoned in villages some miles distant, with only a thin screen of piquets between them rather than close up to the fortress. Some peculiar cannon fire, which was signalling and destruction of guns, alerted Wellington who ordered General Erskine (5th Division) to cover the pass at Barba del Puerco. The order arrived while Erskine was dining and sometime afterwards, having initially proposed to send a corporal's piquet of five men, he sent instructions to Lieutenant Colonel Bevan of the 4th Foot to move 2.5 miles to the pass. Despite dissembling, excuses and lies, it would appear that with his battalion settled for the night, Bevan was persuaded that he 'needn't march till daybreak'. Consequently, when Brennier left the fortress by the north gate he was able to brush aside Campbell's piquets provided by the Portuguese and the 2nd Queen's and head for the unguarded Barba del Puerco.

They were under orders to march as quickly as possible and ignore pursuit, which in the event was provided only by Brigadier General Pack and a handful of men who caused some French casualties and rounded up Brennier's stragglers. A general alert was caused by the explosion of the Almeida but Lieutenant Colonel Iremonger, who was best-placed to intervene, stood the 2nd Queen's to arms but remained on his ground otherwise inactive.

Around dawn Brennier had covered 8 miles to reach Villar de Ciervo where a troop of the 1st Royals mounted a vedette, but a small group of cavalry were only able to delay the French for a very short while. By the time Brennier reached Barba del Puerco and the brow of the hill down to the bridge and safety, the British 36th Foot were closing in from the west, the 4th (belatedly) from the south having been ordered to dump their packs, and a mix of Portuguese infantry and cavalry from the north-west.

Captain Marbot describes the descent to the bridge:

> The last of our columns had to pass through a defile ... The enemy was pressing on from all sides, and several sections of our rear-guard were cut off by the English cavalry. Seeing this, the French soldiers climbed nimbly up the steep sides of the ravine and escaped, only to fall into another danger. The Portuguese infantry pursued them on the heights, pouring a murderous fire into them. When at length our men, on the point of being succoured by Heudelet's division, thought that they were in sight of safety, the earth

General Denis Pack commanding
a Portuguese brigade in 1811.

suddenly failed under their feet, engulfing part of them in a yawning chasm at the foot of a huge rock. The head of the pursuing Portuguese column incurred the same fate, rolling pell-mell into the gulf with our people. Heudelet's division succeeded in forcing the allied troops back beyond the sight of this disaster, and when the foot of the precipice was explored, a fearful sight appeared.

Wellington was furious, and complained: 'I am obliged to be everywhere, and if absent from any operation, something goes wrong.' Of Erskine, he said 'that there is nothing on earth so stupid as a gallant officer.' Colonel Bevan was to be court-martialled but shot himself, allowing Erskine to escape his large portion of the blame, while Napoleon promoted Brennier to lieutenant general.

Meanwhile, on 12 May Marshal Marmont arrived at the Army of Portugal which was in cantonments around Ciudad Rodrigo and replaced Masséna who was recalled to Paris, never to serve again in an active capacity, his last command being in Marseilles.

Chapter Ten

The Combats of Espeja and El Bodón

The Battle of Fuentes de Oñoro had demonstrated the weakness of the Army of Portugal and that it would take Marshal Marmont some months to provision, re-equip and re-clothe. It was, however, equally apparent that although the tide was gradually turning, the allies were not yet strong enough to take the battle to the French in Spain as the emperor's armies would surely unite to outnumber Wellington. Therefore, the British were to switch their focus further south against Marshal Soult in Andalucía. The result was the bloody Battle of Albuera and the second failed siege of Badajoz. Meanwhile, further north Wellington's troops, ably assisted by Julián Sánchez's guerrillas, began to blockade Ciudad Rodrigo. This, for instance, drew the Light Division back into Spain and across the Águeda to the east of Sabugal.

During July Marmont, who had marched south to join Soult in raising the siege of Badajoz, returned north to a central position astride the River Tagus centred on Almaraz from where he could support the French armies to the north and south should Wellington attack. The marshal used the time well to continue the reconstitution of his 36,000-strong army that he had begun on taking command in May.

During August Wellington, who maintained his forces in the south on the River Caia until Marmont and Soult had dispersed, now marched his seven divisions north to the Águeda area and began a blockade of Ciudad Rodrigo, this time by the Light and 3rd divisions plus cavalry. Wellington's headquarters were established at Fuenteguinaldo just 16 miles to the south-west of Ciudad Rodrigo, having carried out a close reconnaissance of the fortress on 11 August. There was no immediate French reaction as the fortress was well-supplied, a convoy having reached the city in early August with enough food to last the garrison into October. Wellington's other divisions were in cantonments to the rear at rest.

Receiving intelligence that Wellington was assembling a siege train and that other preparations indicative of an intent to mount a siege were being made, Marmont was stung into action, starting to move troops north. Wellington was well-informed as usual by his network of spies, guerrillas and exploring officers and was able to monitor French preparation at Salamanca to assemble a large convoy of supplies for Ciudad Rodrigo and to mass troops to break the blockade.

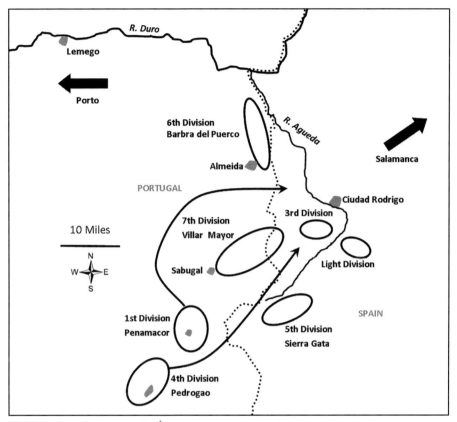

Wellington's deployment on the Águeda front, September 1811.

Wellington knew that a French force of 50,000 men, including Dorsenne's Army of the North with a superiority of cavalry, would be impossible to stop on the open plains around Ciudad Rodrigo and, consequently, he would decline battle unless the French pushed forward to ground more suitably defensive where positions could be prepared. He gave instructions to Generals Picton and Craufurd that only if pressed was the 3rd Division to fall back to El Bodón and the Light to positions beyond the Vadillo stream. Marmont, however, eventually developed grander aims beyond just resupplying Ciudad Rodrigo, as a Wellingtonian error presented him with an opportunity.

The much-heralded advance began on 22 September when the French drove in the 5th Division's piquets who were watching the passes over the Sierra de Gata to the south. Matters initially proceeded as expected with French cavalry arriving on the 23rd and the convoy of supplies being escorted into Ciudad Rodrigo on 24 September, escorted among others by a division of the Imperial Guard. This

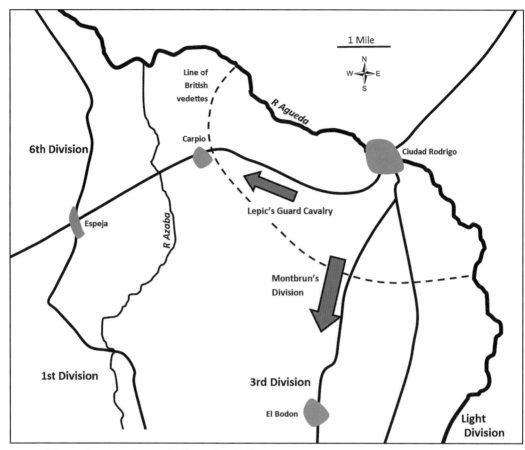

Marmont's reconnaissance, 25 September 1811.

division was a part of Dorsenne's Army of the North, which was co-operating in the enterprise. The large French force remained inactive on the plain about the city during the 24th. Marmont's quiescence, rather than posing a threat, would seem to have indicated to Wellington that he need not concentrate his army from their scattered piquets and cantonments. At the same time, however, the French marshal, in addition to curiosity over Wellington's intentions at Ciudad Rodrigo, may have realized that his opponent's force was dispersed and therefore vulnerable. Consequently, Marmont with four divisions and the 4,000 cavalry available was provoked into action to see if preparations to besiege Ciudad Rodrigo were evident and launched two reconnaissances in strength. One was to the west towards Carpio and the River Azaba and the second larger force was sent south towards the El Bodón Plateau.

Combat at Carpio and Espeja

General Dorsenne provided elements of Lepic's Guard Cavalry and the attached German Lancers of Berg totalling in excess of fourteen squadrons of between 1,500 and 2,000 sabres, supported by two horse artillery pieces for the advance

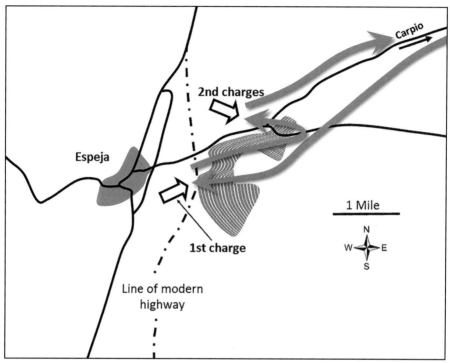

Combat at Espeja.

on Carpio. On the morning of 25 September, they were seen deploying by vedettes of the 14th Light Dragoons. They fell back to the Azaba and beyond, as the French continued to advance across the river leaving a reserve at Carpio. Once across, the French detached another three squadrons to secure the ford.

Meanwhile, Captain Cocks of the 16th Light Dragoons was sent forward and described in a letter home what happened:

> Between Carpio and Espeja is a wood. When our piquets were driven from the line of the former I was ordered to support them in the wood with two small squadrons. They [the French] advanced with 500 men, leaving the rest in support [at the Azaba and Carpio]. I kept them in check a little but was obliged to retire thro' the wood, as they attempted to surround me. On getting through the wood I found three more [friendly] squadrons formed. I made my arrangements and the instant the head of the enemy column had cleared the wood and begun to deploy, Hay, who had come up with one Squadron, myself and Brotherton of the 14th charged with complete success. The enemy – pikemen [lancers] and chasseurs – scarcely awaited the shock and we drove them to their supper.

Our men were broke [disorganized]; but they are no longer ignorant barrack soldiers and they re-formed constantly. We retired, again drawing on the enemy to the top of the wood. He had the imprudence again to come through. He got a volley from the light company of the 11th [Foot] which had by this time come up and was again charged by us.

With the Guard Cavalry reeling from the unexpected volley, the British squadrons' charge was met at the halt and the French were thrown back.

Napier records an incident during the fighting at El Bodón between the opposing cavalry: '... it was in one of the cavalry encounters that a French officer, in the act of striking the gallant Felton Harvey of the 14th Dragoons, perceived that he had only one arm, and with a rapid movement brought his sword down into a salute, and passed on.'[1]

Amid the gruesome carnage of a hand-to-hand combat, a remarkable chivalry could still exist among the cavalry of the Imperial Guard.

Wellington in his dispatch only mentions the 61st but other sources state that all three light companies of Hulse's brigade (11th North Devon, 2/53rd and 61st Foot) and presumably their company of the 5th 60th Rifles were deployed to

Lieutenant Colonel Sir Felton Harvey, commanding officer of the 14th Dragoons.

create the conditions in which the enemy could be overthrown by four squadrons of Light Dragoons. This was the first occasion on which British cavalry confronted lancers. Captain Cocks continued:

Captain Cocks.

> We drove him all way through the wood and he never afterward advanced but, after waiting till evening near Carpio, returned to Rodrigo.
>
> I was only personally engaged once with a Chasseur and had the fortune to kill him the first blow. We had eight men of the 16th wounded and some horses killed; the 14th had an Officer and a dragoon wounded. It is difficult to judge the loss of the enemy because as fast as his men were cut down, if not quite dead they crawled into the thickets and could not be found. We took up a *chef d'escadron* and fifteen men, all wounded. Eight or more lay dead on the road and we afterwards learnt that twenty-one, including four officers, were brought back to Carpio in blankets unable to sit on their horses. The total loss in killed, prisoners and badly wounded was probably seventy or eighty men.

Among the 'French' dead was an Irishman, Colonel O'Finn, who had fled to France in 1799 following the previous year's rebellion in which he played a significant part in County Cork and entered French service.

Combat at El Bodón

Wellington in his dispatches to Lord Liverpool wrote of the events that same day:

> About 8 in the morning they moved a column, consisting of between thirty and forty squadrons of cavalry, and fourteen battalions of infantry, and twelve pieces of cannon, from Ciudad Rodrigo in such a direction that it was doubtful whether they would attempt to ascend the hills by La Encina or by the direct road of El Bodón.

General Montbrun advanced his division of dragoons and two of light cavalry down the Fuenteguinaldo Road towards El Bodón and Picton's widely-spread 3rd Division. The French were soon tangling with Alten's 500-strong brigade consisting of five squadrons of the 11th Light Dragoons and 1st Hussars KGL who had been rushed forward to support the infantry. With 2,500 sabres plus two batteries of guns, the French drove straight through the British outpost line in the centre. In front of them were Picton's men, who it is widely acknowledged had been deployed in positions far too close to Ciudad Rodrigo, with his brigades spread out on a frontage of 6 miles, as well as being on less than favourable ground.

Major Henry Ridge of the 2nd Battalion 5th Foot, the senior officer at El Bodón, wrote of the opening of the action:

> ... having received no orders, whether to retire if attacked (by a superior force), or to defend our post to the last extremity, I thought it prudent, in the first instance, to take the best means in my power to prevent a surprise, and planted the pickets [*sic*] accordingly. Feeling myself in a very responsible situation, I visited the pickets at daybreak, when I discovered large bodies of the enemy's cavalry coming out of Ciudad Rodrigo, and crossing the Águeda.

Fortunately, Marmont did not believe that such a dispersed British deployment was not heavily supported with further infantry behind the high ground. Consequently, the marshal did not bring up Thiébault's supporting infantry division but ordered General Montbrun to press on and test the British position with his cavalry.

As the French cavalry continued up the road towards the plateau, Wellington arrived and approved Major Ridge's deployment of the two battalions of Colville's brigade now supported by two batteries of Portuguese guns. The squadrons of Captains Childers and Ridout from the 11th Light Dragoons and a squadron of the 1st KGL Hussars, having had their outposts pushed in, withdrew

Combat of El Bodón.

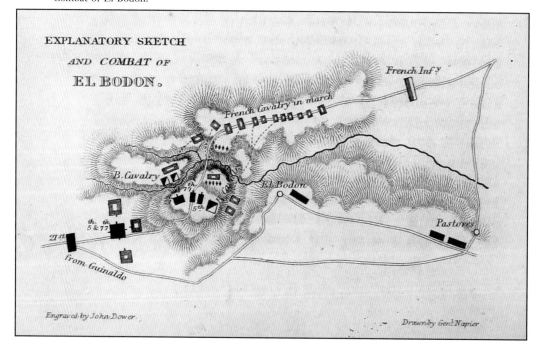

and took up position on either flank. Wellington was clear in his instructions to Major Ridge: to enable other dangerously-exposed brigades and battalions of the 3rd Division to left and right to be drawn back, this central position had to be held! The El Bodón plateau has several crests and is broken by gullies, some with low outcrops of rock, and offered few good avenues of approach for the French cavalry but they had numbers on their side.

Montbrun deployed his force into three brigade columns and a reserve. Each headed for a different part of the plateau, while in the centre the horse artillery took on Picton's Portuguese guns.

As the enemy started to climb the plateau under the fire of the Portuguese 9-pounders, the 11th Light Dragoons and the KGL Hussars charged repeatedly. Captain Childers' own squadron charged eight or nine times in an hour, making use of the extra downhill momentum to drive the French back. By the eighth charge, however, Childers' squadron had been reduced to just twenty troopers and had trouble disengaging from the melee. It is estimated that the French mounted up to forty attacks on various parts of the plateau, but the scale of these was limited by the ground, hence three squadrons prevailing against a force ten times their number. This was a disciplined fight with squadrons retiring and re-forming, covered by another and charging again.

Captain Childers wearing the later 1812 Light Dragoons' uniform.

Meanwhile, the infantry was in action and the duke accompanied by the Prince of Orange and his aide-de-camp Major Alexander Gordon had a lucky escape when a large body of French dragoons erupted onto the plateau, Gordon distinguishing himself and possibly saving his chief as they escaped to the rear. Wellington is reported as going as far as to say at dinner that he would have been captured but for the intervention of Major Gordon.

Eventually the French overwhelmed the battery of Portuguese artillery whose gunners stood to their pieces and fought the enemy with anything that came to hand. Wellington made it clear in a General Order of 2 October 1811 that 'The Portuguese artillerymen were cut down at the guns before they quitted them.' They certainly stood but in fact few were lost and Major Ridge, with reasonably secure flanks thanks to the ground, advanced his 2nd 5th Foot against the blown and disorganized French dragoons. Pausing to fire three volleys at closer and closer range, the 5th, charging out of the smoke with the bayonet, routed the French downhill and the Portuguese gunners were able to resume firing. The 77th Foot also advanced in a similar manner, sending Frenchmen who had at last made it to the crest of their part of the plateau galloping back downhill with the German hussars in pursuit.

During this phase Major General Charles Colville joined his battalions on the high ground having brought up another two squadrons of KGL Hussars and the 21st Portuguese Line who remained in reserve to the south-west of the feature.

In the pause that followed, the French army bombarded the plateau and Montbrun could be seen urging his men into action, but the French cavalrymen were observed to be markedly reluctant to re-enter the maelstrom they had faced at the top of the plateau. Giving up frontal attacks, the French began to feel their way around the flanks and rather than going for the top of the plateau, one brigade made its way to El Bodón along one of the re-entrants that divided the high ground. In addition, French infantry were now marching to support.

At around 1400 hours, having gained two hours, Wellington, seeing that the plateau was about to be enveloped and that the other elements of the 3rd Division had extricated themselves, ordered Colville back. Later he wrote in the General Order:

> The post would have been maintained, if the Commander of the Forces had not ordered the troops to withdraw from it, seeing that the action would become still more unequal, as the enemy's infantry were likely to be engaged in it before the reinforcements ordered to the support of the post could arrive.

Covered by the cavalry, the guns were extricated and the infantry started to pull back, but once off the plateau and onto the low ground and the road back to Fuenteguinaldo the country was open and highly favourable for the French cavalry. In this circumstance the infantry had to retire in squares: the Portuguese

General Colville.

21st Line formed one and the 5th and 77th, both being about 500-strong, the other. Movement in square was slow and they were repeatedly charged, but the French were unable to break them.

The British cavalry, who had also benefited from the ground up on the plateau, were now similarly more vulnerable to a much larger force. Having covered the withdrawal of the infantry, with the KGL squadron being the last to leave, according to Captain Childers: 'They fled at the gallop for almost a mile, saved by musket fire from the 5th and 77th.' The 11th lost ten men killed and twenty-one wounded, including the commanding officer Lieutenant Colonel Cumming.

As the KGL and the 11th would have been overwhelmed, the allied infantry were now on their own. Wellington's General Order goes on to add more detail and award praise:

The troops then retired with the same determined spirit, and in the same good order with which they had maintained their post ... supported by Major General Alten's cavalry and the Portuguese artillery. The enemy's cavalry charged three faces of the square of the British infantry, but were beaten off, and finding from their repeated fruitless efforts that these brave troops were not to be broken, they were contented with following them at a distance, and with firing upon them with their artillery, till the troops joined the remainder of their division, and were afterwards supported by a brigade of the Fourth Division.

Although the 21st Portuguese Regiment were not actually charged by the cavalry, their steadiness and determination were conspicuous, and the Commander of the Forces observed with pleasure the order and regularity with which they made all their movements, and the confidence they showed in their officers.

The Commander of the Forces has been particular in stating the details of this action in General Orders, as, in his opinion, it affords a memorable example of what can be effected by steadiness, discipline, and confidence. It is impossible that any troops can at any time be exposed to the attack of numbers relatively greater than those who attacked these troops under Major General Colville and Major General Alten, on the 25th September; and the Commander of the Forces recommends the conduct of these troops to the particular attention of the officers and soldiers of the army, as an example to be followed in all such circumstances.

Eventually, the two battalions joined the rest of the 3rd Division that had converged on the road into a single column that the French continued to harass. Lieutenant Grattan of the 88th Connaught Rangers recalled:

For 6 miles [4 miles would be more accurate] across a perfect flat, without the slightest protection from any incident of ground, without their artillery, and almost without cavalry ... did the 3rd Division continue its march. During the whole time, the French cavalry never quitted them: six guns were taking the division in flank and rear, pouring in a shower of round shot, grape, and canister. This was a trying and pitiable situation for troops to be placed in, but it in no way shook their courage or confidence: so far from being dispirited or cast down the men were cheerful and gay. The soldiers of my own corps, the 88th, told their officers that if the French would only charge, every officer should have a nate [nice] horse to ride upon. General Picton conducted himself with his usual coolness. He rode on the left flank of the column, and repeatedly cautioned the different battalions to mind their quarter-distance ... We had at last got close to the entrenched camp at Fuenteguinaldo when Montbrun, impatient that we should escape from his grasp, ordered his troopers to bring up their right shoulders and incline towards our marching column. The movement was not exactly bringing his squadrons into line, but the next thing to it, and they were within half pistol-shot of us. Picton took off his hat, and holding it over his eyes as a shade from the sun, looked sternly but anxiously at the French. The clatter of the

General Sir Thomas Picton.

horses and the clanking of the sabres was so great, when the right squadrons moved up, that many thought it the preliminary to a general charge. Some mounted officer called out, 'Had we not better form square?' 'No,' replied Picton, 'it is only a ruse to frighten us, and it won't do.'

The 3rd Division withdrew on its own until the Fusilier Brigade (7th, 23rd and 48th Foot) marched forward from Fuenteguinaldo to assist in *ordre mixte*. According to Lieutenant Robert Knowels: 'Our regiment advanced in line with the 23rd and 48th in close column on each flank.' This formation, with the threat posed by the cavalry on the plain, provided a combination of security with columns on the flanks and firepower with the 7th in line in the centre. With the 3rd Division supported, Montbrun's cavalry stopped following them and gave up hoping for an opportunity to pounce.

It wasn't only the 3rd Division that had been caught in a dangerous position but the other blockading division as well. The Light Division was on the right bank of the Águeda, and with Marmont pressing forward on both sides of the river, forcing Picton back, General Craufurd could have been cut off and destroyed in detail. Consequently, on the afternoon of 25 September, Wellington ordered him to cross the river and join the army but Craufurd, believing that there was no threat to his own position, delayed. He eventually assembled the division at Agallas and according to Lieutenant Simmons of the 95th marched 'just after dark', extricating himself from an increasingly difficult situation via Robleda, and forded the Águeda. According to Lieutenant Cooke of the 43rd, the troops during the night suffered from the cold and that 'The march was much impeded owing to a trifling stream in the road, and other obstacles, which the soldiers could not at first surmount for the extreme dark.'

The Light Division eventually joined Wellington and such divisions of the army within marching distance of the half-finished entrenchments at Fuenteguinaldo in the mid-afternoon of 26 September. Wellington said: 'I am glad to see you safe.' Craufurd replied 'Oh, I was never in any danger I assure you' and got the sharp confessional reply 'But I was, from your conduct!' Craufurd was heard muttering as he returned to his division 'He's dammed crusty today.'

Meanwhile, by nightfall on 25 September Marmont had four infantry divisions totalling some 20,000 men over the Águeda, with the rest of his army moving up behind. Wellington had, however, at that stage only managed to assemble the 3rd and 4th divisions, Pack's Portuguese brigade and part of his cavalry in the entrenched camp at Fuenteguinaldo; around 15,000 men. The arrival of the Light Division the following day barely brought the numbers to parity but Marmont, despite assembling 40,000 of his troops during the morning of the 26th, did not attack. It seems that the French defeats at Buçaco and Fuentes de Oñoro and their experience before the Lines of Torres Vedras were casting a shadow that made Marmont hesitate at the crucial moment, unwilling to risk attacking Wellington in a prepared position, even a half-finished one, saying: 'The English position is impregnable – the thing that proves it so is that Wellington is offering us battle upon it. We shall never make an end of him by running at it head down; that would have no good result.'

What was in effect a Wellingtonian bluff got him out of trouble that he subsequently described as a 'bustle'. Nonetheless, with more French troops arriving Wellington decided to withdraw to his next strong defensive position 9 miles to the rear beyond Aldeia da Ponte. The army marched after dark, leaving the Light

Division and KGL Hussars to keep up patrols and maintain the fires until after midnight.

Dawn on 27 September found Wellington's army assembled on a 6-mile front and in a strong defensive position but Marmont, after some skirmishing, pulled back and there was to be no general engagement.

By the beginning of October Marmont had returned to Salamanca and Dorsenne to the north. The blockade of Ciudad Rodrigo could be resumed but with French forces able to concentrate against Wellington if needed, mounting a siege in the autumn of 1811 was simply not a practical proposition.

Note

1. Colonel Felton Harvey, commanding officer of the 14th Light Dragoons between 1811 and 1819, had lost his right or sword arm in battle earlier in the war.

Chapter Eleven

Preparations and Investment

As early as 18 July the Duke of Wellington wrote: 'The next operation which presents itself is the siege of Ciudad Rodrigo, for which I have so far prepared as to have our battering train on the Douro' and concluded by saying 'I am tempted to try this enterprise.'[1] The opportunity, however, did not present itself in the summer of 1811 as Marmont and the other French armies remained within concentrating distance. Nonetheless Wellington, with Ciudad Rodrigo in mind, had put in train preparations for a siege that could begin quickly when the moment was right.

If the allies were to advance into Spain and join in taking the war to the country's French occupiers, Wellington would have to have the two border fortresses of Ciudad Rodrigo and Badajoz in his hands. He would need one for his entry into Spain and the other held to guard against intervention by one or other of the French armies, who would be able to threaten his line of communication. To Wellington, these fortresses were 'the Keys to Spain'.

On 28 July, the engineer officer attached to Picton's 3rd Division, Captain Burgoyne, received instructions 'to train 200 men of the division in the art of sapping and other rough field work operations.'[2] Burgoyne commented:

> … to our disgrace and misfortune, we have no regular establishment [of sappers] equal to, notwithstanding the repeated experience of the absolute necessity of such a corps, to act under the Engineers in a campaign. For want of such an establishment we are frequently led to the loss of valuable officers, and very undeserved discredit. The undertaking I am set about will be only temporary, and will supply very imperfectly this deficiency.

Burgoyne was, of course, correct and it wasn't until after the third siege of Badajoz that the Royal Engineer Establishment was founded at Chatham in 1812 and the following year the small Corps of Royal Military Artificers was enhanced and renamed the Corps of Royal Sappers and Miners. In the meantime, those volunteers and pressed men from across the battalions of the 3rd Division which was clearly earmarked for the siege would have to do.

Back in May 1811 Wellington, who had chosen not to use the siege train at Badajoz, now ordered Vice Admiral Barkley, on board whose ships the guns had been lying at anchor in the Tagus for months, to sail it to Oporto. Consequently, seventy-eight heavy guns, howitzers and mortars reached the River Douro in

The Duke of Wellington.

Major Alexander Dickson.

mid-July. Commander of the reserve artillery Major Dickson[3] was given sixty-two days in which to offload the train, plus the myriad of artillery and engineer siege stores, onto barges and to reach Almeida. The river had been made navigable as far as Peso da Régua but beyond that point the train would have to be moved by draft animals and carts (400 pairs of bullocks and 900 country carts). A considerable amount of labour was necessary, particularly in making road repairs for the carts, mass of stores, equipment and ammunition. By the middle of September, the train was gathered in Dickson's artillery park at Vila da Ponte near Lamego, nearly 70 miles from Almeida and just under 100 miles from Ciudad Rodrigo.

Major John Jones recorded in his siege journal that the following quantities of guns and ammunition were in the artillery park:

Ammunition Rounds, grape, case, &c. included:

	GUNS	AMMUNITION
24-pounders iron	4	644
18-pounders "	4	440
10-inch mortars "	8	525
5-inch howitzers "	20	348
5-inch mortars brass "	10	48
8-inch howitzers "	2	215
Total	48[4]	

While the divisions earmarked for the siege were having their men trained as sappers, others were repairing the defences of Almeida. Jones continued:

… on the 12th November, Almeida being again rendered defensible, orders were sent for the battering train and siege stores to move forward from Vila

A 24-pounder mounted on a fortress carriage.

da Ponte. On the 22nd the stores and first division of guns entered the fortress under the pretext of being intended for its armament, though really to be in readiness to commence the siege of Rodrigo at the favourable moment.

With the same view, the several divisions of the army again moved forward their cantonments into the country between the Águeda and Côa, and every possible exertion was made to bring forward the ammunition to Almeida.

In all, twenty-five heavy guns were brought forward along with their round shot.

The majority of Wellington's army had remained dispersed on the Côa/Águeda front after Marshal Marmont's revictualling and had gone into winter quarters on 1 October 1811. Its commander, however, continued to be closely informed of French intentions, which developed significantly during the autumn months. In September Marmont and the Army of Portugal had clearly been Napoleon's chosen instrument for progress in subduing the peninsula, with a proposed attack on Elvas which he believed would bring Wellington marching to its relief and defeat. Marshal Suchet was, however, making significant progress in Valencia on the Mediterranean coast and Napoleon switched his attention there and gave orders for the transfer of troops to reinforce his success. Marmont's contribution numbered some 15,000 men; a transfer made possible in the emperor's mind by grossly over-estimating the number of British sick. The reverse was true; even though a large proportion of the British reinforcements received during the summer, many with lingering Walcheren fever, had broken down in the Iberian heat and the rigours of campaign, with cooler weather and winter quarters the health of the army was rapidly improving.

During the autumn, the British cavalry and Julián Sánchez's guerrillas were active right up to the walls of Ciudad Rodrigo. On 15 October Sánchez rounded up 200 head of cattle that the garrison had turned out to graze from under the noses of the French and also captured the governor of the city, General Renaud and five officers who had ventured out of the fortress to inspect the cattle with only a small escort. Major Gordon, one of the duke's aides-de-camp, commented that General Renaud

> ... after staying with us some days, has been sent to England. I have given him a letter of recommendation to you, and will be obliged to you to show him some attention, the more so as he probably will land at Portsmouth. He is esteemed an excellent officer, and is a very intelligent fellow. He will give

A miniature of Major Alexander Gordon.   Uniforms of a general and his aides-de-camp in 1812.

you a great deal of information upon our campaigns here, and of the state of the French Armies in Spain, of the Emperor, etc. provided you give him enough wine to drink at table. I have made it a point to be very kind to him, as has Lord W; indeed, the civility I have constantly received from the French Army is very great, and the way they all know and speak of me is something ridiculous.

Clearly, despite brutal fighting this was still a war between professional gentlemen! In a letter of 23 October Gordon wrote of the thoughts in Wellington's headquarters:

With respect to Rodrigo, notwithstanding the capture of its Governor and half his livestock, we have abandoned the intention of blockading it, as it does not appear they are reduced to that state of distress as to allow us to hope any decided good would be gained by the effect of a strict blockade. We have some idea of attempting an escalade of the town, which from the badness of the Garrison (mostly Italians) and the capture of the Governor became a consideration with us, but I scarce think we shall, under every view of the case, either attempt or succeed in such a plan of attack.

On 2 November, the British learned that a French column was speeding down from Salamanca. Lieutenant Simmons recorded:

Information had been received that a body of French troops were escorting a new Governor to Rodrigo. The Light Division moved towards the fortress this morning, and the 3rd Division also made a forward movement to support us to Fuenteguinaldo. It soon was ascertained that the Governor had entered it, as the enemy were in bivouac two leagues in the rear. Their purpose being effected, they returned to Salamanca.

The new governor, General of Brigade Jean Léonard Barrié, was the only available general of the appropriate rank at Salamanca. He was far from an active officer of the type described by Major Gordon and was reluctant to take on the command at Ciudad Rodrigo, regarding it as a poisoned chalice. Nonetheless, with a siege imminent, as much as possible was done to prepare, including making the burned-out and battered convents of Santa Cruz and San Francisco defensible and creating an additional redoubt on the forward slope of the Greater Teson named Fort Renaud after Barrié's predecessor.[5]

Throughout the late autumn a loose blockade of Ciudad was maintained, with one of the tasks allocated to Lieutenant Simmons being to prevent the leakage of food into the fortress. He recalled being 'ordered to reoccupy Fradamora and keep a good look-out. Succeeded in capturing a number of peasantry that were going to the French garrison with wine, onions, bread, and eggs for sale. I purchased what I wanted, and then sent them under escort to our Commissary.'

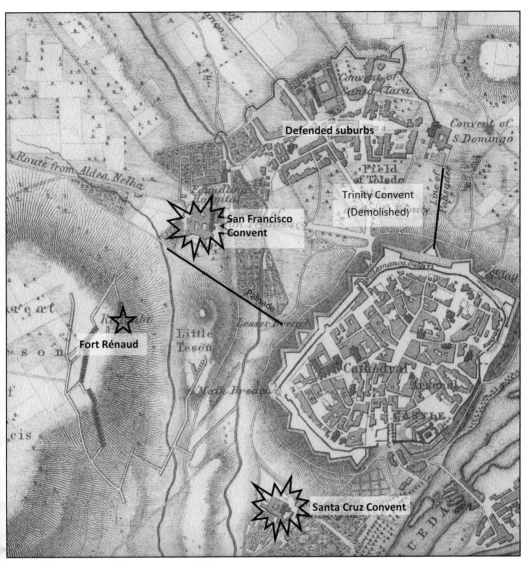

Convent of Santa Clara

Defended suburbs

Convent of S.Domingo

Route from Aldea Netha

Field of Toledo

Trinity Convent (Demolished)

San Francisco Convent

Palisade

Lesser Teson

Fort Rénaud

Little Teson

Main Breach

Cathedral

Arsenal

CASTLE

Santa Cruz Convent

The defences of Ciudad Rodrigo 1812.

As autumn changed into winter, it was noted that the Imperial Guard Cavalry had crossed the Pyrenees back into France and that the two divisions of Guard Infantry, all of which had been under General Dorsenne's command, were marching east. Once back in France it was no great secret that they would join the preparations for the coming Russian campaign. In addition, the Polish regiments that had been such an important part of the French peninsular armies were also withdrawn. All these largely veteran troops were to be replaced – eventually – but by poorly-trained and equipped conscripts. As word of these moves came, in addition to the redeployment of some of Marmont's divisions to the successful Suchet, the chance of taking Ciudad Rodrigo grew and Wellington was on the

Wellington's headquarters at Freineda. Once the investment was complete, he moved forward to Gallegos.

alert. In a letter on 18 December Major Gordon wrote 'the Lord Wellington will lay siege to Rodrigo, but it will be at least three weeks before we can break ground.' That same day the duke started to issue orders.

During Marmont's operations around Ciudad Rodrigo back in September his troops had found and burned fascines and gabion baskets in the bivouacs of the 3rd and 4th divisions but with the French moves to the east, Wellington ordered another set to be made:

G. O.   Adjutant General's Office,
                                         Freineda, 18th December 1811.

1. The Commander of the Forces begs that the soldiers of the regiments of the 1st, 3rd, 4th and Light Divisions and Brigadier General Pack's brigade may be employed in making fascines [bundles of sticks] and gabions [baskets for rock and soil] and pickets [stakes] of the following dimensions:

2. Fascines of one foot thick and six feet in length.

3. Gabions three feet in height by two feet three inches diameter, of the same numbers that there will be of the fascines.

4. Twice as many pickets as there will be fascines, three feet six inches long.

A gabion basket woven from rods of green growth.

5. These articles when made are to be kept at the headquarters of the several regiments; an officer of engineers will be sent round to inspect them, and will pay those who shall have made them, for the larger fascines two Vinteens each, for the gabions four Vinteens each, and for the pickets half a Vinteen each.

6. Lieutenant Colonel Fletcher will send with the engineer officer to the headquarters of each division a proportion of tools for the purpose of making fascines and gabions, which will be distributed to the several regiments and will be returned when the work shall be finished.

7. The engineer officers will report on the progress of the work every third day.

The ever-critical Captain Burgoyne recorded in his journal that this was not straightforward as the country had in accessible places already been stripped of suitable materials:

This arrangement appears bad, as the parties will be so dispersed it will be impossible to superintend them well. The distance to Ciudad Rodrigo is in many instances five leagues and in some as much as seven; in many places, the materials are bad or scarce, whereas about Espeja and Campillo, within two leagues of good road, is plenty of stuff to employ the whole.

In a letter home Lieutenant Robert Knowles of the 7th Fusiliers recorded that 'Detachments from each regiment in the 4th Division are employed making gabions and fascines for the erection of batteries, and the battering train have orders to be in readiness to march at an hour's notice.'

Preparations went on apace with Burgoyne again recording on 30 December: 'I am cutting planks for [gun] platforms at Puebla de Azaba. The number of gabions proposed to be made in the first instance is of gabions 2,500, of fascines 2,500, and of pickets 10,000.' In addition, preparations for a bridge of trestles to be thrown across the Águeda by the staff corps were begun. Captain Jones recalled: 'Major Sturgeon and 148 soldiers [and] artificers, selected from the army, were assembled at Almeida for this service.' The work was secretly performed in the arsenal at Almeida and had been nearly completed in mid-December.

In the New Year, Napoleon's attempt to command from Paris resulted in the final dislocation of the French armies in western Spain and, seizing the opportunity that Wellington had awaited so long, on 1 January 1812 he issued his orders for operations against Ciudad Rodrigo. According to Major Jones, this was 'notwithstanding the mortar ammunition being still at Vila da Ponte, to commence the siege instantly with guns only, and directed the bridge for the heavy ordnance to be put down forthwith and the stores immediately to move forward.'

This decision to mount the siege immediately when only days earlier Wellington had been predicting that all would be ready in ten days' to two weeks' time, when the mortar and howitzer ammunition would be at Almeida, is probably borne out of the long wait and what could have been a fleeting opportunity to launch operations against Ciudad Rodrigo. The duke, with limited transport and time, was going to risk the siege with guns only, but in contrast to those guns used in the two failed sieges of Badajoz they were well-founded new iron guns. He also had a sound logistic plan and the necessary enablers in place or nearly so. Overnight, however, on 1 January heavy snow fell, 'which lay on the ground to a considerable depth, and the weather became very inclement; during the night of the 3rd the snow increased considerably, and on the 4th it blew a violent gale with much sleet.'

The Investment

With the staff corps' trestle bridge ready and the stores being loaded onto carts and waggons, despite delays occasioned by the snow, the investment could begin. On 4 January, preparations were far enough advanced for orders to be issued to the siege divisions – the 1st, 3rd, 5th and Light Divisions, plus Pack's Portuguese Brigade – to march and take up positions as shown on the map opposite.

Lieutenant William Grattan of the 88th Connaught Rangers recorded the details of a miserable march:

> The morning of the 4th of January was dreadfully inauspicious. The order for marching arrived at three o'clock, and we were under arms at five. The rain fell in torrents, and the village of Aldeia da Ponte, which the brigade of General Mackinnon occupied, was a sea of filth; the snow on the surrounding hills drifted down with the flood and nearly choked up the roads, and the

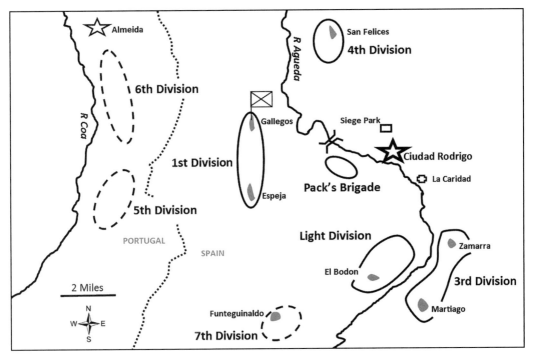

Wellington's deployment before Ciudad Rodrigo, January 1812.

appearance of the morning was anything but a favourable omen for us, who had a march of nine leagues to make ere we reached the town of Robleda on the river Águeda, which was destined to be our resting-place for the night.

At half-past six the brigade was in motion, and I scarcely remember a more disagreeable day; the rain which had fallen in the morning was succeeded by snow and sleet, and some soldiers, who sunk from cold and fatigue, fell down exhausted, soon became insensible, and perished; yet, strange to say, an Irishwoman of my regiment was delivered of a child upon the road, and continued the march with her infant in her arms.

Charles Boutflower, surgeon of the 40th (2nd Somersetshire) Regiment of Foot, wrote in his diary:

We march to-morrow morning to San Felices el Chico, a small village to our left, for the purpose of making room for Head Quarters and the Guards who come here. This place is a scene of the utmost hurry and bustle; nothing to be seen but Engineers, & all the Implements requisite for a Siege.[6]

At the same time the 5th and 6th divisions moved forward across the Côa, followed several days later by the 7th Division. The cavalry and Julián Sánchez provided a screen of outposts towards Salamanca and the east. There was no need to deploy an infantry division in that area as well, as Wellington was confident that the French were in no position to break the siege with Dorsenne or Marmont having so few men immediately available.

Lieutenant Simmons recorded a miserable march on 4 January to El Bodón:

A stormy cold, incessant rain during the day. The Águeda much swollen. Forded it nearly up to the shoulders. The men obliged to put their pouches upon the knapsacks and hold on to each other to prevent being forced down with the current. Some time exposed before there was any possibility of getting lodged. Officers, men, and all huddled together. Got our men better regulated and had three houses for the company.

The divisions were to use the small scattered villages rather than bivouac closer to the city due to the lack of tents in 1812 and the winter season.

Ciudad Rodrigo's garrison on the day of investment was as follows:

34th Leger, one battalion	975
113th Ligne, one battalion	577
Artillery, two companies	168
Engineers	15
Non-combatants (civil officers, etc.)	36
Sick in hospital	163
Staff	3
Total	1,937

This figure is much lower than that of the Spanish garrison in 1810. Marmont was taking a risk that in mid-winter, with the British supposedly wracked with sickness, Wellington would not attempt a siege and that the stores thrown in during September and November would last until the spring of 1812.

On 6 January Wellington's headquarters moved from Freineda to Gallegos, which was approximately 8 miles from Ciudad Rodrigo. From here on the following day, according to the Royal Engineers' historian: 'Lord Wellington, accompanied by his Commanding Engineer, Lieutenant-Colonel Fletcher, and other officers of his staff, made a close and careful reconnaissance of the place, and decided upon the plan of operations.'

They had crossed the Águeda by the fords of La Carbonara 2 miles below the city, and 'unattended by any escort, reached several points from which they obtained a sufficient view of the defences to decide on the attack.' Wellington and his staff, mounted on corn-fed horses, were in much better condition than the French cavalry horses and did not need to fear enemy pursuit or ambush in the open country around Rodrigo.

Wellington and Fletcher elected to attack from the Greater Teson towards Ciudad Rodrigo's north-west corner – the same direction from which Marshal Ney had launched his siege in 1810. This would enable some of his trenches to be reused but above all, even though the French breach had been repaired, it was believed that the soil and rock would not have fully compacted yet and would be more quickly susceptible to destructive fire from the British heavy guns.

Infantryman of a French *légère* regiment, the main difference between *ligne* and *légère* was the colour of the trousers and front of the jacket.

Lieutenant Colonel Fletcher, Wellington's chief engineer.

On returning from the reconnaissance, Major Gordon wrote summing up the mind of the headquarters and the risk that they were taking:

> Rodrigo will be invested tomorrow. The trenches will be opened either that night or the 9th ... I am in great hopes of our getting it; altho' I think we have but eighteen or twenty days to spare. If in that time we are able to make a practicable breach, I think we shall certainly take the town, but after that period I am of opinion the enemy will be able to collect here in force and oblige us to raise the siege. There is a very weak garrison which is much in our favour but the season of the year is such as to render our operations very precarious and uncertain.

With the divisions in place around the city, along with the stores and necessities for a siege to form the Engineer Park loaded on carts at Gallegos, Wellington could begin the siege. By 8 January 1812 the staff corps' bridge for the crossing of the heavy equipment was in place adjacent to the ford of Marialba and the Light Division was ordered to march from El Bodón. Lieutenant Simmons was among them and was

> ordered to move before day, and crossed the Águeda at a ford above the convent of La Caridad [Ford of Cantarranas]. Our march was conducted out

Portuguese bullock carts were the mainstay of Wellington's transport and logistics.

of range of shot from the town to the north side, and behind a hill in the vicinity of San Francisco [the Greater Teson] ... Several French officers made their appearance and politely took off their hats and spoke to us. They were of course very anxious to know what this meant.

Captain Leach commented that 'The weather being very sharp the process was not a pleasant one.' He continued:

The necessary dispositions for the investment of the place were soon completed, under the immediate direction of Lord Wellington. Here was some cannonading from the town as the regiments advanced to take up the different posts allotted to them. General Pack's Portuguese brigade invested the town on the left bank of the river and was in position on the heights above the bridge which leads onto it.

Rifleman Costello, having had a good look at the fortifications, commented that they 'afforded only a subject for jest; as I believe at that time, such was the confidence that filled the ranks of our division, it would have been difficult to persuade the men that they could not beat the French under any odds.' Costello and his fellows settled down in temporary bivouacs some 2 miles north of the city. They made crude shelters and constructed ladders for that night's operations.

Meanwhile, Lieutenant Grattan described the scene and activity around Ciudad Rodrigo as the divisions set up camp and took over houses:

The number of Spaniards, Portuguese and soldiers' wives in the character of sutlers was immense, and the neighbourhood, which but a few days before was only an empty plain, now presented the appearance of a vast camp. Wretches of the poorest description hovered round us in hopes of getting a morsel of food, or of plundering some dead or wounded soldier: their cadaverous countenances expressed a living picture of the greatest want, and it required all our precaution to prevent these miscreants from robbing us the instant we turned our backs from our scanty store of baggage or provisions.

Assault on Fort Renaud

Fort Renaud was one of three significant outworks that covered the north-east through to west faces of Ciudad Rodrigo. The city walls had been rendered vulnerable by the march of artillery technology that meant siege artillery on the dominating Teson features could batter the walls. Resources had not been forthcoming to produce more than basic protective enhancements to the defences and the three outworks were an attempt to address this problem.

Fort Renaud was a well-built redoubt sited on the southern slope of the Greater Teson just below the crest where it could be mutually supported by cannon mounted on the walls of Ciudad Rodrigo (525 yards) and those on the upper surface of the San Francisco convent (450 yards). Its fire overlapped that from the Santa Cruz convent on the western end of the Teson features. Its significance in Wellington's mind was that a similar work had caused considerable difficulty at the failed siege of Badajoz the previous year and consequently its capture would be of importance.

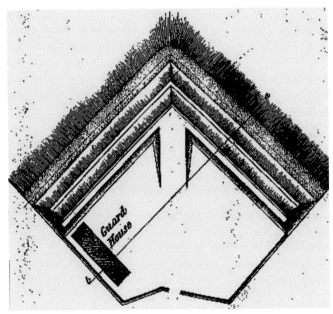

Major Jones' sketch of Fort Renaud.

Mounting two cannon and a howitzer, Fort Renaud was a relatively simple construction; essentially an earthen fleche with a palisaded/revetted 20ft-deep ditch to the front followed by a protective rampart. The rear, however, was just a loop-holed light brick wall. This was normal procedure for outworks to prevent it, if taken, being easily used by the enemy, as the brick wall would provide little protection from the fire of the main fortress's heavy guns. The fort is incorrectly marked on the top of the Teson on maps in some histories and also as being square. Modern air and satellite photography reveals Fort Renaud was lower down on the Greater Teson to the south. The work often incorrectly marked is in fact the post-1812 siege redoubt built by the British, and the now overgrown but obvious outwork built on the northern side of the Teson was constructed by the Spanish later in 1812.

Wellington decided that Fort Renaud was to be taken by escalade without a preliminary bombardment, which would enhance surprise and save the five days that both Colonel Fletcher and the French estimated it would take to reduce the place with artillery fire. The attack to be mounted on the night of 8 January was entrusted to Colonel Colborne of the 52nd Light Infantry with 450 men from across the Light Division, each of the 43rd, 1/52nd and 2/52nd providing two companies and the 1st and 3/95th Rifles along with the 1st and 3rd Caçadores providing one company each. The 95th would also provide guides in the form of an officer and two sergeants to ensure that the attack, which was to be launched under cover of darkness from dead ground on the northern slope across the crest, was correctly directed towards Fort Renaud.

Colonel Colborne wrote that the whole of 'the Light Division marched from El Bodón, or near, early on the 8th and reached the ground in front of the Upper Teson about noon.' He continued: 'The detachments intended for the assault of the redoubt were not volunteers; they were companies commanded by the senior captains of each battalion; two from the 43rd, four from the 52nd Regiment, two from the 95th, and one from each of the Portuguese battalions.'

The plan was that four companies, including the two Rifle companies, the whole being under Major Gibbs, would form the advance guard and were directed to take up position on the crest of the fort's glacis and open a suppressive fire. A group of sappers with ladders commanded by engineer Captain Thompson would follow behind and place the ladders for the assault. Colborne recounted:

> In the rear of the whole [advance guard] the companies destined for the actual escalade followed. In this order we started and advanced, after a caution had been given by me in respect to silence, and each captain had been instructed *precisely* where he was to post his company and how he was to proceed on arriving near the redoubt.

The two companies of Caçadores brought up the rear of the ten companies.

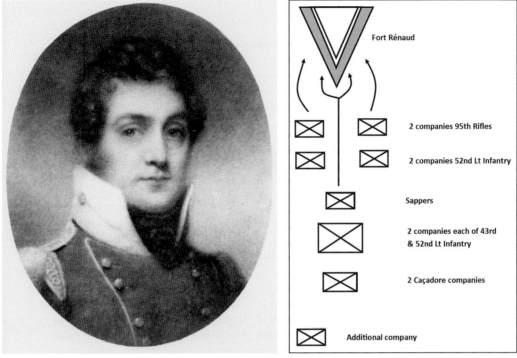

Fort Rénaud

2 companies 95th Rifles

2 companies 52nd Lt Infantry

Sappers

2 companies each of 43rd
& 52nd Lt Infantry

2 Caçadore companies

Additional company

Colonel Colborne commanding the 52nd Light Infantry and his plan.

Major Jones of the Royal Engineers wrote:

During the day everything was kept as quiet as possible, and an equal examination made of every side of the town so as to prevent any suspicion of an immediate effort, or of the point about to be attacked; but soon as it became dark a force formed under arms and a working party of 700 men paraded in two divisions.

Several hours after dark with the guides in place, the assault force formed up in close column of companies with the Teson ahead of them. Over the crest and down the slope beyond lay the fort in silence. At 2000 hours the escalade force moved forward with Colonel Colborne and Major Napier mounted on their chargers. The colonel recalled: 'When we reached the point marked by the officer of the 95th, I dismounted and again called out the four captains of the advance guard and ordered the front company to occupy the front face and the 2nd the right, etc.'

Lieutenant Harry Smith was sent back by Colborne to get an additional company to enhance the attack, while the riflemen and the two companies of musket-armed red-coated men of the 52nd Light Infantry began their move forward towards their designated position at the foot of the fort's short glacis slope:

When about fifty yards from the redoubt I gave the word 'double-quick'.
This movement and the rattling of canteens alarmed the garrison; but the

defenders had only time to fire one round from their guns before each company had taken its post on the crest of the glacis and opened fire. All this was effected without the least confusion, and not a man was seen in the redoubt after the fire had commenced.

The signal for the next phase of the attack to begin was a shout of 'England and Saint George'. This brought the infantrymen who had been trained as sappers forward with ladders and fascines:

> The party with the ladders soon arrived and placed them in the ditch against the palisades, so that they were ready when Captain Mein of the 52nd came up with the escalading companies. They got into the ditch by descending on the ladders and then placing them against the fraises [tree branches forming a protective entanglement].

Major Jones adds some detail on the crossing of another part of the ditch:

> Lieutenant Jones, who accompanied the detachment with a party of sappers carrying scaling ladders, fascines, axes, etc. on arriving at the counterscarp, finding the palisades to be within three feet of it and nearly of the same height, immediately placed the fascines from one to another and formed a bridge, by which a part of the storming party walked over the palisades and jumped into the ditch; where finding the scarp without revetment they readily scrambled to the top of the parapet and came into contact with the bayonets of the defenders.

So effective was the suppressive fire from musket and rifle that the only enemy fire received by the sappers and the assault companies of the 52nd and 43rd was in the form of shells and grenades randomly thrown over the rampart into the ditch. The fuses of most of these were snuffed out and casualties were light.

While the escalade was being made to the front Lieutenant Gurwood of the 52nd with little for his marksmen to do followed the ditch around to the rear of the redoubt and reported that the ladders could be used there to mount an escalade. As he and his men began their climb of the wall at the rear of the fort, its gate opened and a French sergeant appeared lighting a shell. He was promptly shot but the shell, fuse burning, rolled towards Gurwood's men, who could do little to the fizzing object but kick it away. Fortuitously the shell rolled back against the gate and, exploding, it demolished the gate, providing an easy route into Fort Renaud for the 52nd.

With the British both in front of them and behind them as well as being out-numbered four to one, the French promptly surrendered, with forty-eight of the approximately seventy-three-man garrison being taken prisoner, having run hastily to the guardhouse where they had barricaded themselves in to escape bayonet and sword. Only four French soldiers escaped back to the city. French

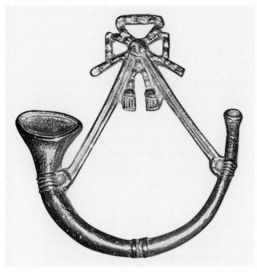

The generic period brass light infantry bugle-horn badge worn by rifles, light infantry battalions and light companies of line regiments. Examples have been found in the UK, the Iberian Peninsula and in North America.

Major John Jones: a later engraving of him as a general.

soldiers taken by the Caçadores were treated badly by the vengeful Portuguese soldiers, with many being not only robbed but stripped and beaten as well. When one considers the brutal French behaviour during their invasions of Portugal (1807–1808 and 1810–1811), it is easy to appreciate how such behaviour by Portuguese troops resulted.

Officers who had been stripped naked were taken to the rear for questioning, with their modesty being restored with handkerchiefs and greatcoats. Meanwhile, Major Jones and his sappers had a task to perform:

> Instantly the redoubt was carried, the precaution was taken of making its rear perfectly accessible by breaking down the gates and forming openings in its rear enclosure but in a very short time the garrison directed such a quick fire into the enclosure that it was thought right to withdraw everyone from its interior.

The garrison of Ciudad Rodrigo, who had clearly not expected an attack so soon, responded with a heavy fire primarily, as indicated by Jones, against the fallen redoubt. So much so that Colborne deployed his assault force, now a part of the guard force, in the small valley between the two Teson features where they were out of the worst of the enemy fire and could discharge their duty as 'cover party', standing ready to repel any counter-attack or attempt to recapture the redoubt. Colborne wrote:

> It was pitch dark that night, and the firing went on so long that the rest of the army thought we should not take the fort, and were very anxious about it. We were firing into the fort from the glacis across the ditch, but our men could not be seen. The only danger was of our firing on each other. The firing was so steady and continuous that I could not see any sign of the enemy on the ramparts.

The swiftness and style of the capture of Fort Renaud added to the still-growing reputation of the Light Division and helped the newly-arrived Colonel Colborne begin to establish his reputation as one of the finest commanding officers in the Peninsular Army. In summary George Napier wrote:

> The Colonel formed his party and gave his orders so explicitly, and so clearly made every officer understand what he was to do, that no mistake could possibly be made. The consequence was that in twenty minutes from the time he moved to the attack the fort was stormed and carried.

Wellington and General Craufurd were anxiously awaiting the attack and were much relieved when they heard the cheer of success, which was apparently even more of a relief to the brigade commander Colonel Barnard of the 95th Rifles. Apparently 'Barnard, unable to restrain his emotion, threw himself on the ground in the vehemence of his delight so that General Craufurd, who was at a little distance and did not see who it was, exclaimed: "What's that drunken man doing?"'

Craufurd, who was not known for fulsome praise of subordinates or even expressions of approval, later said to his staff: 'Colonel Colborne seems to be a steady officer.'

The siege of Ciudad Rodrigo had got off to a good start.

Notes

1. Letter to Lord Liverpool, 18 July 1811. Wellington, however, cautioned that 'I beg your Lordship to observe that I might be obliged to abandon it.'
2. Major General Whitworth Porter, *History of the Corps of Royal Engineers*, Vol. 1 (Longmans, 1889).
3. Dickson had come to Wellington's attention as a major attached to the Portuguese army during 1811 where he commanded the allied siege artillery at Olivença with energy and enterprise.
4. J.T. Jones, *Journals of sieges carried on by the army under the Duke of Wellington, in Spain, between the years 1811 and 1814*.
5. The redoubt of Fort Renaud is the source of some confusion. In French sources it is referred to as the San Francisco Redoubt, which is not to be confused with the defended convent of San Francisco. Fort Renaud is today only visible from air photography and is often confused with a redoubt built by the British on the crest of the Greater Teson and a substantial Spanish redoubt on its northern slopes, both dating from after the siege.
6. Charles Boutflower, *The Journal of an Army Surgeon During the Peninsular War*.

Chapter Twelve

The 1812 British Siege of Ciudad Rodrigo

Immediately the capture of Fort Renaud was completed, much of the remainder of the Light Division, some 700 men who had been told off as labourers and trench guards, were to break ground on the Greater Teson. According to Major Jones[1] the first division of 400 labourers, with Colborne's force covering their front, 'were to open a trench [the first parallel] on the flank of the redoubt and the second division opened up the communications[2] to it from the rear across the crest of the Greater Teson.' This was successfully accomplished 'with little loss as the garrison directed nearly all their fire into the redoubt throughout the night.' Lieutenant Simmons of the 95th Rifles, however, who was supervising work up on the Teson, was not so sanguine, commenting: 'I became perfectly familiar with the difference of sound between the missiles, shot and shell, long before dawn.'

The Royal Engineers suffered their first casualty that night. Captain Ross, the duty director,[3] was killed by grapeshot fire from the guns in the San Francisco convent while superintending the night's work 'which unfortunate event caused considerable interruption to the work … A row of gabions had to be placed

A protective wall of gabion baskets.

between the battery and the place, which served to conceal the workmen in the front ditch, a portion of the relief continued to be employed there.'

9 January 1812: Day 1

Captain Leach commented that 'without intermission, throughout the night, we worked liked rabbits.' Consequently, the first parallel was about 600 yards long, 3ft deep plus a parapet and was 4ft wide, the work at this early stage providing 'tolerable cover'. Around dawn, as the enemy's fire became more accurate, the first division of labourers was marched back and, according to Major Jones, 'a relief of fifty men was sent in to improve the lodgement, and 350 men to perfect the approaches.' Due to the winter season Wellington not only decided that the troops should be based in villages, but that they should work in rotation. Jones explains

> ... that the duties of the siege should be taken by the Light, 1st, 3rd and 5th Divisions alternately; each remaining for four and twenty hours on the ground, to furnish the guards of the trenches and the working parties. The division coming on duty [was] to march from its cantonments so as to arrive on the ground at mid-day, when the division relieved should return home.

This had been specified in Wellington's orders issued during the previous day. Consequently, it was these instructions that the 1st Division followed when they marched to relieve the Light Division:

> When a division is ordered for duty ... it is to march from its cantonments before daylight in the morning ... The troops will be able to cross at the fords ... [The trestle bridge was reserved for the battering train, ammunition and siege stores.] The troops are to have with them a day's provisions cooked, and they are to be followed by two days' spirits, and no other baggage.
>
> A sufficient number of men to cook the provisions for the day the division is relieved are to be left in the cantonments ... A hot meal waiting for them.
>
> Each regiment is to take along with it the entrenching tools belonging to it.
>
> The Engineers will order to the ground a sufficiency of cutting tools to enable those men not immediately on duty to supply themselves with firewood.

It was noted that the garrison 'fired a good many shells throughout the day but with little effect'. During the 9th the French gunners had clearly not got the range to the British trenches.

The relief in the trenches duly took place at midday and the 1st Division continued the work started by the Light Division. Later that day Colonel Fletcher, Wellington's chief engineer, was able to look out from the first parallel or

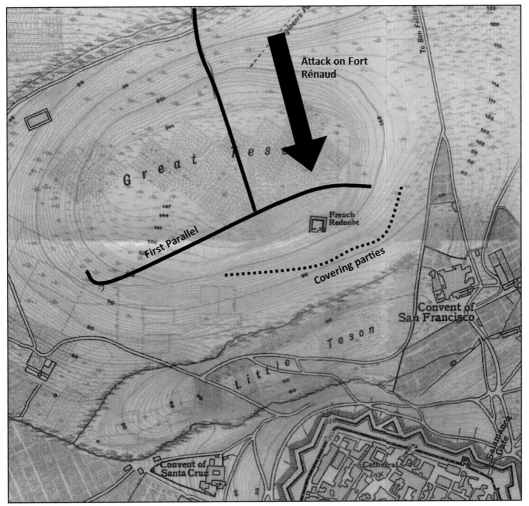

Work by the Light Division, 8–9 January 1812.

lodgement and 'was enabled to decide on the best trace for the parallel and the best sites for the batteries and had picketed them out.' This vital task he carried out under the cover of the failing light at dusk. The drill was laid down in the *Journal of Sieges*:

> In order to discover the trace of works to be erected in the night, it is very desirable that a light-coloured line[4] should be used to mark their outline. Stripes of white coarse cotton, about two inches broad, answer very well for such purpose, and are visible on the ground in the darkest night.

At this early stage in the siege the majority of the work would be carried out in darkness; in this case batteries Nos 1 to 3 were begun forward of the parallel. On the night of 9/10 January 1,000 members of the 1st Division were detailed as labourers and another 500 would act as cover party or guards. After dark, they

Plan view

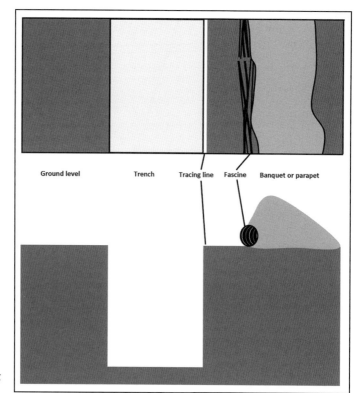

Ground level   Trench   Tracing line   Fascine   Banquet or parapet

Section view

Diagram of breaking
fresh ground.

headed up onto the Teson where the procedure for breaking fresh ground for the
batteries was as follows:

> Each man on marching out of the [Engineer] park carried a fascine four foot
> in length, which, on the division halting, he placed down parallel to the
> white line, at two feet in front of it; and as he afterwards only opened the
> ground to the white line, and threw the earth beyond the fascine, a space of
> two feet was left for the banquette. The workmen were placed four feet
> apart, and were expected at that distance to complete before the hour of
> being relieved a trench three foot in depth by three feet six inches wide at
> bottom, being something more than a cubic yard and a half of excavation.

10 January 1812: Day 2

Although entire divisions typically 3,000 to 4,000 strong were ordered to the
trenches, not only were men left behind to guard their camp and prepare a meal,
but also to guard the Engineer Park and the bivouac area. The remainder, according to the number required by the engineers, were split into two shifts: one resting

and the other in the trenches. The number of men labouring at night, certainly in the early phases, was typically greater. The changeover of shifts was normally at 0100 hours. The *Journal of Sieges* for the night of 10/11 January records:

> Working party, 1,000 men. The guard of the trenches was this day, and during the whole siege, regulated by the number of workmen employed, so that their united force should form a body of men in the trenches, of at least 1,500, which was supposed to be equal to two-thirds of the garrison; and under all circumstances, the workmen were kept prepared to act with the guard of the trenches.

During 10 January, it was realized that an error had been made in tracing out a part of battery No. 1. Jones explained that it

> was so much shut in by the redoubt in its front, that it was thought less labour to remove five of the guns [gun positions only at this stage] to the left of No. 3 battery, than to cut away the redoubt; and that battery was accordingly lengthened to contain sixteen guns.

Uniform of a Royal Engineer officer.

A substantial proportion of the two days' work on the battery had been wasted but siting defences, particularly in the dark, after the attack on Fort Renaud is and was fraught with difficulty.

At midday the 4th Division took over from the 1st for its initial turn in the trenches. Lieutenant Robert Knowles of the 7th Fusiliers commented that they were in the trenches 'and opened communications from the parallels to the batteries'. Charles Boutflower, the surgeon of the 40th Foot, also coming forward for his first period of duty on the Teson, recorded in his diary:

> During the twenty-four hours our casualties amounted to three killed & twelve wounded, which was more than a half of the loss of the whole Division. There appeared much despondency at the commencement of the business on the part of the Engineers, though they seem since to think better of it; it is however rumoured that Marmont is assembling a formidable force, and many are of opinion he may succeed in raising the siege.

The work on trenches and batteries had progressed but there was still much to do on the night of 10/11 January:

> Working party, 1,200 men. Five hundred workmen were employed to open the communication from the parallel to the batteries, to form a trench of communication and support between No. 1, 2 and 3 batteries, and to excavate for the magazines. The remaining 700 were employed on the batteries, parallel and approaches. The garrison kept up a well-supported fire of shells throughout the night, and threw many light balls.

'Light balls' were early illuminating rounds made up of turpentine and tar. The Royal Engineers' history[5] records the method for dealing with them:

> Two or three bold men of the Engineer brigade were always in readiness to run up and extinguish the light balls as they fell, and generally succeeded in a few seconds in smothering them with filled sand bags or by shoveling earth over them. The garrison always directed their fire on the men whilst so occupied, which diverted it altogether from the working party, employed, perhaps, at a few yards distance from the ball to its right or left. Some casualties occurred to the men thus employed, but generally they had extinguished the light ball before a second discharge of artillery could be brought upon them.

11 January 1812: Day 3

The routine changeover on this day saw the 5th Division wading the Águeda to relieve the 4th and General Leith's men came under the direction of the Engineers, not all of whom were professionals.

A part of the preparations for the siege had not just been the training of 200[6] infantrymen from the 3rd Division as sappers, but also twelve volunteer officers

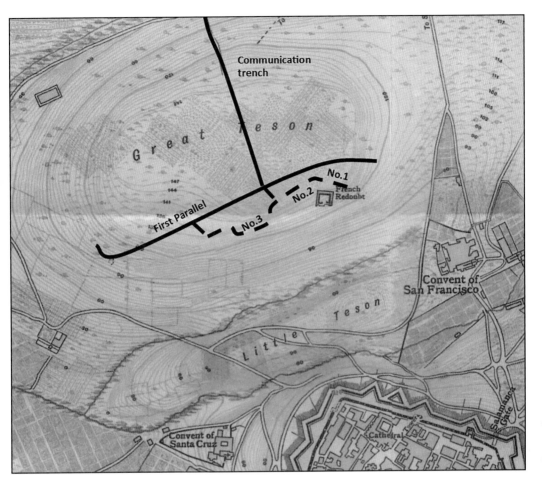

Tracing of the batteries.

to act as additional engineers. Their jobs under the control of the duty siege director and Royal Engineer officers was to oversee the work and ensure that it was technically correct, for instance ensuring that the glacis slope in front of a battery was at the correct angle and thick enough to ensure that they were shot-proof. The Royal Engineers' history explains:

> Being under fire of the powerful artillery of the fortress, at a distance of less than 600 yards, it was absolutely necessary that the parapets should have a minimum thickness of eighteen feet. In order to provide the mass of earth required for such a profile, it was determined to make the batteries half sunken, part of the earth being taken from the ditch in front, and part by lowering the terreplein to the rear.

All men employed as engineers or sappers received extra pay. Jones records:

> The officers acting as engineers, and those in charge of the sappers from the line, were paid 1 shilling per day. The soldiers acting as sappers and miners,

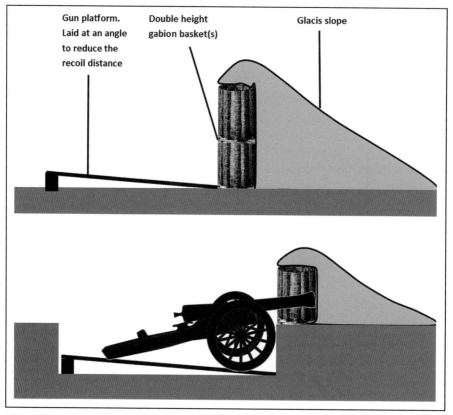

The profile of a typical battery.

and those working as artificers, were paid for their daily labour according to the rates laid down in the King's regulations for military working parties.

Major Jones goes out of his way to praise the temporary engineers:

> It would be highly unjust to close these Journals without adverting to the merit of the officers of the line who volunteered as engineers and sappers at these sieges. All of them were zealous, gallant, and highly useful; many intelligent, and some acquired considerable practical knowledge. They shared the fatigues and dangers of the trenches and assaults equally with the other engineers; and as, like them, some untimely fell and many were severely maimed.

No amount of praise can obscure the fact that with the death of Lieutenant Skelton, who had been standing in danger on the parapet to encourage the men, the lack of senior and experienced engineers was keenly felt. Captain Burgoyne, amid a list of complaints in a private letter, observed 'We go on most miserably, no superintendents, no arrangements, it is said that Wellington objects to give any assistance the Colonel proposes.'

It is further recorded that there were '20 miners and 60 carpenters, selected from the troops generally[7] and there were present 18 rank and file of the corps of Royal Military Artificers.' As the siege began, further engineers and artificers who had been continuing to work on the Lines of Torres Vedras were ordered to march to Rodrigo. However, they had not arrived by the end of the siege.

During 11 January the siege guns finally arrived at Ciudad Rodrigo, having had a slow and painful journey from Almeida, and formed an artillery park alongside that of the Engineers. There were thirty-four 24-pounders and four 18-pounders, all thirty-eight guns being mounted on travelling carriages along with 'a proportion of spare carriages, forges, gins, &c., complete. Two days' expenditure of ammunition for the thirty-eight pieces was deposited in the park, and a similar proportion was left in an entrepot at Gallegos.'

Ammunition would be brought up on a daily basis from Almeida to Gallegos and on to the batteries from the Artillery Park north of the Greater Teson.

12 January 1812: Day 4

The 12th, a day of 'extreme cold' but clear weather, saw the return of the Light Division to the trenches in soaking clothes that froze on them but firewood was available to warm and dry those who were waiting their turn to go to the trenches. Lieutenant Cooke of the 43rd Light Infantry remarked that three days on from their previous trench duty, not only was French fire more accurate but 'the land is arable, and bestrewn with loose stones, which were flying on all sides from the impulse given by the cannon balls, and the bursting of shells, which were exploding on every side, killing and maiming many soldiers.'

This was the stage of the siege where the garrison's abundant artillery started to come into its own. There were plenty of targets for them, and what is more the relatively few French artillerymen, supplemented by infantry, had now got the range of the British workings. Jones recorded:

> The artillery fire of the place, however, became so hot and so accurate, that it was impossible to continue the excavation of the ditches. Shells were constantly dropping into them, and exploding amongst the party employed there. After many casualties had been thus occasioned the men were retired, and cover had to be obtained by extending the rear excavation. Another great impediment was caused by the salvoes of shells fired by the garrison, which, bedding themselves in the earthwork, and exploding more or less simultaneously, acted like small mines, frequently blowing away large masses of parapet, and undoing in a moment the work of hours. In spite of all these difficulties the Engineers succeeded in pushing forward, and on the night of

the 12th the emplacements were ready for the carpenters, who began to lay the gun platforms.

As much work was now being carried out repairing existing entrenchments as digging the new ones. Captain Leach of the 95th Rifles also records that it was not just material damage to the trenches done by the French artillery: 'The garrison kept up, as usual, an eternal fire of shot, shells, and grape, by which we lost many men.' Rifleman Costello commented of this day's work:

Now was the time to cure a skulker, or teach a man to work for his 'life'. There we were, in twos, each provided with a pickaxe and shovel; now digging with a vengeance into the frozen mould, and then watching the glances of shot; and again, sticking to work like devils, or perhaps pitching ourselves on our bellies to avoid being 'purged' with grapeshot.

Stone-built gun platforms and embrasures up on the walls of Ciudad Rodrigo were far more resilient than the earthen ones on the Greater Teson that required constant repair.

With the enemy artillery being far more active and the batteries not yet being ready, Leach continues to describe a new phase of the siege for the sharpshooters of the 95th Rifles:

> Some companies of our regiment were sent out of the trenches, after it was dark, to get as near the town as possible, and to fire at the artillerymen through the embrasures. If this operation was a disagreeable one to the enemy, it was far from a delectable one for us: they threw fire-balls among us, which were composed of such combustible matter, that they could not easily be extinguished, and made everything near them as visible as at broad day. The moment we were perceived, musketry and grape were served out with no sparing hand. When relieved by the 1st Division on the 13th, we went through the same fiery ordeal again, from every piece of ordnance which the garrison could make use of.

The Riflemen performed this sniping duty from cover enhanced by shallow pits, depending on the lie of the ground either on the lower slope of the Lesser Teson or at the foot of the glacis slope. The range was between 100 and 200 yards. While only the 95th Rifles are recorded carrying out suppressive fire as described above, it is fair to assume that the companies of the 5th 60th Rifles attached to the brigades of the other divisions performed a similar function on a daily basis for the remainder of the siege. This assumption might be extended to rifle-armed companies of Caçadores battalions and King's German Legion light troops.

The *Siege Journal* recorded that overnight '1200 men [were] employed on the batteries, parallel, and communications, and in filling up shell-holes, the number and depth of which were found very inconvenient during dark', also the carpenters began to lay the heavy wooden platforms that were to bear the weight of the 18- and 24-pounders and to place the splinter-proof timber of the battery magazines.

The Covering Force

While the divisions earmarked for the siege were taking their turn in the trenches before Ciudad Rodrigo, those cavalry and infantry units providing the covering force were also astir. Private Wheeler of the 1st Battalion, 51st Regiment of Foot, a part of the 7th Division, were detached and he described in a letter home how they deployed across the border into Spain, marching

> to the mountains of Sierra de Gata, in the neighbourhood of Ciudad Rodrigo [some 30 miles to the south]. We were quartered in the village of Pio; this place contains a few miserable dwellings. We were stationed here to prevent the enemy from rendering assistance to the garrison while the siege was going on. Our duty was very severe, it consisting of furnishing piquets in the passes of the mountains, the nearest to Pio being about two leagues. The country all round was covered with snow. To shelter ourselves from the keen

An impression of a 'chosen man' of the 5th Battalion, 60th Royal North American Regiment (Rifles). In respect of their German origins, they were one of the few units of the army permitted to grow facial hair.

frosty air that continued during our stay in this part, we dug a large hole in the snow; in the centre, we kept a good fire, round which sat the men on duty; our fuel consisted of furze and fern. Of this we had abundance from places where the snow had drifted, but in collecting it we wanted snow pattern, for often we would sink over our heads, into some hole or burrow, when we expected we had firm footing.

The men on sentry were not only exposed to the cold winds but were much annoyed by the frequent visits of wolves; this I think for the short time it lasted it has been the severest duty we have yet performed.

We were on duty every other night, our clothes worn thin and wrecked by the fatigues of the former Campaign. It was difficult to tell to what regiment we belonged, for each man's coat was like Joseph's 'coat of many colours'.

Wheeler concluded that as the siege went on 'We could hear the roaring of the guns at Rodrigo, and we heartily wished the place reduced.'

13 January 1812: Day 5

During 12 January Wellington heard that two messages from General Barrié explaining the situation and appealing for help had been intercepted. It is not known whether other copies got through to Salamanca, but on that day word had also arrived of what was believed to be the expected French reaction to the siege. All was not, however, as it seemed. Marshal Marmont at Talavera had received a series of letters from General Dorsenne at Salamanca dated 1, 3, and 5 January warning of imminent moves by Wellington but the marshal, having become inured to similar reports over the previous six months, was slow to react. Without having heard of the siege until as late as 15 January, Marmont started on his return journey to Salamanca and at the same time set two infantry and a heavy cavalry division in motion, but they moved slowly and would not be within a

A cross-belt plate of the 51st Foot.

General Dorsenne.

distance to intervene at Rodrigo soon. Wellington, however, had become aware of some French movements nearer at hand and assumed they were intended to lift the siege. Consequently, on the morning of the 13th after his inspection of the trenches Wellington conferred with Colonel Fletcher, his chief engineer. The question was whether the progress of the siege be hurried. The duke's original intention was to mount a more conventional siege with thirty-three guns in three batteries on the Greater Teson, a second parallel and trenches being dug up onto the glacis slope. These batteries on the Lesser Teson would reduce the counter-scarp and faussebraye in the conventional manner.

This was, however, likely to be a protracted business, with work progressing more slowly the closer the trenches came to the walls. Jones recorded that these difficulties were already manifesting themselves:

> To oppose this heavy fire, it became necessary to persevere in making the parapets of the batteries of the thickness originally traced, and all the excava-tion being confined to the interior both night and day, the progress of the work was very unsatisfactory; particularly as the batteries being on the slope of the hill it required considerable height of parapet to screen their rear.

Time was the one thing Wellington did not have, especially as the mortars and howitzers had not arrived and much of the ammunition was still at Vila da Ponte and en route and with the information that led him to calculate that Marshal Marmont would advance to relieve Ciudad Rodrigo before the shot could be brought. According to Jones, Wellington enquired of Colonel Fletcher

> as to the practicability of forming a breach from the first batteries. His opinion being in the affirmative, his lordship decided to use them for that purpose, and that the work should in other respects proceed according to the original plan; when, as the movements of Marshal Marmont should render it expedient, he would either storm the place with the counterscarp entire, or wait till it should be blown in.

Orders were given to mount the batteries as quickly as possible and to start breaching, while the infantry would continue to sap away up onto the Lesser Teson where the second parallel would be dug, but to execute this the guns in the Santa Cruz convent would have to be neutralized.

The Santa Cruz Convent

During the 1810 siege one of the key aspects was the capture of the Spanish con-vents, which had been converted into the outworks of San Francisco and Santa Cruz. While Fort Renaud had been attacked as the opening move of Welling-ton's siege, the much-battered and burned convents had been repaired, made reasonably defensible and garrisoned by the French. Both convents mounted two cannon and a howitzer and those in Santa Cruz would be able to enfilade the trenches once the British started to dig a flying sap down from the crest of the Greater Teson which was due that night.

Consequently, Wellington ordered the 1st Division to mount an attack on Santa Cruz on the night of 13 January. General Campbell chose Baron Löwe's brigade of King's German Legion (KGL) infantry battalions for the task. Schwertfeger wrote: '... for this purpose, three hundred men, composed of the corps of skirmishers and detachments of the line battalions of the legion, with one company of the sixtieth; the whole under the command of Captain Laroche de Stackenfels of the first line battalion of the Legion.'

The 'sixtieth' were fellow Germans from the 5/60th Rifles who were to support the KGL with suppressive fire against any of the defenders that showed themselves over the walls.

The large gaps in the stone wall of the convent dating from the 1810 siege had been repaired by the French with wooden palisades but General Barrié could only spare a relatively few defenders for the outwork. There is little recorded detail of the assault on Santa Cruz, but it is assumed that the break-in described below was a surprise to the enemy as the attack was supported by an effective deception plan:

> Under a heavy fire from the fortress, the advance, consisting of the skirmishers of the first line battalion under Lieutenant Charles von Holle, forced the palisades by which the convent was surrounded, and, appearing

The old bull ring now stands on the site of the Santa Cruz convent. This is a view from the walls.

unexpectedly in the place, surprised the defenders, who fled, leaving behind their arms, baggage and accoutrements.

The cost of the capture of Santa Cruz was three men killed, and Lieutenant Lewis von Witte and thirty-four men were wounded. Most were hit by fire from the walls of the city.

That night, with the batteries nearly completed, Jones records that

it was decided to push the approaches forward this evening, and form part of the second parallel: 500 men were allotted for this duty, and opened the approaches and a sufficient length of the parallel ... by the flying sap with trifling loss, although the garrison by means of light-balls discovered the workmen and kept up a continued fire on them. The remaining 300 men were employed to open the embrasures of the several batteries.

The second parallel now ran along the top of the Lesser Teson within 200 yards of the walls and the batteries were made ready for the guns. Most of the twenty-three 24-pounders and four 18-pounders were brought up overnight.

The second parallel, the completed batteries and the French sally.

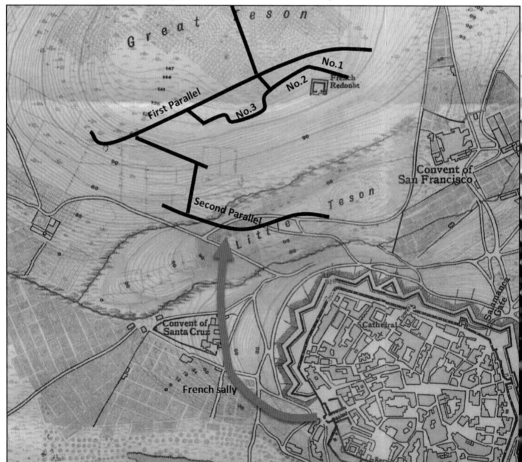

14 January 1812: Day 6

After a grim twenty-four hours on duty the 1st Division was due to be relieved once again by the 4th Division. Instructions for the procedures to be adopted during the relief were laid down in De Lancey's orders:

> As soon as the first battalion of the relieving division shall move on the ground, the general officer commanding the division which has performed the duty for the preceding twenty-four hours will commence the relief by sending off to their cantonments a proportionate number of troops, those of course first which have the greatest distance to go to their cantonments, and the relief will proceed in proportion as the troops shall arrive.

The French had, however, noticed from their vantage point in the cathedral tower that over the preceding days as the relieving division approached, those

A British 1802 pattern regimental cap often referred to as the 'stovepipe shako' (*left*) and a French centre company shako of the period (*right*).

troops working in or guarding the trenches moved back as a body rather than awaiting relief in place. This left the trenches extremely vulnerable to a French sortie, which unlike General Herrasti's practice in 1810, had hitherto been noticeably absent as a part of General Barrié's 1812 defence.

The French timed their sortie well. With the departure of the working and guard parties at 1100 hours as they saw the 4th Division's reliefs approaching, there were only gunners, engineer officers and sappers left in the trenches to face 500 French infantry. They swept out of the Puerta de la Colada, overwhelmed the defenders in Santa Cruz and headed a matter of hundreds of yards further on to the second parallel. Here they tipped gabion baskets into the trench, undoing much of the previous night's digging. Jones provides an account of the sortie:

> The danger was imminent that the assailants would penetrate to the batteries and succeed in spiking the guns. This, however, was obviated by the bravery and promptitude of an Engineer officer [probably Jones himself], who collected as many of the workmen not belonging to the retiring division as he could get together, and manned the parapets, keeping up such a steady fire that the advance was checked sufficiently long to enable the relieving division to rush forward to the rescue. The column was driven back into the town, the damage done by them being confined to the overthrow of the gabions fixed on the previous night.

The labourers were from the 2/24th and 1/42nd Foot but the timely arrival of General Graham and the leading reliefs brought matters to a close and, satisfied with their partly-successful sally, the French withdrew to the fortress taking many of the digging tools left in the second parallel with them. This had been a dangerous moment and much more damage could have been done if a significant number of guns had been spiked, which were already the bare minimum. This sortie could have badly delayed the siege and given Marmont those few extra days in which to intervene.

Opening Fire

Despite the sally, Batteries No. 1 to No. 3 up on the Greater Teson were finally established, equipped and provided with ammunition and opened fire at 1600 hours. Lieutenant Robert Knowles of the 7th Fusiliers wrote:

> I was on duty in one of the batteries at the time, and consider myself a lucky fellow to escape without a scratch, as my party had the dangerous duty of opening the embrasures for the guns, and the enemy's fire was directed altogether at us. A very fine young man, a lieut. in the Engineers, was mortally wounded when standing by my side.

In breach of convention, which normally called for the initial fire from the besiegers' cannon to focus on dismounting as many enemy guns as possible in the first fire, Wellington ordered twenty out of twenty-seven guns to concentrate on the same north-west corner where the French had breached the walls in 1810. Two of the 18-pounders engaged the San Francisco convent. Jones's table below, shows that the artillery was only able to fire for an hour before darkness fell. It also gives details of the weather and the way it interrupted the bombardment:

Time of firing at Ciudad Rodrigo

On the 16th Jan. 1810 at this place the sun rose at 16 minutes past 8 o'clock, and set at 54 minutes past 4, giving 8 hours and 38 minutes for the time of firing, or for calculation 8 hours and a half.

	Hours
Jan. 14, 1812. Firing from 20 24-prs. and 2 18-prs.	1
15. The whole day, from 23 24-prs. and 2 18-prs. to form the great breach	8½
16. Foggy weather, firing from 23 24-prs. and 2 18-prs.	1
17. Foggy weather, firing from 23 24-prs. and 2 is-pro. but cleared up at noon	5
18. Clear weather, from 30 24-prs. and 2 18-prs. to form large and small breach	8½
19. Clear weather, from 30 24-prs at 4 P.M. both breaches considered as practicable, fire turned on defences, and place assaulted at 7 P.M.	8½
Total	32½

The firing by the two 18-pounders against San Francisco was to soften up the convent for an attack that evening. Corporal Lawrence of the 40th (Somersetshire) Foot wrote:

We had to commence throwing up our batteries and breastworks under a particular annoyance from three guns, situated on a fortified convent a little distance from the town, near where our brigade's operations were in progress, so our colonel for one volunteered to storm the convent, which offer was accepted.

Several companies, therefore, including my own, advanced under him unobserved by the enemy in the darkness of the night, and succeeded in effecting an entrance into the convent, the garrison being taken by surprise, but managing to decamp.

Surgeon Charles Boutflower recorded in his diary that 'Considerable resistance was expected, but, on the men appearing on the walls of the Convent, the enemy fired a volley, and fled to the town with precipitation.' Lawrence continued:

I then volunteered with a few men to march on up to the tower where the guns were situated, a priest being made to show us the way, as the path which

Royal Artillery siege
train gunners.

we had to tread was so winding. When we arrived at the top, which must
have taken us at least ten minutes, we found no French there, but the three
shattered cannon still remained, which we were ordered to pitch down, not
much improving their condition thereby, and so we gained the object for
which we had come. All the French that were left in the convent, or at least
all I saw there, were two of their wounded, but they were good enough to
leave us a room full of cabbages, which came in very handy.

The surgeon had a much easier task than he expected with 'only three men
wounded in this affair' and went on to record that 'We (the 40th) remained in
possession of the Convent and Suburbs during the remainder of the siege, instead
of returning to our cantonments, as was the case with the remainder of the Army.'

That night the 4th Division found a working party of 500 men. Their task, as
recorded by Major Jones, was as follows:

The approaches to the second parallel destroyed by the garrison during the
sortie in the morning were reinstated, and 150 gabions were placed in con-
tinuation of the second parallel. Some strong gabions, supported by cross-
pieces in their interior, were laid on their sides along the bottom of the small
rivulet, to allow the water to run under the parapet of the sap.

This latter bit of engineering was to cross the stream that ran between the two
Tesons and stop water flooding the approach trench.

15 January 1812: Day 7

There was much work to be done in addition to that in the trenches. On the morning of the 15th Corporal John Spencer Cooper of the 7th Royal Fusiliers recalled:

> I volunteered out of my turn for the trenches, and fell in about three a.m. 'Twas bitterly cold, and there was no breakfast in those days. The adjutant called me out of the ranks and ordered me to take a party of batmen and mules, and carry pine logs to the bivouac before Rodrigo. But where were the logs? They were growing in a neighbouring wood. It was a pretty job I had with six lazy batmen, six stupid kicking mules, and only two or three blunt tomahawks. At last we got loaded and under way, but the loads were never content to ride decently: they were continually forming triangles or gravitating to earth. After much vexation I got to camp, and found the officers sitting in shallow pits round burning logs, but the men had neither shelter nor fires.
>
> At this moment a relief for the trenches was falling in. 'Corporal xxxx [*sic*], where are you?' No answer. I snatched up my piece and marched off in corporal somebody's place to fill sandbags, etc., for a nearly-completed battery. An engineer gets on the top of the battery to superintend the laying of the bags, a shot comes and cuts him in two. His dollars fly about. At this time the French were firing most furiously to destroy the battery.

The weather on the 15th continued fine and clear, allowing a full day's bombardment of the walls with the last five available 24-pounders being brought into action in Batteries 1 and 2. The fact that Wellington was pursuing the siege with guns only was the cause of some comment in the army. Captain Cocks is one who recorded his thoughts:

> It is a principle of his to avoid the use of mortars: 'The way to take a place,' I heard him say, 'is to make a hole in the wall by which the troops can get in and mortars never do this, they are not worth the expenditure of transport they require.' Well this all very well against such a place as Ciudad Rodrigo, but it would sacrifice men against a more respectable fortress.

Wellington's view is expressed in a letter written during the siege of Badajoz which sums up his reasoning:

> In all the sieges which I have carried on in this country I have used only the fire of guns, principally from entertaining an opinion that the fire of mortars and howitzers has an effect upon the inhabitants of a town alone; and that a French garrison in a Spanish or Portuguese town would be but little likely to attend to the wishes or feelings of its habitants. By this measure I have diminished considerably the excesses and difficulty of these operations, and

A representation of a British infantryman of the period.

at all events, whether successful or not, I have done no injury to the Spanish or Portuguese inhabitants.

Major Jones later commented on the peer's views on the lobbing of shells from howitzer or mortar into enemy-held fortresses: 'The feelings above expressed no doubt influenced Lord Wellington in deciding upon the equipments for the several sieges in Spain; and it is very much to be regretted that his Lordship, in dreading the abuse, should have overlooked the use of vertical fire.'[8]

In the case of Ciudad Rodrigo, however, with its snap investment when the opportunity presented itself the mortars, howitzers, their ammunition and equipment simply couldn't be brought forward in time. Wellington, it can be argued, made a political virtue of not killing the very people who resented his inability to raise the 1810 siege.

After a successful day's firing throughout the 15th, Jones recorded that

In the evening both the main scarp and faussebraye walls were so much shaken and injured as to give hopes of speedily bringing them down,

Batteries 4 and 5, plus the advanced sap which was never completed.

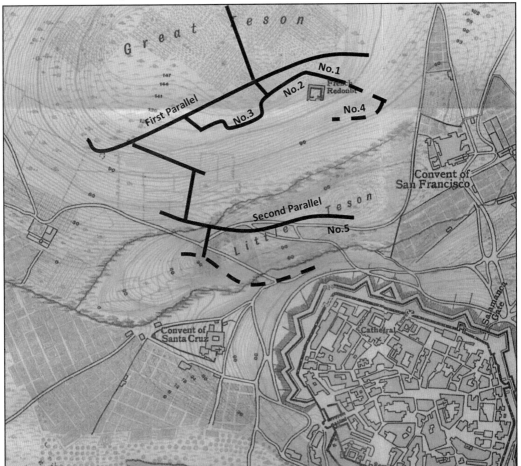

therefore, to be prepared to form a second breach speedily in the tower, Battery No. 4, for seven 24-pounders, was marked out in a favourable and more advanced situation. The garrison kept up a heavy fire, particularly of shells, throughout the day, which occasioned many casualties.

The tower had been identified as a potential weak spot at the beginning of the siege that could be readily demolished by gunfire to form a steep ramp of rubble over at least a part of the faussebraye, which would become a second or lesser breach:

> To avoid the loss attendant upon forcing retrenchments as the garrison might make behind the main breach, it was determined to attempt to form another opening in the scarp wall just before the conclusion of the attack, by unexpectedly bringing a heavy fire on a small projecting tower seen to its base over the faussebraye, and represented to be excessively weak and bad, and requiring but little battering to bring it down.

Lieutenant Grattan of the 88th who took over the works with the 3rd Division at midday recorded:

> In some instances, the soil was so unfavourable, it was next to an impossibility to make head against it; instead of clay or gravel, we frequently met with a vein of rock, and invariably when this occurred our losses were severe, for the pick-axes, coming in contact with the stone, caused sparks to issue that plainly told the enemy where we were, and, as a matter of course, they redoubled their efforts on these points.

The *Siege Journal* records the night of 15/16 January as being busy for Picton's men:

Night between 15th and 16th January

700 workmen were employed. 400 on No. 4 battery and its communications, 100 to repair the batteries, and 200 to improve the second parallel and the approaches to it.

The sappers were employed to extend the second parallel.

16 January 1812: Day 8

The following day dawned clear and fire was opened, but after an hour at 0930 hours a thick fog that persisted all day settled on Ciudad Rodrigo. Consequently, the opportunity was taken to improve the trenches and batteries with 700 men working at a time: 'One-half was employed on the new battery No. 4, and the other half in perfecting the second parallel and the approaches to it ... The engineers however took advantage of the fog to place fifty gabions in prolongation of the second parallel.'

The view down from the walls to the area where the second parallel was dug.

As an indication of just how much of a logistic burden the siege was on the never-ending mule and bullock convoys on the 50-mile route over difficult and mountainous terrain, the expenditure of ammunition thus far was 2,790 rounds of 24-pounder and 340 rounds of 18-pounder shot.

With the creation of a practicable breach being imminent, that evening Wellington summoned General Barrié to surrender the fortress. Being well-informed as to the condition of the garrison and its weak commander as well as Marshal Marmont's movements, the duke was clearly hoping that the fortress would capitulate, with Ciudad Rodrigo thus falling into allied hands days earlier than it otherwise would. Napoleon had, however, given instructions that fortress commanders were not to surrender on summons but only after at least one assault. Consequently, Barrié refused to capitulate.

The Light Division on their third turn in the siege works provided a working party of 700 men during the foggy night of 16 January. Their task was to work on the embrasures and gun platforms, all of which needed general repair. The embrasures in particular, not being of stone, became rounded, open and more vulnerable to enemy shot. In addition, there was a task more to the liking of the men of the Light Division:

As many infantry as could be posted in the parallel without materially impeding the workmen were employed to keep up an incessant fire of

The area of the Greater Breach from the city side as it is today.

musketry on the breach. ... Riflemen were placed in pits in front of the workmen along the face of the hill, to fire into the embrasures and keep under the artillery of the place, which at this short distance was found to destroy every gabion opposed to it.

A sergeant of the 43rd Light Infantry employed among the trench guards recalled that

the bellowing of eighty large guns shook the ground far and wide; the smoke rested in heavy columns upon the battlements of the place; the walls crashed to the blow of the bullet; and when night put an end to this turmoil the quick clatter of musketry was heard like the pattering of hail after a peal of thunder.

With the summons rejected, the target for much of the French fire overnight, so close that they could see it despite the fog, was Battery No. 5, for six 24-pounders. Work was commenced should the main batteries on their own fail to create a breach at over 500 yards. In the event, the other battery that was being built, Battery No. 4, was only used on the 19th at the very end of the siege.

During the day Private John Cooper of the 7th Royal Fusiliers had a duty that took him to the siege works. He recalled: 'Hearing that my brother

George, who belonged to the 43rd, was in the trenches, I sought and found him under fire setting up gabions. Though balls were whizzing unpleasantly about their ears, some were amusing themselves by throwing clods of earth at each other.'

17 January 1812: Day 9

The fog of the previous evening persisted throughout the morning and provided the French an opportunity to carry out repairs to the section of the walls that the British were breaching and to put in place additional defensive measures. The Riflemen of the 95th in their pits in front of the second parallel were, during the morning, subjected to 'well-directed fire of grape and the enemy obtained an ascendancy over the riflemen in the pits, but two or three cool fellows steadily persevering in firing at the gunners, the discharges of grape became less correct, and in the afternoon, were only kept up from the distant embrasures.'[9]

The fog, however, burned off around noon and

as soon as it was sufficiently clear to point the guns accurately, the fire recommenced as yesterday, and was continued without intermission till dark, when a considerable portion of both walls had been beaten down. The garrison was equally active, and by an incessant fire of shot and shells occasioned many casualties: a 24-pounder in No. 2 was rendered unserviceable by being struck in the muzzle; several of the wheels of the 24-pounder carriages were demolished, and many of the platforms blown up by shells.

Work continued slowly throughout the day on the saps forward of the second parallel. After relief of the Light Division by the 1st Division it is recorded that the French artillery up the ramparts 'knocked over the gabions nearly as fast as they could be placed.' Jones commented on this latter period of the sieges:

The third period is, when it approaches close to the place – when every bullet takes effect – when to be seen is to be killed ... when the space becomes so restricted that little or no front of defence can be obtained ... Then the work becomes truly hazardous, and can only be performed by selected brave men who have acquired a difficult and most dangerous art called sapping, from which they themselves are styled sappers.

Corporal Lawrence of the 40th Foot was one of his battalion that remained holding the San Francisco suburb, which proved to be scarcely less dangerous than taking turns in the trenches:

Now and then the garrison would greet us with a cannon-ball, which often did some little mischief; a sergeant was killed by one, which at the same time took another's arm off, and I myself had a narrow escape one day whilst in the breastworks, from a six-pounder which having struck the convent, rebounded and caught me in the chest. Luckily it was nearly spent, but as it was it knocked me down, and it was some time before I could recover my breath, and that not until my comrades had poured some rum and water down my throat. My chest was much discoloured and swollen, through which I was ill for nearly a week.

During the night of 17/18 January the 1st Division laboured on laying the platforms for Battery No. 4 along with completing its magazine and opening the embrasures, while the gunners brought seven 24-pounder guns up through the trenches and were in position before daylight. It is fortunate that the French focused their attention on delaying work on Battery No. 5 in the extension of the second parallel rather than Battery No. 4 on the Greater Teson.

Once again light troops, this time of the 1st Division, no doubt including their two companies of the 5/60th Rifles, were in action now that the second parallel was within musket range of the walls: 'The guard in the second parallel kept up a continued fire of musketry on the breach throughout the night, to prevent its being cleared.'

18 January 1812: Day 10

The day was clear, cold but sunny, giving the perfect opportunity to complete the breaching and create the lesser breach by collapsing the tower with the newly-commissioned seven 24-pounders of Battery No. 4. A full eight and a half hours' firing was possible with the 24-pounders firing at a rate of just over seven rounds per hour. This sustained rate of fire wore out the 541 British and Portuguese gunners and by the 18th casualties, sickness and injury had added to their difficulties. Consequently, gunners from the field batteries of the divisions were drafted in to serve the guns and maintain the volume of fire on this vital day of the siege.

The 4th Division who took over at midday suffered greatly; so heavy was the fire of French cannon and musket from the city walls that the 'guards forward of the second parallel were annihilated'. Wellington had persisted throughout the siege in the policy of concentrating the fire of his siege guns on creating a breach rather than reducing the defenders and their defences to the flanks. During the night, however, Lieutenant Ingilby in charge of a 6-pounder and a 5.5in howitzer from one of the field artillery brigades were installed in Battery No. 5 during the night and would do their best to prevent the French repairing or retrenching the breaches once the sun rose.

On the 18th the 3rd Division were in their camps. Lieutenant Grattan described the scene as the siege was approaching its climax:

Our bivouac, as may be supposed, presented an animated appearance – groups of soldiers cooking in one place; in another, some dozens collected together, listening to accounts brought from the works by some of their

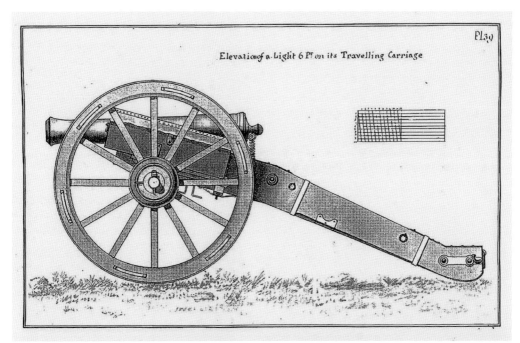

Pl.30

Elevation of a Light 6 Pr on its Travelling Carriage

A diagram of a British 6-pounder gun and a howitzer. (*Firepower Museum*)

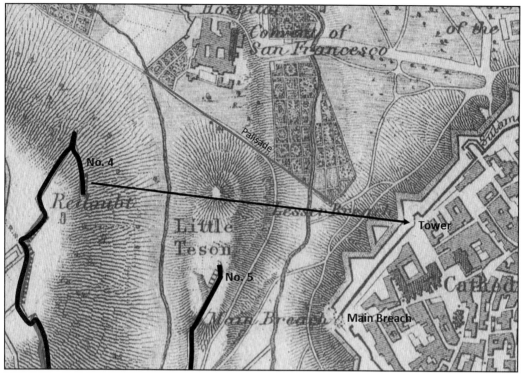

Creating the lesser breach.

companions whom curiosity had led thither; others relating their past battles to any of the young soldiers who had not as yet come hand to-hand with a Frenchman; others dancing and singing; officers' servants preparing dinner for their masters; and officers themselves, dressed in whatever way best suited their taste or convenience, mixed with the men, without any distinguishing mark of uniform to denote their rank. The only thing uniform to be discovered amongst a group of between four and five thousand was good conduct and confidence in themselves and their general.

19 January 1812: Day 11

The bombardment continued at dawn and, as expected, with gunfire from the seven 24-pounders in Battery No. 4 able to strike the base of the tower, the whole western face came tumbling down. The guns fired away for a total of eight and a half hours during the day improving the breaches, while the 5.5in howitzer and 6-pounder were during the final day and evening before the storm engaging French troops at the top of the breaches as they struggled to repair their defences and make them untenable for assault.

During the afternoon Wellington toured the trenches with Colonel Fletcher and Major Dickson, and after a good look at the walls declared the breaches practicable. In doing so he was accepting that the glacis slope and faussebraye had not been broken down as much as was desirable. Consequently, reaching the foot of the breaches would be an additional and difficult challenge. The peer sat in the trenches and with a pencil wrote his orders for the storm, which was to take place that very evening. (see Appendix II for a full transcript of Wellington's orders.)

Notes

1. J.T. Jones, *Journal of Sieges*, Vol. 1.
2. The terms 'approaches' and 'communication trenches' are synonymous and both are used freely in accounts of the siege.
3. Colonel Fletcher commanded the engineer works, Major Jones was brigade major and Ross and Burgoyne were to take it in turns to be the duty siege director.
4. 'Tracing line' was cotton tape very similar to the cotton 'mine tape' of the twentieth century and its modern plastic equivalent.
5. Major General Whitworth Porter, *History of the Corps of Royal Engineers*.
6. Reduced to 180 during training.
7. Ordinary infantrymen with the requisite skills from across the divisions.
8. J.T. Jones, *Journal of Sieges*, Vol. 3. Published after the original volumes in 1856.
9. Ibid.

Chapter Thirteen

The Storm of Ciudad Rodrigo

Having declared the breaches practicable during the afternoon of 19 January 1812, Wellington developed a plan that made use of his superior numbers to pull the unfortunate General Barrié and his all-too-few defenders in multiple directions. In addition, the urgency with which Wellington ordered the storm probably helped achieve a level of beneficial surprise. With the 4th Division exhausted from working in the trenches since the previous day, the assault was to be delivered by Picton's 3rd Division who took over in the trenches as normal at midday, while the Light Division was summoned from El Bodón to storm the lesser breach.

It is said that against advice General Barrié considered the lesser breach to be too small and too steep to be practicable and he believed that the bombardment would continue for at least another day. In short, he considered a storm of the city on the night of the 19th unlikely. Therefore the assault was to him, at least, a surprise.

The final act of the siege of Ciudad Rodrigo was to take place under cover of night at 1900 hours, a time at which it was dark enough to conceal movement of the assault troops and yet not give the French much time to repair their defences once the big guns of the siege train ceased fire at dusk. Thanks to the fire from the gun and howitzer in Battery No. 4, the French were unable to do much to repair the greater breach but they had already been able to dig retrenchments, lay mines and site flanking cannon behind the breach, just inside the city wall, with which to receive the British forlorn hope.

The main assault was to be preceded by two attacks at 1850 hours to draw General Barrié's reserves away from the main effort at the breaches. Colonel O'Toole, leading the 2nd Caçadores and the Light Company of the 2/83rd (County of Dublin) Regiment, had the task of removing a threat posed by the two cannon below the castle that could enfilade the 3rd Division's attack, particularly that of the 2/5th Foot of Campbell's brigade. Meanwhile, General Pack's Portuguese brigade was to demonstrate at the San Pelayo Gate[1] on the eastern side of the city.

The assault on the greater breach was to be delivered by the 3rd Division. General Picton was directed in Wellington's orders[2] to deploy the 2/83rd (less its Light Company) to provide covering fire from the second parallel. It is again likely that the sharpshooters of the division's company of 5th/60th Rifles would

The uniform of a British Light Company officer.

have joined the 83rd. The peer also specified that the attack was to be delivered by Mackinnon's brigade (left) and Campbell's brigade[3] (right). Both brigades were to converge on the greater breach via different routes; Mackinnon's in a direct assault from the second parallel with the support of close-range fire from the three companies of the 3/95th Rifles detached from the Light Division. Campbell was to fight his way from the west through the complex combination of glacis slope, ditches, faussebraye and obstacles set up by the French towards the greater breach. The 77th (East Middlesex) Regiment was to be his brigade reserve. The 3rd Division's overall reserve was to be provided by Power's Portuguese brigade who would occupy the second parallel once vacated by Mackinnon's brigade.

The assault on the lesser breach was to be delivered by General Craufurd's Light Division, from a forming-up point in cover on the low ground beyond the convent of San Francisco. With a smaller breach and with the division having only two brigades the assault would be by Vandeleur's brigade, while Barnard's brigade would follow up and provide the reserve (mainly 1/43rd). This brigade would also detach, as already mentioned, the three companies of 3/95th Rifles to give fire support to the main attack on the greater breach.

Altogether to storm Ciudad Rodrigo Wellington intended to use 10,700 troops, giving a superiority of five to one over the defenders, but gaining the breaches even with a favourable numerical balance was never a given certainty in siege warfare.

Wellington's plan for the storming of Ciudad Rodrigo.

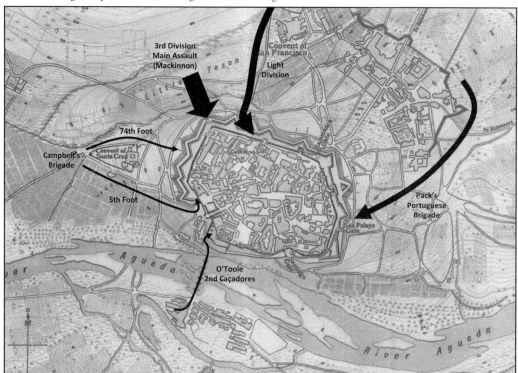

Procedure

While Wellington deviated from the traditional approach to the bombardment, the method of the storming of Ciudad Rodrigo was conventional. With the advent of the rifle-armed infantryman in the British army, if not the first to close on the enemy's defences, the Rifles would be towards the head of the column, with the task of getting to a position where they could effectively take on any French infantryman or gunner brave enough to show himself over the walls or in an embrasure.

As the glacis slope had not been reduced in the abbreviated bombardment, the assault force was preceded by sappers or infantry carrying hay bags, which would be dropped from the glacis slope into the ditches to help break the fall of those who had to jump down into them.

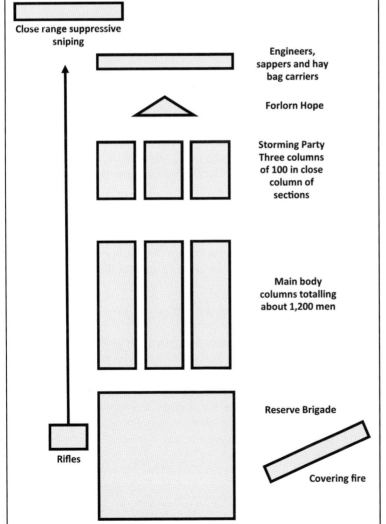

Diagram of a typical procedure for a storm.

Both 12ft and 25ft ladders were also made and were distributed among the troops of the storming party. The former were for climbing down into the outer ditch and scaling the lower bastions, while the latter were for use where the faussebraye was at its highest.

The actual attacks on the breaches were to be spearheaded by forlorn hopes: a group of twenty-five volunteers headed by a junior officer. The custom was that if he survived he would gain promotion without purchase and of all the officers who volunteered, the commander normally selected the most deserving candidate. The benefits of volunteering for the forlorn hope for the rank and file were less clear-cut.[4] Men were prepared to take the first blast of the enemy's fire for glory, possible advancement and often to be first at the plunder!

The forlorn hope was followed by the stormers, normally led by a field officer, usually a major. The size of the storming party, also made up of selected volunteers, was in the case of Ciudad Rodrigo 300-strong. Their task was scarcely less dangerous than that of the forlorn hope and again there was no shortage of volunteers from across a brigade or division. If all went well they would scale the breach and then clear and secure the immediate area for the main body of the assault troops. In the worst case the stormers were to simply overwhelm the enemy with numbers. The main body following behind would deploy according to the width of the breach. In reality all of these neatly-organized bodies broke down as they, under fire, scaled the glacis slope and jumped down into the ditches; success depended on the bravery and determination of the stormers to get up the breach in the face of all that the enemy could use to confront them.

The essence of the main body's task again was to provide weight of numbers but specifically it was to clear the walls and other key defences, secure the remaining resources of a fortress and to round up prisoners of war. The main effort was, however, scaling the breach and taking the adjacent walls.

Preparations

During 19 January the Light Division was summoned from their camps around El Bodón and marched the 6 miles to their ford of the Águeda. According to Cooke of the 43rd Light Infantry:

> During the greater part of the day we remained cooking behind the convent of Norbortins [La Carida] ... 3 miles S.E. of the town. Soon after three o'clock we moved towards the ground occupied by the foot guards [actually part of the 3rd Division], who were halted one mile and a half from the suburbs of Ciudad Rodrigo. These troops came forward to wish us success, and our band struck up *The Fall of Paris*. The third division occupied the trenches, and the garrison must have observed the march of the Light Division from the ramparts – extra troops! The governor should have pondered on it! If he had kept a sharp look-out, he must have been expecting the assault.

Lieutenant Grattan of the 88th (Connaught Rangers) commented that 'On our march we perceived our old friends and companions, the Light Division, debouching from their cantonments, and the joy expressed by our men when they saw them is not to be described; we were long acquainted, and like horses accustomed to the same harness, we pulled well together.'

While awaiting orders for the assault during the afternoon, Grattan also recalled the 43rd Light Infantry passing the 88th's bivouac to the north of the Greater Teson:

> They had no knapsacks – their firelocks were slung over their shoulders – their shirt collars were open, and there was an indescribable something about them that at one and the same moment impressed the on-lookers with admiration and awe. In passing us, each officer and soldier stepped out of the ranks for an instant, as he recognised a friend, to press his hand – many for the last time; yet, notwithstanding this animating scene, there was no shouting or huzzaing, no boisterous bravading, no unbecoming language; in short, everyone seemed to be impressed with the seriousness of the affair entrusted to his charge.

General Mackinnon, having been given his orders, asked Major Thompson to provide a subaltern of the 88th to command the forlorn hope, who, if he survived, would receive promotion to captain and command of a company. An account of the process was written by Captain John Davern who

> was present when the Commanding Officer (Major Thomson), assembled the officers of the 88th Regt. together, and asked if any of them would volunteer the forlorn hope, your poor brother immediately came forward in the most gallant manner, dropping his sword, and saying he was ready for that service and a number of private soldiers of the regiment came forward as volunteers with him.
>
> The officer who had volunteered and was selected was Lieutenant Mackie.

A subaltern officer of the 88th Connaught Rangers.

During the afternoon General Picton addressed every unit from horseback. To the 88th he said: 'It is not my intention to expend any powder this evening. We'll do this with cold iron!' According to Lieutenant Grattan:

> The soldiers listened to the communication with silent earnestness, and immediately began to disencumber themselves of their knapsacks, which were placed in order by companies and a guard set over them. Each man then began to arrange himself for the combat in such manner as his fancy or the moment would admit of, some by lowering their cartridge-boxes, others by turning theirs to the front in order that they might more conveniently make use of them; others unclasping their stocks or opening their shirt-collars; others oiling their bayonets; and more taking leave of their wives and children.

Major Thompson wished his men luck and 'his eye filled, his lip quivered, and there was a faltering in his voice'. However, he instantly regained his composure, drew himself up and gave the word, 'Gentlemen, fall in', and at this moment it is recorded that 'Generals Picton and Mackinnon, accompanied by their respective staffs, made their appearance amongst us.'

As the hour approached, the generals dismounted and led the forlorn hope into the trenches. They were followed by the 300-strong storming party commanded by Major Manners of the 74th Highland Regiment (later the Argyles) and the

A contemporary print of a company and their camp followers on the march.

SOLDIERS on a MARCH.

remainder of the 45th, 88th and the 74th, with Power's Portuguese brigade bringing up the rear.

Meanwhile, the Light Division had assembled behind the convent of San Francisco where Lieutenant Simmons of the 95th Rifles was rueing some over-zealous volunteering:

> ... when Lieutenant Smith, Brigade-Major, came to a fire near which I was standing and said, 'One of you must come and take charge of some ladders if required,' at the impulse of the moment I took with me the men required, and followed him to the Engineers' camp, where the ladders were handed to me. I marched with them to General Craufurd, who was with the advance. He attacked me in a most ungracious manner. 'Why did you bring these short ladders?' 'Because I was ordered by the Engineer to do so, General.' 'Go back, sir, and get others; I am astonished at such stupidity.' Of course, I went back, but was sadly crestfallen. This is what I deserved for over-zeal. I returned with the ladders. A Portuguese captain and his company were waiting for something to do, so I said, 'Here, my brave fellows, take these ladders', and handed them over with every necessary instruction for the good of the service. I then instantly returned to the company I belonged to, which was posted at the head of the column ready to proceed.

Earlier General Craufurd also had the task of selecting officers to lead the forlorn hope and storming party. The commanding officer of the 40th Foot had already volunteered to provide them, arguing that he and his men knew the approaches to the lesser breach better than anyone else thanks to their time in the San Francisco suburbs since the evening of 14 January. This offer was, of course, rejected by Craufurd in favour of his own officers and men, among whom there was as usual no shortage of volunteers.

Among the hopefuls was Lieutenant Harry Smith of the 1st 95th Rifles. He wrote:

> I was senior subaltern of the 95th, and I went to General Craufurd and volunteered the forlorn hope that was [later] given to Gurwood.
>
> Craufurd said: 'Why, you cannot go; you, a Major of Brigade, a senior Lieutenant, you are sure to get a company. No, I must give it to a younger officer.'

Craufurd did, however, grant a similar request from Major George Napier[5] of the 52nd Light Infantry who wanted to lead the storming party. As the hour was wearing on, Napier called for volunteers from the 43rd, 52nd and 95th: 'Soldiers, I have the honour to be appointed to the command of the storming party which is to lead the Light Division to the assault of the small breach. I want 100 volunteers from each regiment; those who will go with me step forward.'

Lieutenant Harry Smith in later life.

So many stepped forward that there was no possibility in the time available of selecting the Light Division's stormers. Major Napier was summoned to speak to Wellington as daylight failed. He was told 'Now you do understand the way you are to lead, so as to arrive at the breach without noise or confusion?' Consequently, Napier decided not to have his men load their muskets and rifles in case a negligent discharge alerted the enemy. A staff officer commented 'Why, your men are not loaded; why do you not make them load?' Napier later wrote:

> I replied, 'Because if we do not do the business with the bayonet without firing we shall not do it at all, so I shall not load.'
>
> I heard Lord Wellington, who was close by, say 'Let him alone; let him go his own way.'

As darkness fell and the hour for the storm approached, a British officer[6] recalled

> It was by this time half-past six o'clock, the evening was piercingly cold, and the frost was crisp on the grass; there was a keenness in the air that braced

our nerves at least as high as concert pitch. We stood quietly to our arms, and told our companies off by files, sections, and sub-divisions; the sergeants called over the rolls – not a man was absent.

... the moon occasionally, as the clouds which overcast it passed away, shed a faint ray of light upon the battlements of the fortress, and presented to our view the glittering of the enemy's bayonets as their soldiers stood arrayed upon the ramparts and breach, awaiting our attack; yet, nevertheless, their batteries were silent, and might warrant the supposition to an un-observant spectator that the defence would be but feeble.

Colonel O'Toole's Escalade

No doubt the same pre-attack emotions were present in Lieutenant Colonel Bryan O'Toole and his men as they waited in cover south of the Águeda. He was commanding the 2nd Caçadores, a battalion detached from the 7th Division, for the storm of Ciudad Rodrigo. Along with his own battalion he had under command the Light Company of the 83rd Foot for what was an ambitious and dangerous mission. With scaling ladders, they were to dash across the Águeda bridge, which was dominated by guns mounted around the castle high above it, and take on a lower, outlying battery. With its two guns, this position could sweep with grapeshot the 2/5th (Northumberland) Regiment's approach to the

The view from the castle of the bridge across which Colonel O'Toole led the assault.

Colonel Bryan O'Toole.

glacis slope from the area of the Santa Cruz convent. If successful and the situation allowed, O'Toole's force was to attempt an escalade attack on the main city defences.

Heading along the road in cover of vegetation and the houses of the suburb on the southern bank of the Águeda, led by the 83rd's Light Company, O'Toole's men reached the end of the bridge, paused and at 1850 hours led the charge across it in the face of growing fire from the castle above them. Setting up their six 12ft scaling ladders they were up the rocky outcrop and wall, and scrambled into the battery. Here they overwhelmed the defenders and captured the two artillery pieces that could have turned the 5th of Foot's escalade onto the faussebraye into a disaster. All this was achieved in just a few minutes.

The city walls towered above them, far too high for their short scaling ladders, but the assault troops were not done and located a stout iron-studded wooden door, which they hewed down with pioneer axes and the Caçadores and the company of the 83rd were into the city. Such was the speed of their attack it is entirely conceivable that O'Toole's Portuguese and Irishmen were the first allied troops into Ciudad Rodrigo! One observer from the Light Division, however, recorded that they were still attempting to escalade when he arrived at the castle.

The rock face and wall up which O'Toole's men escaladed to capture the gun position.

The Greater Breach

At the same time as Colonel O'Toole was rushing across the Águeda bridge, Campbell's brigade started to move forward from cover to the right of the ruins of the Santa Cruz convent. Major Sturgeon of the staff corps led the 2/5th of Foot towards the Puerto de la Colada gate where nearby it was possible to gain entry through a substantial gated and palisaded gap to the outer ditch from where, using their dozen short scaling ladders, they would be able to climb up onto the faussebraye.

Major Sturgeon led the battalion stealthily forward unobserved by the French who concentrated on firing cannon and musket in the direction of the breach and trenches. Reaching the palisaded gate, with their twelve heavy pioneer axes they began cutting their way through. Despite the thud of the axes they remained undetected because of the noise of firing. On breaking through, however, a young officer gave a cry of 'huzzah', which was taken up by the soldiers and a shower of grenades from the walls above resulted, but using their 25ft ladders the 5th Foot were quickly up on the faussebraye where according to Wellington's orders they were 'to proceed along the faussebraye, in order to clear it of the enemy's posts on their left, towards the principal breach.'

Staff officers, in addition to their administrative function, were expected to help direct from the front during the period.

Within five minutes Major Ridge led his battalion towards the greater breach clearing a few small enemy groups as they went. Up on the faussebraye the 5th were strung out and very exposed to enemy fire from the walls, which partly explains why, with ninety-four casualties, they suffered the heaviest losses of all units involved in the storm of Ciudad Rodrigo.

The 77th Foot was supposed to have remained in reserve behind the Santa Cruz convent but in the event, they followed the 5th in a misunderstanding indicative of the speed with which the storm was mounted. Wellington's orders were a little contradictory, 'to support the first party, which will have entered the ditch.'

At the same time as the 5th started forward, the 74th Foot (Argyle Highlanders) who were to form in two columns to the left of the convent of Santa Cruz also advanced. Each column consisted of five companies headed by nine unarmed soldiers carrying three 12ft ladders, with which they were to descend from the glacis slope into the outer ditch.

Here the 74th were to clear any obstacles as they headed north to the greater breach. The Scots met with little resistance and arrived at the breach where 'the faussebraye and inner wall had been battered into one common mass of debris.'[7]

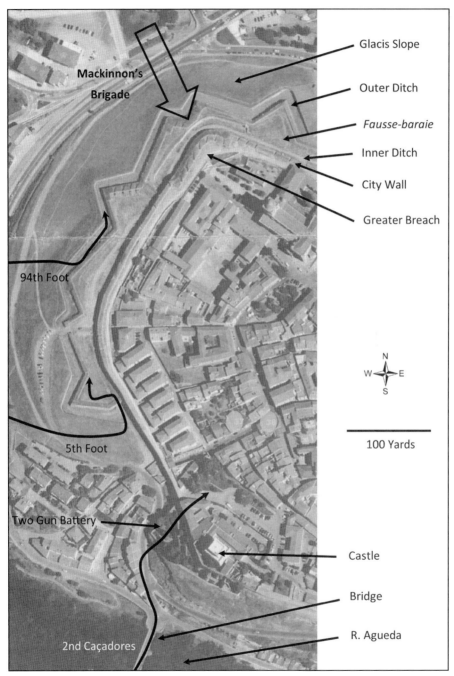

The assault on the eastern walls.

The entry point of the 5th Foot to the outer ditch and the faussebraye.

To their surprise they had reached the foot of the breach before the 3rd Division's forlorn hope and were very shortly joined by the 5th of Foot.

Mackinnon's brigade began the main assault on the greater breach when a signal rocket arced up into the night sky at 1900 hours. Major Jones describes their advance:

> At the appointed hour the attack commenced ... and immediately a heavy discharge of musketry was opened from the trenches, under cover of which 150 sappers, directed by Captain Macleod and Lieutenant Thomson, Royal Engineers, and Captain Thompson of the 74th Regiment, advanced from the second parallel to the crest of the glacis, each man carrying two bags filled with hay, which they threw down the counterscarp into the ditch, and having reduced its depth from 13½ to 8 feet, fixed the ladders upon the bags.

The 3rd Division's columns were immediately under a deluge of fire from the defenders, who General Barrié had concentrated around the breach. Their artillery was 'charged to the muzzle with case shot and opened a murderous fire on the columns.' Not only did Picton's men have to brave the enemy's fire, but they had to scramble out of the trenches, attempt to gain some cohesion, and head down the slope of the Lesser Teson into a rough boggy area at the foot of the glacis. Consequently, by the time that the sappers, Lieutenant Mackie's forlorn hope and Major Manner's stormers arrived at the breach, some men of the 5th and 94th were already on their way up the slope of rubble and soil.

Several companies of the 5th of Foot to the right of the breach and the three companies of 3/95th Rifles to the left were in position on the faussebraye providing the all-important covering or suppressive fire while the breach was scaled. The Rifles had started from behind the San Francisco convent and, as the 5th had, they needed ladders, in this case three of them to descend into the ditch and then climb up onto the faussebraye where they opened fire.

At about this stage there was the first of two major explosions; this one was almost certainly an expense magazine being ignited up on the walls rather than a mine as shells were showered by the explosion onto soldiers of both sides.

The greater breach is reported by Captain Cocks to have been some 30ft wide, forming a bank of crumbling earth at a 50-degree angle. Up it struggled

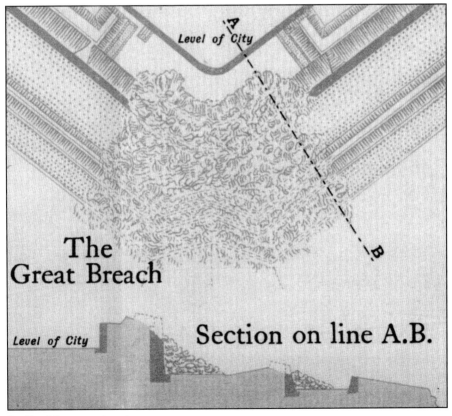

Profile of the greater breach.

The storming of the greater breach at Ciudad Rodrigo.

Campbell's brigade, the forlorn hope and the stormers, all mixed together. Grattan described the demeanour of the 3rd Division's soldiers:

> In place of that joyous animation . . . a look of severity, bordering on ferocity, had taken its place, there was, most unquestionably, a savage expression in the faces of the men that I had never before witnessed. Such is the difference between the storm of a breach and fighting a pitched battle.

Officers and men shouted 'huzzah' but the French 'were in no way daunted by the shout raised by our soldiers – they crowded the breach, and defended it with a bravery that would have made any but troops accustomed to conquer, waver.' Men fell and were trampled by the onward rush of the fighting division. Lieutenant Mackie and Major Manners were borne on at the head of the assault by a tide of soldiery up to the lip of the breach. Here a volley of musket fire greeted them from the ranks of the French infantry drawn up to face them. Bayonets flashed and thrusted but '. . . two guns of heavy calibre, separated from the breach by a ditch of considerable depth and width, enfiladed it, and as soon as the French infantry were forced from the summit, these guns opened their fire on our troops.'

The stormers, having secured the top of the breach, found themselves hemmed in by a 16ft drop into the city in front of them, with chevaux de frise below, while to their flanks the broad city wall had been retrenched with deep wide ditches and

An example of one of the many types of chevaux de frise. They are made up of anything sharp: swords, bayonets and sharpened stakes, in this case deployed to deter the stormers from jumping down to city level.

banks of soil that gave cover to the two cannon and numerous musketeers. Even though the greater breach had been carried, the storm of Ciudad Rodrigo hung in the balance!

Brigadier General Pack's Escalade

Meanwhile, to the east and south-east of the city Pack was in action. Wellington's orders to the independent Portuguese brigade were 'Brigadier-General Pack, with his brigade, will make a false attack upon the outwork of the gate of St. Jago [St Pelyo], and upon the works towards La Caridad.' This was to be a demonstration against the complicated set of outworks in order to attract French force to this quarter and it was not expected to result in an escalade of the city wall.

Following the palisade from behind the Santo Domingo convent, under cover of darkness five battalions from the 1st and 16th Portuguese regiments and the 4th Caçadores were over the glacis slope, down into the ditches and quickly up the scaling ladders into the defences around the gate. Jones records in the *Journal of Sieges* that

the Portuguese, under Brigadier-General Pack, spiritedly escaladed the small bastion in front of the gate of St. Jago, defended by a small guard,

General Denis Pack.

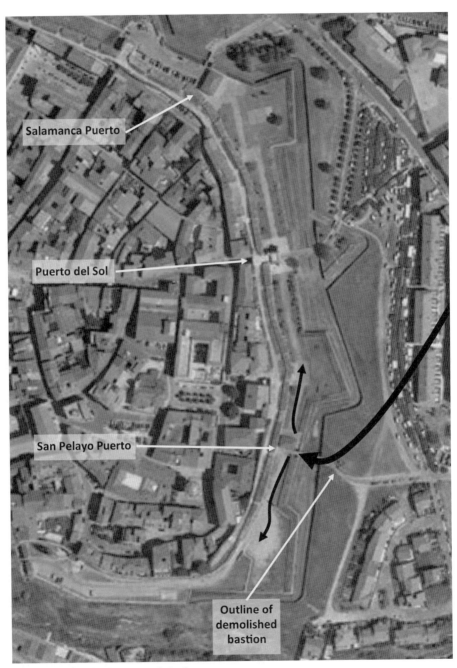

The attack of Pack's Portuguese brigade.

The area of the Portuguese attack.

which they overpowered and bayoneted; but no attempt was made to escalade the main rampart, on account of its great height, and the double obstacle created by the faussebraye.

The attack around the south of Ciudad Rodrigo sounds easy but the Portuguese suffered a total of 114 casualties during the storm, which out of a total bill of 560 is a significant proportion. The majority were suffered by Pack's brigade.

The Lesser Breach

With three companies of the 3/95th Rifles having been detached to the 3rd Division, the plan that General Craufurd developed for the Light Division was as follows:

(1) Four companies of the 1st Battalion 95th Rifles under Major Cameron to line the crest of the glacis and fire on the rampart [astride the breach].

(2) One hundred and sixty men of the 3rd Caçadores carrying hay and straw bags, twelve 12-foot ladders and some axes.

(3) The 'forlorn hope' consisting of an officer and twenty-five volunteers under Lieutenant Gurwood of the 52nd.

(4) The storming party; three officers and 100 volunteers from the 43rd, 52nd and Rifles under Major George Napier of the 52nd.

(5) The main body of the Division under Craufurd consisting of the remainder of Vandeleur's Brigade, namely the two Battalions of the 52nd and some companies of the Rifles.

(6) Barnard's Brigade, consisting of the 43rd, some companies [two of the 2nd Battalion] of the Rifles and the 1st Caçadores to remain in reserve and to close on Vandeleur's Brigade when it reached the breach.

(7) Barnard is to detail four companies of the [1/95th] Rifles to man the 2nd parallel at 180 yards from the walls and keep up a sharp fire on the defenders.[8]

Once the breach was carried, the 43rd was to clear the walls to the left and the 52nd to the right. The Salamanca Gate was to be captured and opened as a matter of priority.

General Craufurd addressed his men: 'Soldiers! The eyes of your country are upon you. Be steady, be cool, be firm in the assault. The town must be yours tonight. Once masters of the wall, let your first duty be to clear the ramparts, and in doing this keep together.'

Surgeon Charles Boutflower of the 40th Foot had a grandstand seat on the roof of the convent for the assault of the Light Division and beyond that of the 3rd. He wrote: 'The first conflict was terrible. No description however, can do justice to the grandeur of the scenery; the rapid fire of the musketry, the infinite number of hand grenades, and the explosion of two mines, presented a Coup d'Oeil beautifully awful.'

The Light Division was also to attack when the rocket signal was fired. Bugler Green of the 1/95th recalled:

My regiment was formed behind a convent about 300 paces from the right breach; we had made a wide ditch from this convent in the night by our working party that led straight to the breach, and the enemy had a 6-pounder at the top of it. The moon had risen, the word was given to form sections and double-quick time; off we started.

Craufurd led the division forward, with Cameron's four companies of riflemen who were to make their way with ladders onto the faussebraye either side of the lesser breach in the lead. The route taken was below the northern end of the Lesser Teson and to the right of the gardens of San Francisco, following the remains of the palisade wall where some cover had been dug. They too had to cross the stream and boggy area at the foot of the glacis slope, but do not seem to have been impeded as much as the 3rd Division. As the forlorn hope reached the glacis slope, Rifleman Costello recalled Craufurd shouting 'Now lads, for the breach.' Hitherto the enemy's fire had been concentrated on Picton's men to their right, but all that was about to change. Lieutenant Simmons later wrote of the approach to the breach:

> A tremendous fire was opened upon us, and as our column was entering the ditch an expense magazine [one of the 'mines' referred to above] on the ramparts near the large breach blew up and ignited a number of live shells, which also exploded and paid no sort of difference to friend or foe. The night was brilliantly illuminated for some moments, and everything was made visible. Then as suddenly came utter darkness, except for the flashes from cannon and muskets, which threw a momentary glare around.

With the loss of their night vision the Light Division's stormers were disorientated and not only that, the hay bags that should have been brought forward by the Caçadores had not arrived. Consequently, the men of the 43rd, 52nd and 95th mostly without hay bags had to jump the 12ft down into the darkness of the outer ditch. Once down in the ditch, according to Cooke of the 43rd:

> There was a sort of check, but no longer than might be expected, as they had to scramble in and out of the faussebraye, and then to jump into the dry ditch; but having gone too far to the left, the advance got on the wrong side of the tower, which was not breached, and the soldiers, for a few seconds, were knocking with the butt-ends of their fire locks against the wall, crying out 'Where's the breach?' For although the enemy were firing – rapidly from

The assault on Ciudad Rodrigo and the explosion of one of the 'mines'.

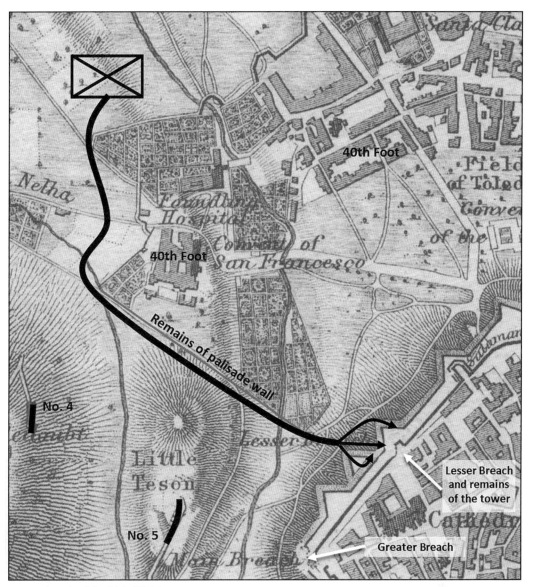

Assault of the Light Division.

the top of the wall, still the troops, on first descending to the bottom of the ditch, were in total darkness. This state of suspense lasted, however, a very short time, for two soldiers, stumbling on the loose rubbish, called out 'Here's the breach.'

The confusion in the darkness had not only seen the forlorn hope gone too far to the right, but Lieutenants Harry Smith and John Kincaid, among others, at the head of the stormers had scrambled up what they thought was the breach only to find that it was the battered wall of a ravelin. While some were called back and redirected by Colonel Colborne and the Engineer officers, Lieutenant Simmons took a more direct approach. He explains:

> In my hurry, after descending into the ditch, I mistook the traverse for the top of the breach, and as the ladders were laid against it, I ascended as well as many others, and soon found our mistake. We crossed it, and slid down directly opposite the breach, which was soon carried.

The lesser breach was reported by Captain Cocks to have been steeper than the greater and only 10 to 15ft wide at the top, but being made up of the collapsed tower's stone blocks it offered better footing for the assault. In addition, it had been created with such rapidity during the final thirty-six hours of the bombardment that the French garrison had not had the opportunity to retrench the top of the breach. All they had managed in the hour of darkness since the siege guns ceased fire was to position an artillery piece that virtually blocked the top of the breach. Major George Napier probably fell victim to that gun:

> When about two-thirds up, I received a grapeshot which smashed my elbow and great part of my arm; and on falling, the men, who thought I was killed, checked for a few moments, and forgetting they were not loaded commenced snapping their muskets. I immediately called out 'Recollect you are not loaded; push on with the bayonet.' Upon this the whole gave a loud 'huzzah' and driving all before them, carried the breach.

The 'maze of walls and trenches' below from the top of the lesser breach.

Rifleman Costello as an officer in later life.

Rifleman Costello, who was mixed in with the stormers at the top of the breach, also recalled the incident:

> I had got up among the first, and was struggling with a crowd of our fellows to push over the splintered and broken wall that formed the breach, when Major Napier, who was by my side encouraging on the men, received a shot, and, staggering back, would in all probability have fallen into the trench, had I not caught him. To my brief inquiry if he were badly hurt, he squeezed my hand, whilst his other arm hung shattered by his side, saying, 'Never mind me – push on, my lads, the town is ours!' And so indeed it was, our men entering it pell-mell.

Major Napier was severely wounded, losing his right arm. Meanwhile, Rifleman Green had also survived the gun's first blast of canister and wrote:

> Some of us got up to the gun, it was loaded again, and the French gunner was in the act of applying the match, when one of our men knocked him down

with the butt of his rifle. If we had been one moment later many of us would have been sent into eternity, as we were close up to the muzzle.

Lieutenant Cooke recalled that the gun was angled to fire down the breach and partly blocked the way onto the walls: 'however, there was a clear yard from the muzzle of the gun to the wall, a sufficient space for one or two soldiers to enter at a time, besides those who could pass underneath the muzzle of the gun and over the wheels of the carriage.'

Even though they had not been in the forlorn hope, Captain Uniacke and Lieutenant Johnson were first up through the breach and onto the walls, Uniacke almost certainly in command of one of Major Cameron's four companies which had been giving covering fire from the faussebraye. Duty done there, they had headed for the breach.

Although the Light Division carried their breach with élan, after their first rush up to the city walls, on the glacis slope below light balls were burning and the approaches to the breach were swept with enemy fire.

General Craufurd had led the division's main body up onto the glacis slope, where he stood, bellowing orders and encouraging his men. He was all too clearly a commander and as such was targeted by French marksmen on the walls less than 50 yards away. Willoughby Verner records in the Rifle Brigade's history that

General Craufurd urging his men on up the breach.

Craufurd 'was struck by a musket ball which passed through his arm, broke through his ribs, passed through a part of his lung and lodged in his spine.' The impact of the lead ball was so great that it spun the general over and back down the glacis slope. His ADC Captain Shaw-Kennedy dragged his general 'and half carried him to a spot where an inequality of ground protected him from direct fire from the place.'

Also with the main body, Brigadier Vandeleur was hit and seriously wounded while climbing the steep rubble-strewn breach, as was Lieutenant Colonel Colborne who was hit in the shoulder. Both were seriously wounded and command of the Light Division devolved on Colonel Barnard.

The Final Phase

Both breaches had been carried and the Portuguese were in the town in small numbers to the south, but the main assault by the 3rd Division had been checked by the French retrenchments behind the greater breach.

Picton's soldiers had cleared the French infantry from the top of the breach but had immediately been raked by the two 24-pounders double-loaded with

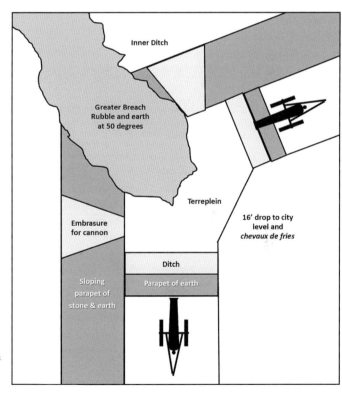

Diagram of the French retrenchments at the greater breach.

grapeshot fired into the flanks of the throng now reaching the top of the breach. Few of the men who led the way up the breach and reached the top survived. This was the critical moment when a storm could fail and it is easy to appreciate how even heavily outnumbered defenders of a fortress could prevail.

There was a short pause before impetus was regained by the stormers, but in that time French gunners, working feverishly, had reloaded and a second discharge had a similar devastating impact but men continued to arrive at the top of the breach. Lieutenant William Grattan of the 88th provides us with a glimpse of the nature of the fighting to break out of the breach to the left:

> The French cannoniers, five in number, stood to, and served their gun with as much sangfroid as if on a parade … but this was of no avail. Men going to storm a breach generally make up their minds that there is no great probability of their ever returning from it to tell their adventures to their friends; and whether they die at the bottom or top of it, or at the muzzle, or upon the breech of a cannon, is to them pretty nearly the same!

With more men coming up into the breach and no way forward, the stormers turned to left and right, down the deep ditches and over the earth and rubble parapet that the French had hastily built to protect the two cannon and bar the way onto the walls. The French fired again but more troops were pressing on up the breach. The first of the next wave to reach the top after the last discharge were three men of the 88th: Sergeant Brazil and two of his soldiers, Privates Swan and Kelly:

> … the three men passed the trench in a moment, and engaged the French cannoniers hand to hand; a terrific but short combat was the consequence. Swan was the first, and was met by the two gunners on the right of the gun, but, no way daunted, he engaged them, and plunged his bayonet into the breast of one; he was about to repeat the blow upon the other, but before he could disentangle the weapon from his bleeding adversary, the second Frenchman closed upon him, and by a *coup de sabre* severed his left arm from his body … he fell from the shock, and was on the eve of being massacred, when Kelly, after having scrambled under the gun, rushed onward to succour his comrade. He bayoneted two Frenchmen on the spot, and at this instant Brazil came up; three of the five gunners lay lifeless, while Swan, resting against an ammunition chest, was bleeding to death. It was now equal numbers, two against two, but Brazil in his over-anxiety to engage was near losing his life at the onset; in making a lunge at the man next to him, his foot slipped upon the bloody platform, and he fell forward against his antagonist, but as both rolled under the gun, Brazil felt the socket of his bayonet strike hard against the buttons of the Frenchman's coat. The remaining gunner, in attempting to escape under the carriage from Kelly, was killed by some

The top of the now-repaired breach.

soldiers of the 5th, who just now reached the top of the breach, and seeing the serious dispute at the gun, pressed forward to the assistance of the three men of the Connaught Rangers.

Grattan recalled that 'At the same instant a frightful explosion near the gun to the left of the breach, which shook the bastion to its foundation, completed the disorder':

> Mackinnon, at the head of his brigade, was blown into the air. His aide-de-camp, Lieutenant Beresford of the 88th, shared the same fate, and every man on the breach at the moment of the explosion perished ...
>
> Others were so stunned by the shock, or wounded by the stones which were hurled forth by the explosion, that they were insensible to their situation; of this number I was one, for being close to the magazine when it blew up, I was quite overpowered, and I owed my life to the Sergeant-Major of my regiment, Thorp, who saved me from being trampled to death by our soldiers in their advance, ere I could recover strength sufficient to move forward or protect myself.

This second large explosion was not as Grattan believed a magazine exploding, but a mine that was sprung by the French. It wasn't, however, just the 3rd Division that suffered casualties.

The Light Division, having forced their way through the breach and onto the walls with scant opposition from the buildings of the town, duly turned left and right to clear the way. The lesser breach was only about 150 yards from the greater breach and it took no time for them to reach the area where Sergeant Brazil was fighting when the mine was sprung. Bugler Green wrote:

> Although dark, among the first I saw on mounting the ramparts was my own Captain, Uniacke, rushing along with a few men to the right of the breach. Though not on the forlorn hope, this gallant soldier was determined to be first in the town. This was the last time he was doomed to be at our head. A few moments afterwards the French sprung a mine, by which the whole party were killed or maimed.

Captain Uniacke was mortally wounded. Lieutenant Cooke provides more grim detail:

> I ran towards the large breach, and met an officer slowly walking between two soldiers of the Rifle Corps. I asked who it was, when he replied, 'Uniacke' and walked on. One of his eyes was blown out, and the flesh was torn off his arms and legs. He had taken chocolate with our mess an hour and a half before! He died in excruciating agony!

Lieutenant Harry Smith, as major of brigade, speaking with the authority of his commander, led troops down towards the greater breach following the Riflemen. He later wrote: 'I seized a company of the 43rd and rushed on the flank, and opened fire which destroyed every man behind the works. My conduct caused great annoyance to Captain Duffy, with whom I had some very high words.'

Harry Smith was badly singed by the explosion of the mine; with his uniform rendered to rags he headed on towards the breach. Here Major Wylde, General Mackinnon's major of brigade, had found some planks to bridge the ditch to the right of the breach. Over these the 45th Foot stormed, still under heavy fire from the city below. They went across the parapet of earth and onto the walls beyond, overwhelming the defenders in similar hand-to-hand combat as Sergeant Brazil. Some of the British infantry fired into the streets and neighbouring houses; others scrambled down into the city to take on the wavering French.

Since Napier published his history in 1828 there has been much futile discussion over the extent to which the Light Division helped the 3rd Division overcome opposition at the top of the greater breach, a debate that was noticeably absent between the two divisions at the time.

In carrying the lesser breach, the leading elements of the Light Division were undoubtedly the first British troops into the city but their breach was more easily taken. It must be borne in mind that, unlike the 3rd Division, they had only been subjected to heavy fire once they were in the act of jumping down into the outer ditch. Their breach was also less well-defended but on the other hand the speed

The grave of Lieutenant Beresford who survived the blast but died of his wounds at Almeida.

Major William Napier, officer of the 43rd and Peninsular Wars historian.

and élan with which, despite some disorientation in the ditches, the breach was carried was remarkable and it is, however, only fair to conclude that those light infantrymen and rifles coming up behind the left retrenchment must have helped significantly.

Notes

1. Referred to in Wellington's orders as St. Jago.
2. For the full transcript of Wellington's orders for the storm of Ciudad Rodrigo see Appendix II.
3. Colonel Campbell of the 94th was commanding the brigade in the absence of General Colville.
4. The French name for the forlorn hope is more descriptive: *les enfants perdus* or 'the lost children'.
5. Not to be confused with his brother William Napier of the 43rd (Monmouthshire) Light Infantry.
6. Lieutenant Grattan.
7. Sir Charles Oman, *A History of the Peninsular Wars*, Vol. 5.
8. William Willoughby Verner, *History and Campaigns of the Rifle Brigade, 1800–1813*, Vol. 2.

Chapter Fourteen

Aftermath

With the victorious allies swarming up the breaches and into the city, the French garrison fell back to the Plaza Mayor and laid down their arms. Some 200 British soldiers, including William Lang of the 74th at their head, were first on the scene and 60 French officers and 1,300 men were duly taken prisoner. The seeds of the subsequent disorder were, however, already apparent. Costello wrote that the stormers '... next took possession of the market place, where they commenced huzzahing and fringing the air. In the midst of this the ceremony of planting the colours was gone through.'

Meanwhile, General Barrié and his staff had barricaded themselves in the castle. This was not for some heroic last-ditch defence, but for safety as they had no illusions as to their fate if captured by British or Portuguese soldiers in the first flush of victory before their blood cooled. The story of the surrender has been another source of argument between the 3rd and Light divisions and their forlorn hope commanders, who both survived. Gurwood was knocked over and stunned

The Plaza Mayor and the City Hall.

The castle of Ciudad Rodrigo and the entrance where these events were played out.

while climbing his breach, and the 5th and 94th Regiments of Foot were of course in the greater breach ahead of Mackie, hence, unusually, both officers living to argue over the tale!

Both Gurwood of the 52nd Light Infantry and Mackie of the 88th Connaught Rangers independently arrived at the castle within minutes of each other and both believed that they took the formal French surrender, signified by the handing over of a French officer's sword. In brief from reconciling witness testimony, the consensus is that Mackie probably arrived first and was handed a sword of surrender. Minutes later Lieutenant Gurwood (he had been wounded) formally received General Barrié's surrender and sword.[1] This he took to present to Wellington, who directed Lord Fitzroy Somerset to buckle it on the young officer. Thus it was Lieutenant Gurwood, described by Harry Smith as 'a sharp fellow', who had the honour of being mentioned in the peer's dispatches as taking the surrender.

Meanwhile, the wounded were lying largely unattended. Among those on the slope up to the lesser breach was the commander of the storming party, Major George Napier. He wrote:

> During all this time the troops of the Light Division kept pouring into the place through the breach, and I kept cheering them on as well as I could, but

William, Prince of Orange, who
served as an aide-de-camp to
Wellington during the siege.

I got terribly bruised and trampled upon in the confusion and darkness.
However, very soon 'Victory! England forever!' was shouted by thousands,
and then I knew all was right, and I waited patiently in the breach till all had
passed, when I heard my name called several times, and upon answering ...
with the help of a sergeant and some men I got down and proceeded to the
old ruined convent, where I found numbers wounded and the surgeon very
busy with his knife.

His rescuers were Wellington's ADCs, the Prince of Orange, Lord Fitzroy
Somerset and Lieutenant the Earl of March of the 13th Light Dragoons who had
volunteered to join the 52nd in the storm. Napier was carried in a specially
sprangled maroon officers' sash that when spread out doubled as a stretcher. He
continued:

It soon came to my turn to have my arm amputated, and I then reminded my
friend Walker, who was there, of his promise to me a few hours before, and
begged he would be so good as to perform the operation; but he told me he
could not, as there was a staff surgeon present, whose rank being higher, it
was necessary he should do it, so Staff Surgeon Guthrie cut it off. However,

for want of light, and from the number of amputations he had already performed, and other circumstances, his instruments were blunted, so it was a
long time before the thing was finished, at least twenty minutes, and the pain
was great. I then thanked him for his kindness, having sworn at him like a
trooper while he was at it, to his great amusement, and I proceeded to find
some place to lie down and rest, and after wandering and stumbling about
the suburbs for upwards of an hour, I saw a light in a house, and on entering
I found it full of soldiers, and a good fire blazing in the kitchen.

The Sack of Ciudad Rodrigo

Back in the centre of the city discipline was breaking down, led by the 'incor-
rigible rogues, scoundrels and criminals that every regiment in the army had to
the tune of a good dozen or more.' Some prisoners were shot; Kincaid recalled
that some purported to be Italian

> and endeavoured to excite our pity by virtue of their being 'Pauvres
> Italianos'; but our men had, somehow, imbibed a horrible antipathy to the
> Italians, and every appeal they made in that name was invariably answered
> with, 'You're Italians, are you? Then, d—n you, here's a shot for you'; and
> the action instantly followed the word.

A soldier of the 95th Rifles.

Men slipped away from the ranks and even the 43rd under Colonel Macleod who had come in at the rear of the Light Division and taken up positions on the wall saw his battalion dissolve as men, as in all other battalions in the city, headed into the houses for drink, rape and plunder. Grattan records that 'the troops not selected for [sentry] duty commenced a very diligent search for those articles which they most fancied, and which they considered themselves entitled to by "right of conquest".' Rifleman Costello was among those looking for alcohol:

> The first place I found myself drawn to by some comrades was a large white house that had been used as a commissary's store by the French; here a crowd had assembled to break it open, when they were warned off by a sentinel, a German, who was posted to guard the premises. Not heeding his threat, the throng rushed at the door. The poor sentry, true to his trust, attempted to oppose their entrance, and the following minute was run through the body by a bayonet.
>
> The house contained several puncheons of spirits, which the men present immediately tapped, by striking in the heads. All now soon became madly drunk; and several wretches, especially those mounting the steps that had been placed against the butts, to enable them to obtain the rum, fell into the liquor head-foremost and perished, unnoticed by the crowd. Several fights took place, in which the drunkenness of the parties alone prevented mischief; and to crown the whole, a light falling into one of the barrels of spirit, the place was set on fire, and many poor wretches, who from the quantity of liquor they had swallowed, were incapable of moving, were consumed in the flames.

A sergeant of the 43rd Light Infantry recorded that there were three or four fires including around the great magazine which if it had ignited the powder '... the town, and all in it, would have been blown to atoms, but for the energetic courage of some officers and a few soldiers, who still preserved their senses.'

Meanwhile, according to Lieutenant Grattan of the Connaught Rangers:

> There were, nevertheless, several minor combats in the streets, and in many instances the inhabitants fired from the windows, but whether their efforts were directed against us or the French is a point that I do not feel myself competent to decide; be this as it may, many lives were lost on both sides by this circumstance, for the Spaniards, firing without much attention to regularity, killed or wounded indiscriminately all who came within their range.

Grattan continued to explain how the 88th broke into Spanish houses with locks

> remarkable for their strength, and resembled those of a prison more than anything else; their locks are of huge dimensions, and it is a most difficult task to force them. The mode adopted by the men of my regiment (the 88th)

The sack of Ciudad Rodrigo.

in this dilemma was as effective as it was novel; the muzzles of a couple of muskets were applied to each side of the keyhole, while a third soldier, fulfilling the functions of an officer, deliberately gave the word, 'make ready' – 'present' – 'fire!' and in an instant the ponderous lock gave way before the combined operations of the three individuals, and doors that rarely opened to the knock of a stranger in Rodrigo now flew off their hinges to receive the Rangers of Connaught.

The fires were often started by increasingly drunk soldiers dropping candles or lanterns as they searched buildings for valuables. The writer continues:

Scenes of the greatest outrage now took place, and it was pitiable to see groups of the inhabitants half naked in the streets – the females clinging to the officers for protection – while their respective houses were undergoing the strictest scrutiny. Some of the soldiers turned to the wine and spirit houses, where, having drunk sufficiently, they again sallied out in quest of more plunder; others got so intoxicated that they lay in a helpless state in different parts of the town, and lost what they had previously gained, either by the hands of any passing Spaniard, who could venture unobserved to stoop down, or by those of their own companions, who in their wandering surveys happened to recognise a comrade lying with half a dozen silk gowns, or some such thing, wrapped about him.

Officers, including Colonel Barnard and Major Cameron, went around the town trying to curb the worst excesses of wanton destruction and round up their men, often having to defend themselves against them and beat soldiers into sensibility

One of the many churches and religious buildings in Ciudad Rodrigo, looted but intact.

with bits of broken musket. Nonetheless, Spanish houses were looted with soldiers taking not just portable wealth but goods and chattels, whatever their worth or practical campaign utility.

It is recorded that by 0100 hours, some four hours after the storm, Barnard had rounded up the Riflemen, formed them by companies on the ramparts and kindled fires.

Disgraceful though the sack of Ciudad Rodrigo was, especially as the worst excesses were vented on the civilian population of an allied country, even if they

Colonel Barnard who commanded a brigade at Ciudad Rodrigo.

had defended their houses against all comers, there are those, including Charles Boutflower of the 40th Foot, who excused the behaviour:

> The Governor had no right to stand the assault; he had not the means after the breaches were practicable of defending himself against our superior numbers. By the laws of war, we should have been justified in putting the whole Garrison to death; they were almost all however suffered to escape with their lives; this was at best but a milk and water humanity, and in point of policy should be severely condemned: we may live to lament the effects of it.

Old martial traditions of siege warfare aside, as has already been recorded, Napoleon had decreed to his army that no fortress was to surrender at first summons or without a fight. There is also evidence from an officer of the 5th Foot who was taken prisoner in the breach early on during the storm and taken to General Barrié who was surprised that the storm had taken place so soon and without a second summons. Perhaps he had intended to surrender?

The behaviour of the two assault divisions at Ciudad Rodrigo was but little in comparison with the three-day orgy of destruction, drunkenness, rape, murder and looting at the culmination of the siege of Badajoz in the succeeding months.

Even though the majority of two regiments of French were captured, their Eagles had either not accompanied them to Ciudad Rodrigo or had been spirited away before the surrender.

Deserters

Among the prisoners taken during the storm were deserters from the British regiments. Many were captured attempting to escape from the fortress, their mix of British and French uniform items exercising the curiosity of their captors. Rifleman Green records what happened to them:

> A little further in the street we met a sergeant of ours with one of our men who had deserted to the enemy. In this place the enemy had all given themselves up as prisoners of war, and among them about forty who had deserted from the British. The French prisoners were escorted to Lisbon and shipped for England; but these forty[2] were sent to the divisions and tried by court martial, for reasons before stated, and three weeks after were shot; seven of them belonged to the Light Division. At their execution *The Dead March in Saul* was played by the band, the caps were drawn over their faces, and the firing party, at the signal, finished the work, with the lives of these traitors to their country and their King, as a warning to all others who might be disposed to join an enemy after having sworn allegiance to their rightful sovereign.

With the result of courts martial being promulgated, Private John Spence Cooper of the 7th Royal Fusiliers of the 4th Division explains the grim process:

> When all was ready the prisoners were drawn to the graveside on a car. One of them was elderly, the other a boy of perhaps nineteen. They kneeled on the new mould facing the guard, and were blindfolded. All were silent. An officer approaches the prisoners and reads the sentence, and then withdraws. A pause. The provost martial [sic] looks toward the General for the signal. 'Tis given. Twelve men fire. Both culprits fall forward. The boy is dead; the elder rolls in agony. More shots are fired through his head and breast, and the deserters are no more. Being laid side by side in the grave, we marched close past it in file; took a look at the bloody remains, and marched away to quarters.

Harry Smith was the duty major of brigade in the Light Division at Ituero:

> The provost Marshal had not told the firing off, so that a certain number of men should shoot one culprit, and so on, but at his signal the whole party fired a volley. Some prisoners were fortunate enough to be killed, others only wounded, some untouched. I galloped up. An unfortunate Rifleman called to me by name – he was awfully wounded, 'Oh Mr Smith, put me out of my misery', and I literally ordered the firing party, when reloaded, to run up and shoot the poor wretches. It was an awful scene.

Several Light Division men had in fact been reprieved and some served with distinction until the end of the war.

20 January 1812

By morning order had been restored and the 3rd and Light divisions started to leave the city, but Captain Jonathan Leach was one of many who walked around the scene of the fighting:

> Daylight of the 20th presented a horrid sight, and unfit to be contemplated in cold blood. Many objects, of both parties, lying near the spot where the magazine had exploded, were frightful to a degree. Bodies without limbs, and limbs without bodies, were scorched and scattered about in different directions; and the houses near the breaches were filled with such of the wounded as were able to crawl away from the ramparts, with a view to find shelter from the severe frost, which numbed their wounds.

Rifleman Costello was also around the greater breach and observed 'a number of Irish women hopelessly endeavouring to distinguish the burnt features of their husbands.' He went on to say:

> Though heartily sick of the morning's mournful perambulation, I yet felt anxious to see Captain Uniacke; his remains lay on the suburbs, in a house

next to that where those of our brave old General were stretched out. Several of the men of his company crowded about his person, hoping – for he was still living, and sensible; that he yet might return amongst us. But his arm had been torn from the socket, and he died some few days afterwards.

There was also a regrettable incident recalled by Lieutenant Simmons:

About nine o'clock in the morning we marched from that part of the rampart where we had been resting for so many hours, seated before good fires. We passed out of the town and then halted. The French prisoners followed, guarded. We had scarcely left the gate when a tremendous explosion took place, which blew up numbers of Frenchmen, and also some Englishmen. Directly under the place we had so recently left were deposited several barrels of gunpowder, which had taken fire from some cause or other. That face of the rampart was a pile of ruins in one instant. I really thought this was a kind act of the Almighty towards us.

Having made their way across the city the 1/95th Rifles left by the Puerto de la Colada gate. They were dressed in French uniforms, breeches and even fine silk dresses, with haversacks bulging and fine Spanish hams hanging from knapsacks. Being unrecognizable as riflemen, Wellington, no doubt looking down his long nose, was heard to incredulously ask a staff officer 'What Corps is that?' The Light Division, crossing by the Águeda bridge rather than fording the freezing river, marched directly across the plain back to their camp at El Bodón.

Captain Jones wrote in the *Journal of Sieges*:

At daylight the Royal military artificers and sappers commenced the destruction of the batteries, and the artillery began to withdraw the guns and send them across the Águeda. About 9 A.M. Lord Wellington came into the town, and having examined the state of the defences, ordered that immediately on the arrival of the troops to form the garrison, a party should be employed to clear away the rubbish from the breaches. Lieutenant-General Leith marched in with his division about mid-day, and in the afternoon the work commenced.

An educated guess at a representation of the 'Valiant Stormer' patch. The only reference to the award of such a badge is to the 52nd Light Infantry.

The impressive Palacio de los Avila in Plaza del Conde used as Wellington's forward headquarters and lodging in Ciudad Rodrigo.

By midday Leith's 5th Division had arrived from their distant cantonments at the city to start hurriedly working on returning it into a state of defence as it was feared that Marshal Marmont, who had been marching to the relief of the fortress, would now attempt to re-take Ciudad Rodrigo by *coup de main* using the British trenches and breaches himself. Putting a fortress back into a state of defence was almost as important as the siege itself. Ciudad Rodrigo had to be in Wellington's hands if he was to be able to pursue his 1812 strategy of invading Spain.

Having been relieved by the 5th Division, on returning to their camp the Connaught Rangers were surprised to find that they were not the only ones who had been in action the previous night:

On reaching the bivouac … I [Grattan] learned, with surprise, that our women had been engaged in a contest, if not as dangerous as ours, at least one of no trivial sort. The men left as a guard over the baggage, on hearing the first shot at the trenches, could not withstand the inclination they felt to join their companions; and although this act was creditable to the bravery of the individuals that composed the baggage-guard, it was nigh being fatal to those who survived, or, at least, too such as had anything to lose except their lives, for the wretches that infested our camp attempted to plunder it of all that it possessed, but the women, with a bravery that would not have disgraced those of ancient Rome, defended the post with such valour that those miscreants were obliged to desist, and our baggage was saved in consequence.

21 January 1812

Jones recorded that '1200 men were employed to level the trenches and clear the breaches ... the engineers' stores were moved from the park into the town, and every exertion was made to render the works immediately defensible.'

He continued that on the 22nd 'A thick fog prevailed all day the working party employed as yesterday. The last of the battering train crossed the Águeda.' Over subsequent days the work continued with the 5th Division supplying a working party of 1,200 men on the 23rd: 'The trenches being in the course of the morning completely filled in, the batteries demolished, and the spare fascines, gabions, and stores brought into the place, a party of workmen was employed to repair, enlarge and improve the redoubt [Fort Renaud] on the great Teson.'

24 January 1812

The front of both breaches was now built up with fascines to the height of the cordon line, and the carpenters commenced laying a row of fraises on that level, preparatory to the parapets being formed. As many men as could work with advantage were employed on the breaches and at every other point, but their exertions were much impeded by a fall of snow.

To say that medical facilities and treatment of the wounded were notoriously bad in the peninsula is to be guilty of understatement, but in the aftermath of the storm of Ciudad Rodrigo they plumbed new depths. Some 400 casualties had

An idealized camp follower.

been moved back into Portugal where 'hospitals' were established around Almeida and as far back as Guarda, but Wellington heard while at dinner that the wounded had been refused shelter and such that was available had been taken over by officers, administrators and hospital staff. That very evening he rode 15 miles to personally order the wounded out of the freezing temperatures into the houses, but when he returned the following day he found that they had been moved out again! Again, he ordered them in and had the officers responsible sent home in disgrace.

25 January 1812

Wellington decreed that the remains of Major General Craufurd, who had died of his wounds after four days, were to be buried in a grave dug in the ditch at the foot of the lesser breach. His coffin was borne out of the city by six sergeant majors from the division escorted by six field officers with several bands playing funeral marches and other 'mournful music'. The 5th Division lined the streets as the dignitaries followed the coffin. Surgeon Charles Boutflower wrote that

> While there I witnessed the funeral of Genl. Crawford [*sic*], who died of his wound the preceding day; it was a very solemn and impressive ceremony, almost every officer of rank in the Army being present; he was buried close to the Small Breach, on the spot where he received his wound; he is considered a real loss to the Service, tho' from the peculiarity of his disposition it is said he had attached but few people to him.

General Craufurd, though flawed and having made some significant and costly errors, was a great loss to Wellington's Peninsular Army. Major William Napier of the 43rd summed him up: 'At one time he was all fire and intelligence, a master spirit in war; at another, as if possessed by the demon, he would madly rush from blunder to blunder, raging in folly.'

Undoubtedly Craufurd had one of the best eyes for ground in any commander, which contributed to an extraordinary ability for outpost work. He had forged the Light Division by training it in a harsh and relentless manner, earning the nickname 'Black Bob' among his soldiers. In death, however, they appreciated and respected what he had done to make them unquestionably the elite division of the army. Out of respect for their fallen leader, as they headed back to El Bodón the representatives of every battalion of the division, as recalled by one unnamed observer, came across a flooded piece of old entrenchment but rather than go around they marched straight through it, just as their erstwhile master would have insisted.

Wellington and the Light Division would miss Craufurd. His successor was General von Alten, who many in the division considered 'very average'. Craufurd was particularly missed, however, when the army had crossed the plains of Spain

General Robert Craufurd.

to the foot of the Pyrenees and the incompetent General Skerret was in temporary command while the Light Division was providing outposts on the River Bidasoa.

During the 25th an advanced redoubt on the Greater Teson was picketed out and work commenced on the ditches. This British redoubt on the crest of the Greater Teson is often incorrectly marked as Fort Renaud on many maps of Ciudad Rodrigo. The original communication trench back to the reconstituted Fort Renaud, which is sited lower down on the feature, was used.

With Ciudad Rodrigo rendered into a state of basically defensible and word coming that Marmont had turned and was marching back to Salamanca, the 150 'sappers' of the 3rd Division, along with the 'volunteer engineers', all of whom had been trained and worked in the trenches throughout the siege, were released back to their regiments with much praise for their performance. Thoughts were also turning to subsequent operations further south and Wellington had returned to his old headquarters at Gallegos where he started planning with both Fletcher and Dickson present.

With regard to proper repairs to Rodrigo, first on the scene were some 'Forty-nine Spanish masons [who] commenced the foundation of a new revetment for the part of the scarp breached.' They also started to deepen the ditches around the now vulnerable north-western corner from 12ft to 13ft to 20ft deep.[3]

31 January 1812

With heavy rain setting in, which did much to impede work that was still mainly being undertaken by the 5th Division, much as it had the French two years earlier, according to Jones:

> Lord Wellington met General Castanos and rode with him along all the defences and the ground around the place, when it was decided, in conse-quence of the great numerical strength which the Spanish General proposed for the garrison, to construct an advanced redoubt on the northern face of the upper Teson, to see into the ravines beyond it, and keep an enemy distant from that side; also, to strengthen and make more considerable posts of the convents in the suburbs.

The additional and substantial 'Spanish Redoubt' is sited below the crest of the Greater Teson on its northern slope. It was connected to the smaller British Redoubt on the crest by the communication trench and thence to Fort Renaud. Its role was to delay the assembly of a besieging army to the north, under the cover of the Teson feature. This would buy extra time for a relief force to march and reach the city.

By the second week of February a 3,000-strong Spanish garrison started to arrive at Ciudad Rodrigo and relieve the 5th Division, and with the works sub-stantially complete the artificers and engineers were finally able to hand over the work of reconstruction on 5 March. Jones recorded for that day:

> On this report Lord Wellington came over to Ciudad Rodrigo, and caused the Spanish governor, General Vivas, and the Spanish chief engineer,

A comparison between the British musket and bayonet and the rifle and sword.

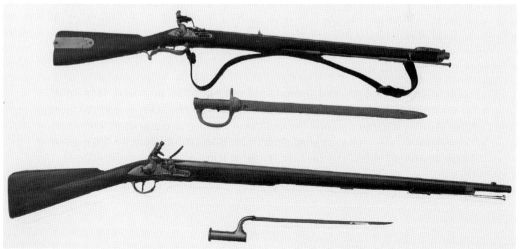

Spanish troops in best uniform.

General Calvet, to attend him around the place, and having pointed out to them the motives for the several changes and additions made to the defences, and having supplied the latter with the necessary funds (12,000 hard dollars) for their completion, directed Lieutenant-Colonel Fletcher to give up the charge of the fortifications to General Calvet.

Reflection

The siege of Ciudad Rodrigo is widely regarded as the most successful British Peninsular War siege, but there was plenty that Captain Burgoyne of the Royal Engineers found to criticize. Though much of it is detail, it does highlight the low level of skill in and organization of siege warfare at the time and how important was the deficiency in engineers, artificers and sappers. On gabion baskets, for instance, he wrote that

> a very small proportion of those made were brought up, those that came were mostly very bad ones, and the gabions of that unwieldy size as to cause the greatest impediment and delay when we got within 200 or 300 yards of the place, that is, under good musketry fire, from the difficulty of getting the men to convey them, particularly at night, when they were most wanted.

Burgoyne's comments on the delivery of equipment and other necessities were as follows:

> There was a great want of arrangement in the bringing up the stores; the fresh working parties were conducted to the engineer depot, whether by day or night, and loaded with platforms, splinter proofs, sandbags, &c., while another part conveyed their arms. These men with the stores would separate even the different parts of the same platform, and come in by ones and twos for an hour after, causing much delay and confusion in telling off the parties, and the stores constantly went wrong.

He went on to complain about the infantry working parties and the slowness of the building of the batteries, but in the case of the latter it was much more to do with the cold and the rocky nature of the Teson. Leaving aside minor difficulties, the Royal Engineers had conducted a highly successful siege and learned a great deal, but at a significant cost of two killed and five wounded out of just nineteen. Wellington's verdict was 'The ability with which these operations were carried on exceeds all praise.'

Of that other intrinsic arm in siege warfare, the artillery, Major Dixon, in an extract from a letter written after the siege, provides a summary of their performance at Ciudad Rodrigo in 1812:

> Lord Wellington has certainly made a most brilliant coup, and, I am convinced, astonished the enemy by the rapidity of his operations. They intended to relieve the place and raise the siege about this day (29th January). We were certainly favoured by the most delightful weather – excessively cold, but perfectly dry. It was not even necessary to put the powder under the laboratory tents, which I was enabled to spare to keep the poor fellows from the pinching frost; for we were nearly without cover.
>
> I am hard pressed for time, but I must say a word in favour of our fine fellows of the Corps. They were (Portuguese and all) at relief and relief, off and on but nothing could exceed their zeal and activity, and their work speaks for itself. Never was better practice made. I had only 430 Artillerymen of both nations, about 130 British, and the rest Portuguese. We had somewhere more than 50 Artillerymen killed and wounded, but no officer materially hurt. The latter days, to make it up, I had some help from our own field Artillery: part of Lawson's company was one day in the trenches, and part of Sympher's German company another.

Some commented that Wellington had ushered in a new form of siege warfare that was far more akin to a *coup de main*, so quick had the attack been, taking just twelve days from investment to fall. The contrasts between the 1810 and 1812 sieges are obvious. In the former the French were slow and deliberate and the governor, General Herrasti, with a large garrison to call upon was both active

Sir Arthur Wellesley
subsequently became the
Duke of Wellington in
1812

and determined. The British siege was conducted at pace but against a smaller garrison with a reluctant commander; nonetheless, events at Ciudad Rodrigo in January 1812 were a well-calculated beginning to a change in British fortunes in Spain.

Having taken and secured the first of that pair of Spanish fortresses known as the 'Keys of Spain' after six weeks in cantonments, Wellington set his army in motion south to the larger and already twice-besieged fortress of Badajoz.

Reward

In the aftermath of the successful siege the Spanish created the title of the Duke of Ciudad Rodrigo, the Portuguese ennobled Wellesley as the Marquis of Torres Vedras and within the British peerage he became Marquis Douro, Earl of Wellington.

Senior officers, field officers and above who commanded battalions, brigades, etc. depending on exact rank received the large or small Army Gold Medal or the Army Gold Cross, along with authorized bars for the principal battles.

Army Gold Medal: the initial qualifying battle was engraved on the reverse, with bars being added for subsequent actions.

The MGSM with bar for Ciudad Rodrigo.

In contrast, surviving junior officers and other rank veterans, against the wishes of the duke, only received the Military General Service Medal (MGSM), which was approved in 1847 and issued the following year.

Notes

1. This sword is today lodged in the Green Jackets' Museum in Winchester.
2. Private John Cooper of the 7th Royal Fusiliers gives the total as seventeen and Harry Smith says eleven at the Light Division's execution.
3. A fact to be borne in mind when visiting Ciudad Rodrigo today. The ditches around the eastern side of the fortress are indicative of what would have faced the besiegers in 1810 and 1812.

Appendix I

Battlefield Tour

Ciudad Rodrigo

There are many ways one can visit the key sites of the sieges of Ciudad Rodrigo but this walking tour encompasses most and is for much of the way picturesque. Allow two and a half to three hours.

Parking is extremely limited within the city walls and around most of the seven gateways. It is recommended that cars are parked at the eastern end of the old city outside the Puerta del Sol gateway where there is plenty of space.

1. **Convent of San Francisco.** Little remains other than the impressive facade.
2. **The Greater Teson.** Take Avenue Portugal west from the San Francisco roundabout and turn first right onto Calle San Martin. This road takes the visitor over the Lesser Teson, which is now covered with apartment blocks. At the end of the road turn right onto Calle Gongora. It is normally possible to park here. At the western edge of the tennis club is a narrow track over the barely-used rail line and up onto the Greater Teson.
3. **3rd Division's Assault position.** Return to Calle Gongora and turn right (west). When the housing gives way to a view of the cathedral, walls and breach turn left. Housing here has been encroaching but hopefully this important vista will be preserved.
4. **The Greater Breach.** Walk on across the road at the foot of the glacis slope and climb. The breach (repaired) is easily discernible.
5. **The Lesser Breach (Puerta de Amayuelas).** The Light Division's lesser breach is located where the Puerta de Amayuelas was put in during the 1820s. Entering the city, on the wall immediately to the right is the plaque commemorating Brigadier General Craufurd.
6. **The Walls to the Greater Breach.** Take the metal stairway up to the walls and turn left back towards the greater breach.
7. **Plaza Herrasti and the Julián Sánchez Memorial.** As far as the Spanish are concerned this is the focus of commemoration of events in 1810. It is worth going down the ramp or stairs to the plaza dominated by the pock-marked facade of the cathedral to view Herrasti's monument in the centre of the tree-lined square, and on the wall beneath the breach a relief memorial to the guerrilla leader Julián Sánchez.

8. **The Castle.** Continue along the walls to the castle, which is now a parador (hotel) and for a euro or two, payable at reception, it is possible to climb the castle's tower.
9. **Plaza Mayor and Town Hall.** Head north through the minor roads to the plaza.
10. **Palacio de Montarco.** Follow the Calle Toro north out of the Plaza Mayor to the Plaza del Conde. The large honey-coloured building with the candy-cane columns flanking its entrance is the residence adopted by Wellington after the 1812 siege. The route back to the recommended car park is out of the Conde Gate and turn right.

Below are the details of driving tours of the outpost actions covered in this book. While the 50,000 Spanish survey maps listed below (Mapa Topográfico Nacional de España) are very handy, it is perfectly possible to use the satnav data to get around. The data below can also be used to conduct a map recce on Google/maps/earth/street view as well. There is, however, limited mobile phone coverage in the more remote places, so it is recommended that visitors have a map or print out their own relevant maps beforehand.

Ciudad Rodrigo to Gallegos de Argañán

Map sheet: MTN50 sheets 525 Ciudad Rodrigo

Start Point: GPS: 40.599844481896184 -6.529998776796901
               GR: 0891977

Via the Azaba bridge near Marialba:
               GPS: 40.624538943545204 -6.661062238100612
               GR: 980999

Finish Point: GPS: 40.63098797237264 -6.702260968569362
               GR: 0891977

There are two routes to Gallegos; the easy one is via the modern A62 motorway towards Portugal/Fuentes de Oñoro stopping off at Carpio de Azaba, the site of one of the cavalry vedettes during much of the siege. Turn off the motorway and head north to Gallegos on the SA-CV-93.

Alternatively there is the route via Conejera, Marialba and the Azaba on the Finca Conejera road (GR-10). Only the first 2 miles of this 10-mile route is tarmacked. The stone road surface is good and takes about an hour to drive, with stops. It is, however, well worth taking this route as one feels that one is stepping back in time and is definitely off the beaten track.

Leave the city heading south across the modern bridge and take the first left after the river; turn right and right again under the highway and onto the GE-10 towards Conejera and follow east to the Marialba bridge and on to Gallegos.

Gallegos de Argañán to the Border via La Alamanda de Gardón

Map sheet: MTN50 sheets 525 Ciudad Rodrigo

Start Point: GPS: 40.63098797237264 -6.702260968569362
                GR: 0891977

Finish Point: GPS: 40.64010674805224 -6.802811620119655
                GR: 859014

Barba del Puerco (Puerto Seguro) Chapel Ermita del Humilladero

Map sheet: MTN50 sheets 500 Villar de Ciervo and 526 Lumbrales

Start Point: GPS: 40.82595524394161 -6.757793424013698
                GR: 892221

Other than overlooking the Águeda Gorge, which was known to the Riflemen as the Valley of the Eagles, this stand requires a walk.

Warning: The walk (there is no vehicle access below the brow of the hill) down to the bridge takes twenty-five minutes but it is about forty-five minutes of very strenuous walking to regain the village. There is no shade and the sun combined with heat presents a serious challenge to the visitor who is not physically fit, properly equipped and provided with ample water. In the event of difficulty, rescue by vehicle is not possible and the authorities would take a long time to arrive. There is also no mobile signal in the gorge.

Park by the chapel at the southern edge of the village. This was used by Captain O'Hare's inlying piquet. Take the concrete road to the left of the chapel. After 300 yards, the now dirt road turns sharply left. Follow the track down to the valley. This is the point where the sergeant's part of the outlying piquet was located.

Follow the track downhill. It is interesting to speculate where the officer's tent would have been pitched but the location for the corporal's piquet is overlooking the bridge and sentry's position.

If one has flexibility with transport there is a walk to a pick-up point at San Felices de los Gallegos, a distance of 4.25 miles, where the castle is well worth a visit. Allow three hours to take in the views and scene of the action. There is a similar steep climb up the French side out of the Águeda gorge.

Villar de Puerco (Villar de Argañán)

Map sheet: MTN50 sheets 500 Villar de Ciervo

Start Point: GPS: 40.673151868750935 -6.713075635317409
                GR: 929053

The scene of the cavalry action can be studied from the road north to Barquilla (SA-CV-93) and the minor road east from the crossroads in the centre of the village towards Sexmiro. The coordinates above take one to the latter.

Espeja

Map sheet: MTN50 sheets 525 Ciudad Rodrigo

Start Point: GPS: 40.56676306859945 -6.711874005678737
GR: 936935

El Bodón

Map sheet: MTN50 sheets 550 Fuenteguinaldo

Start Point: GPS: 40.49337156133055 -6.579694745424831
GR: 053856

A memorial to the combat at El Bodón inaugurated on the 200th anniversary is located to the west of the plateau. It is off the main road at a junction on the earthen Camino Espeja a El Bodón and difficult to find but the accurate long/lat is 40°29'44.19"N 06°36'26.24"W.

Viscount Wellington's Orders

Set out below is the full text of Wellington's orders for the storming of Ciudad Rodrigo on the evening of 19 January 1812:

ARRANGEMENTS FOR THE ASSAULT.

The attack upon Ciudad Rodrigo must be made this evening at 7 o'clock.

The light infantry company of the 83rd regiment will join Lieutenant Colonel O'Toole at sunset. Lieutenant Colonel O'Toole, with the 2nd Caçadores, and the light company of the 83rd regiment, will, 10 minutes before 7 cross the Águeda by the bridge, and make an attack upon the outwork in front of the castle. The object of this attack is to drive the artillerymen from two guns in that outwork, which bear upon the entrance into the ditch, at the junction of the counterscarp with the main wall of the place: if Lieutenant Colonel O'Toole can get into the outwork, it would be desirable to destroy these guns. Major Sturgeon will show Lieutenant Colonel O'Toole his point of attack. Six ladders, 12 feet long each, will be sent from the engineer park to the old French guard-room, at the mill on the Águeda, for the use of this detachment.

The 5th regiment will attack the entrance of the ditch at the point above referred to; Major Sturgeon will likewise show them the point of attack; they must issue from the right of the convent of Santa Cruz; they must have 12 axes to cut down the gate by which the ditch is entered, at the junction of the counterscarp with the body of the place. The 5th regiment are likewise to have 12 scaling ladders, 25 feet long, and immediately on entering the ditch, are to scale the faussebraye wall, and are to proceed along the faussebraye, in order to clear it of the enemy's posts on their left, towards the principal breach.

The 77th regiment are to be in reserve on the right of the convent of Santa Cruz, to support the first party, which will have entered the ditch. The ditch must besides be entered on the right of the breach by two columns, to be formed on the left of the convent of Santa Cruz, each to consist of five companies of the 94th regiment. Each column must have three ladders, 12 feet long, by which they are to descend into the ditch, and they are to have 10 axes to cut down any palisades which may be placed in the ditch to impede the communication along it. The detachment of the 94th regiment, when descended into the ditch, is to turn to its left to the main breach.

The 5th regiment will issue from the convent of Santa Cruz 10 minutes before. At the same time a party consisting of 180 sappers, carrying bags containing hay, will move out of the second parallel, covered by a fire of the 83rd regiment, formed in the second parallel, upon the works of the place, which bags are to be thrown into the ditch, so as to enable the troops to descend the counterscarp to the attack of the breach: they are to be followed immediately by the storming party of the great breach, which is to consist of the troops of Major General Mackinnon's brigade. Major General Mackinnon's brigade is to be formed in the first parallel, and in the communications between the first and second parallel, ready to move up to the breach directly in rear of the sappers with bags. The storming party of the great breach must be provided with six scaling ladders, 12 feet long each, and with 10 axes.

The ditch must likewise be entered by a column on the left of the great breach, consisting of three companies of the 95th regiment, which are to issue from the right of the convent of St. Francisco. This column will be provided with three ladders, 12 feet long, with which they are to descend into the ditch, at a point which will be pointed out to them by Lieutenant Wright: on descending into the ditch, they are to turn to their right, and to proceed towards the main breach; they are to have 10 axes, to enable them to cut down the obstacles which may have been erected to impede the communication along the ditch on the left of the breach.

Another column, consisting of Major General Vandeleur's brigade, will issue out from the left of the convent of St. Francisco, and are to attack the breach to the left of the main breach; this column must have 12 ladders, each 12 feet long, with which they are to descend into the ditch, at a point which will be shown them by Captain Ellicombe: on arriving in the ditch, they are to turn to their left, to storm the breach in the faussebraye, on their left, of the small ravelin, and thence to the breach in the tower of the body of the place: as soon as this body will have reached the top of the breach, in the faussebraye wall, a detachment of five companies are to be sent to the right, to cover the attack of Major General Mackinnon's brigade, by the principal breach, and as soon as they have reached the top of the tower, they are to turn to their right, and communicate with the rampart of the main breach: as soon as this communication can be established, endeavour should be made to open the gate of Salamanca.

The Portuguese brigade in the 3rd division will be formed in the communication to the first parallel, and behind the hill of St. Francisco (upper Teson), and will move up to the entrance of the second parallel, ready to support Major General Mackinnon's brigade.

Colonel Barnard's brigade will be formed behind the convent of St. Francisco, ready to support Major General Vandeleur's brigade; all these columns will have detached parties especially appointed to keep up a fire on the defences during the above.

The men with ladders, and axes, and bags, must not have their arms; those who are to storm, must not fire.

Brigadier General Pack, with his brigade, will make a false attack upon the out-work of the gate of St. Jago, and upon the works towards La Caridad.

The different regiments and brigades to receive ladders are to send parties to the engineers' depot to receive them, three men for each ladder.

W.

Order of Battle, Ciudad Rodrigo 1812

British Army

British units have been annotated with their 1812 county or other titles.

Commander in Chief: Lieutenant General Viscount Wellington
Chief Engineer: Lieutenant Colonel Sir Richard Fletcher
Siege Train Commander: Brevet Major Alexander Dickson

1st Division: Major General Henry Campbell
Fermor's Brigade
1/Coldstream Guards
1/3rd Foot Guards

No. 7 Company 5/60th Rifles
(Royal American Regiment)

Wheatley's Brigade
2/24th Foot (Warwickshire Regiment)
1/42nd Foot (Royal Highland Regiment, Black Watch)
2/58th Foot (Rutlandshire)
1/79th Foot (Cameron Highlanders)
Company 5/60th Rifles (Royal American Regiment)

Baron Löwe's Brigade
1/Line Battalion, King's German Legion
2/Line Battalion, King's German Legion
5/Line Battalion, King's German Legion

3rd Division: Major General Picton
Mackinnon's Brigade
1/45th Foot (Nottinghamshire)
74th Foot (Highland)
1/88th Foot (Connaught Rangers)

Five companies, 5/60th Rifles
(Royal American Regiment)

Campbell's Brigade
2/5th Foot (Northumberland)
77th Foot (East Middlesex)

94th Foot (Scotch Brigade)

Power's Portuguese Brigade
1 & 2/9th Line Regiment
1 & 2nd/21st Line Regiment

12th Caçadores

4th Division: Lieutenant General Lowry Cole
  Anson's Brigade
    3/27th Foot (Inskilling)   Company 5/60th Rifles
    1/40th Foot (2nd Somerset)   (Royal American Regiment)
  Ellis's Brigade
    1/7th Royal Fusiliers   1/48th Foot (Northamptonshire)
    1/23rd Royal Welch Fusiliers   Company Brunswick Oels
  Stubbs' Portuguese Brigade
    1 & 2/11th Line Regiment   7th Caçadores
    1 & 2/23rd Line Regiment

Light Division: Major General Craufurd
  Vandeleur's Brigade
    1/52nd Light Infantry (Oxfordshire)   3/95th Rifles (5 companies)
    2/52nd Light Infantry (Oxfordshire)   3rd Caçadores
    2/95th Rifles (2 companies)
  Barnard's Brigade
    1/43rd Light Infantry   1/95th Rifles (8 companies)
      (Monmouthshire)   1st Caçadores

Independent Brigade
  Pack's Portuguese Brigade
    1 & 2/1st Line Regiment   4th Caçadores
    1 & 2/16th Line Regiment

Overall Anglo-Portuguese strength approximately **26,000**

French Army

Garrison Commander: General Jean Léonard Barrié

Thiébault's Division (detachments of)
  1st Battalion 34th Légère: Major Fourtine
  1st Battalion 113th Ligne: Major Teras
  1 Company Engineers: Captain Cathals
  2 Companies Artillery: Major Husson

Overall strength just under **2,000**

Appendix IV

Wellington's Ciudad Rodrigo Dispatch

Set out below is the full text of Wellington's dispatch concerning the latter days of the siege and storm. It was taken back to London by one of his aides-de-camp, Major Gordon.

To the Earl of Liverpool.   Gallegos, 20th Jan. 1812.

I informed your Lordship, in my dispatch of the 9th, that I had attacked Ciudad Rodrigo, and in that of the 15th, of the progress of the operations to that period, and I have now the pleasure to acquaint your Lordship that we took the place by storm yesterday evening after dark.

We continued, from the 15th to the 19th, to complete the second parallel, and the communications with that work, and had made some progress by sap towards the crest of the glacis. On the night of the 15th we likewise advanced from the left of the first parallel down the slope of the hill towards the convent of San Francisco, to a situation from which the walls of the faussebraye and of the tower were seen, on which a battery for 7 guns was constructed, and these commenced their fire on the morning of the 18th. In the meantime the batteries in the first parallel continued their fire; and yesterday evening, their fire had not only considerably injured the defences of the place, but had made breaches in the faussebraye wall, and in the body of the place, which were considered practicable; while the battery on the slope of the hill, which had been commenced on the night of the 15th, and had opened on the 18th, had been equally efficient still farther to the left, and opposite to the suburb of San Francisco.

I therefore determined to storm the place, notwithstanding that the approaches had not been brought to the crest of the glacis, and the counterscarp of the ditch was still entire. The attack was accordingly made yesterday evening, in 5 separate columns, consisting of the troops of the 3rd and Light Divisions, and of Brigadier General Pack's brigade. The 2 right columns, conducted by Lieutenant Colonel O'Toole of the 2nd Caçadores, and Major Ridge of the 5th regt., were destined to protect the advance of Major-General Mackinnon's brigade, forming the 3rd, to the top of the breach in the faussebraye wall; and all these, being composed of troops of the 3rd Division, were under the direction of Lieutenant General Picton.

The fourth column, consisting of the 43rd and 52nd Regts., and part of the 95th Regt., being of the light division, under the direction of Major General Craufurd, attacked the breaches on the left in front of the suburb of San Francisco, and covered the left of the attack of the principal breach by the troops of the 3rd Division; and Brigadier General Pack was destined, with his brigade, forming the fifth column, to make a false attack upon the southern face of the fort.

Besides these 5 columns, the 94th Regt., belonging to the 3rd Division, descended into the ditch in 2 columns, on the right of Major General Mackinnon's brigade, with a view to protect the descent of that body into the ditch and its attack of the breach in the faussebraye, against the obstacles which it was supposed the enemy would construct to oppose their progress.

All these attacks succeeded; and Brigadier General Pack even surpassed my expectations, having converted his false attack into a real one; and his advanced guard, under the command of Major Lynch, having followed the enemy's troops from the advanced works into the faussebraye, where they made prisoners all opposed to them.

Major Ridge, of the 2nd Batt. 5th Regt., having escaladed the faussebraye wall, stormed the principal breach in the body of the place, together with the 94th Regt., commanded by Lieutenant Colonel Campbell, which had moved along the ditch at the same time, and had stormed the breach in the faussebraye, both in front of Major General Mackinnon's brigade. Thus, these regiments not only effectually covered the advance from the trenches of Major General Mackinnon's brigade by their first movements and operations, but they preceded them in the attack.

Major General Craufurd, and Major General Vandeleur, and the troops of the light division, on the left, were likewise very forward on that side; and, in less than half an hour from the time the attack commenced, our troops were in possession, and formed on the ramparts of the place, each body contiguous to the other: the enemy then submitted, having sustained a considerable loss in the contest.

It is but justice also to the 3rd Division to report that the men who performed the sap belonged to the 45th, 74th, and 88th Regts., under the command of Captain Macleod of the Royal Engineers, and Captain Thompson of the 74th, Lieut. Beresford of the 88th, and Lieut. Metcalfe of the 45th, and they distinguished themselves not less in the storm of the place than they had in the performance of their laborious duty during the siege.

I likewise request your Lordship's attention to the conduct of Lieutenant Colonel Fletcher, the chief engineer, and of Brigade Major Jones and the officers and men of the Royal Engineers. The ability with which these operations were carried on exceeds all praise; and I beg leave to recommend these officers to your Lordship most particularly Major Dickson, of the Royal Artillery, attached to the Portuguese artillery, has for some time had the direction of the heavy train attached to this army, and has conducted the intricate details of the late operation, as he did that of the two sieges of Badajoz in the last summer, much to my satisfaction. The rapid execution produced by the well-directed fire kept up from our batteries affords the best proof of the merits of the officers and men of the Royal Artillery, and of the Portuguese artillery, employed on this occasion; but I must particularly mention Brigade-Major May and Captains Holcombe, Power, Dynely, and Dundas, of the Royal Artillery, and Captains Da Cunha and Da Costa, and Lieut. Silva, of the 1st Regt of Portuguese artillery. I have likewise particularly to report to your Lordship the conduct of Major Sturgeon of the Royal Staff corps. He constructed and placed for us the bridge over the Águeda, without which the enterprise could not have been attempted; and he afterwards materially assisted Lieut.-General Graham and myself in our reconnaissance of the place, on which the plan of the attack was founded; and he finally conducted the 2nd Batt. 5th Regt., as well as the 2nd Caçadores, to their points of attack.

W.

Major Gordon, traditionally the bearer of good news, was promoted to brevet lieutenant colonel, bells were rung in London and Arthur Wellesley was elevated within the peerage from a viscount to the Earl of Wellington.

Index